BRITISH FLAGS

BRITISH FLAGS

WILLIAM GORDON PERRIN

ISBN: 978-93-5614-025-7

Published: 1922

LECTOR HOUSE LLP
E-MAIL: lectorpublishing@gmail.com

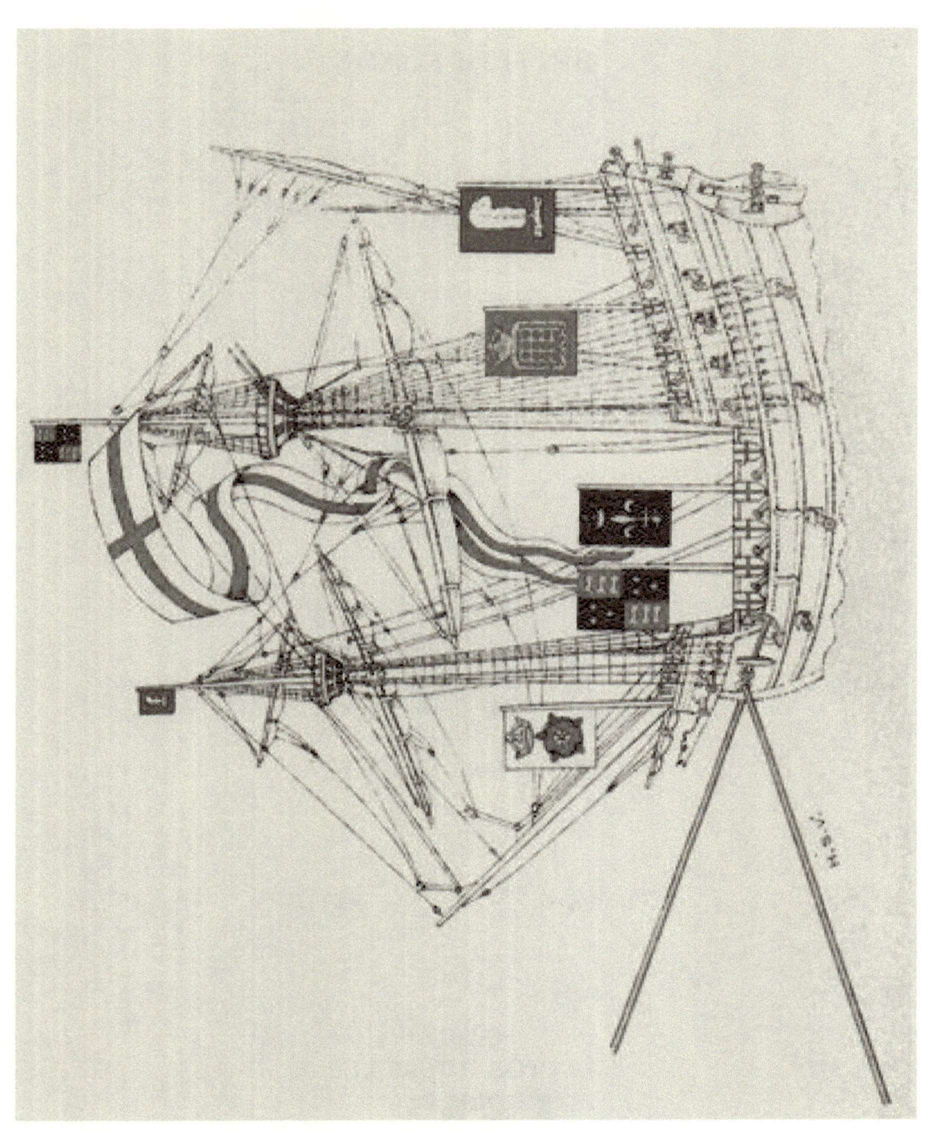

A Ship of Henry VIII, circa 1545

(From a MS. plan of Calais in the British Museum, *c.* 1545)

CAMBRIDGE NAVAL AND MILITARY SERIES

BRITISH FLAGS

THEIR EARLY HISTORY, AND THEIR DEVELOPMENT AT SEA; WITH AN ACCOUNT OF THE ORIGIN OF THE FLAG AS A NATIONAL DEVICE

BY

W. G. PERRIN

ADMIRALTY LIBRARIAN
SECRETARY OF THE NAVY RECORDS SOCIETY
FELLOW OF THE ROYAL HISTORICAL SOCIETY

ILLUSTRATED IN COLOUR BY HERBERT S. VAUGHAN

CHEVALIER OF THE LEGION
OF HONOUR

GENERAL EDITORS
SIR JULIAN S. CORBETT, LL.M., F.S.A.
H. J. EDWARDS, C.B., C.B.E., M.A.

1922

PREFACE

IT might have been expected that the attempt to trace to their origin in the past the institutions and customs in common use upon the sea would from an early date occupy the attention of a seafaring people, but for some obscure reason the British nation has always been indifferent to the history of its activities upon that element on which its greatness was founded, and to which it has become more and more dependent for its daily bread and its very existence. To those who are alive to this fact it will hardly come as a surprise, therefore, to learn that the first sustained attempt at a detailed investigation into the history of the flag at sea was made under the patronage of the German Admiralty by a German Admiral. Vice-Admiral Siegel's *Die Flagge*, published in 1912, was the first book to deal with the development of the flag at sea in a scientific spirit, and although the earlier chapters contain some mistakes due to his employment of translations of early works instead of original texts, and the accounts of the British flags in the later chapters suffer because he had no access to original records, it is a worthy piece of work.

The present book is an attempt to remove the reproach to the British nation which this implies. Its plan is somewhat different from that of the work referred to above. Instead of dealing with the flags of all maritime nations of the world—a task that (if it was to be more than a mere copying or compilation) would entail much work in foreign archives—it seemed more profitable to concentrate upon the history of British Naval Flags, for researches made so far back as 1908 had taught me how much that is inaccurate about their history had received acceptance. But first it seemed necessary to devote some time and space to the inquiry into the origin of the flag and how it became the honoured symbol of nationality that it now is, and for this a general view had to be taken in order that a firm foundation might be laid for the early history of our own flags.

In the first chapter the ground worked over by Admiral Siegel has been solidified by examination of the original authorities, with the result that a few errors have been detected and some new facts brought to light, and the investigation has also been extended further; the most important of the additions being those relating to the standards in the Phoenician and Greek ships of war, forms of the early "standard" and "gonfanon," and the Genoese Standard of St George and the Dragon. For the deduction that the use of a national flag arose in the Italian city states I take the entire responsibility, well aware that further investigations may possibly bring to light fresh facts which will overthrow it.

The chapter on early English, Scottish and Irish flags serves as an introduction to the history of our national flag, which was invented for the use of the mercantile marine, though it was very soon appropriated by the Royal Navy for its sole use. It is very improbable that further research will enable the gap left by the unfortunate destruction of the early 17th century records to be filled, so that the story of the Union Flag may be taken as being substantially complete, but there is still room for further work upon the history of its component crosses. It will be seen that I have been unable to find any solid ground for the common belief that the cross of St George was introduced as the national emblem of England by Richard I, and am of opinion that it did not begin to attain that position until the first years of the reign of Edward I.

The chapters on the flags used to indicate distinctions of command and service at sea give an account of the use (now obsolete) of the Royal Standard at sea by naval commanders-in-chief; of the history of the Admiralty anchor-flag; and of the steps by which the present Admirals' flags were evolved. The history of the ensigns from their first adoption at sea about the end of Elizabeth's reign has been set out in some detail, but further research may bring to light more details of interest in the years between 1574 and 1653. The causes which led to the adoption of a red ensign as the most important British ensign and the steps which led to its appropriation to the Mercantile Marine, and not the Royal Navy, are stated as far as the records availed, though here again further research is needed in the late Elizabethan and early Stuart periods among records that may still survive in private ownership. These chapters may, perhaps, appeal rather to the seaman and the student of naval history than to the general reader, but it is hoped that they may also prove of service to artists who wish to avoid the anachronisms into which some of their brethren have been betrayed.

In order that the development of flag signals may be properly appreciated it has been necessary, when dealing with the earlier years, to take into account what had happened outside the narrow circuit of British waters. The earlier matter, though here examined solely from the point of view of the flags used, offers considerable interest to the student of naval tactics, with which indeed the art of signalling is inseparably connected.

The last chapter, on Ceremonial and other usages, is, from the author's point of view, the least satisfactory. From the nature of the subject, the official records contain very little information about it. It is only by the slow and laborious process of examining contemporary journals, diaries, accounts of voyages, and similar material that facts can be found for any exhaustive treatment of these matters. Something of this has been done, but more remains to do.

In concluding the work which has occupied a large portion of the leisure hours of many years, it is my pleasant duty to express my gratitude to the numerous friends whose encouragement and assistance have enabled me to persevere in what has proved a somewhat arduous task; especially to Sir Julian Corbett, who has read the proofs and given me the benefit of his criticisms; to the officials of the Pepysian Library, Public Record Office, British Museum and London Library for the facilities afforded me; and not least to my friend Mr Vaughan who has spared no pains in the preparation of the coloured plates.   W. G. PERRIN.

January 1922

CONTENTS

LIST OF ILLUSTRATIONS

6. Red Pendant
7. Canada Badge
8. South Africa Badge
9. Indian Marine Badge
10. Lloyds Badge

CHAPTER I

THE ORIGIN OF THE FLAG AND ITS DEVELOPMENT UP TO THE END OF THE THIRTEENTH CENTURY

A FLAG may be defined as a piece of pliable material, attached at one end so as to move freely in the wind, serving as a sign or a decoration. This word is now common to the nations of north-western Europe[1], but it does not appear to have come into use in this particular meaning until the sixteenth century, and the etymology of it is obscure. Perhaps the most satisfactory of the derivations hitherto put forward is that of Professor Skeat, who derives it from the Middle English "flakken" to fly, one of a number of similar onomatopoeic words suggestive of the sound of something flapping in the wind. Its first appearance with a meaning coming within the above definition is as a specific term denoting a rectangular piece of material attached by one vertical edge, flown at the masthead of a ship, as a symbol of nationality or leadership. It was not until towards the end of the seventeenth century that the word began to take on the more general meaning it now has, and indeed the restricted meaning still partially survives in the German language, in which the word "Flagge" is properly applicable only to flags flown at sea, those on land being called "Fahnen." Before the seventeenth century there was no generic term in the English language that covered the various forms—banners, ensigns, streamers, pendants, etc.—that are now generally included under the term "flag."

A somewhat similar change in meaning has, during the course of centuries, affected nearly every flag name, and constitutes one of the great difficulties in the way of a clear exposition of the early history of flags. Moreover, the early writers are neither consistent in their use of terms nor accurate in their application. This renders the correct interpretation of many passages a matter requiring caution and discrimination and, it may be added, experience. As a guide to the reader we shall set down the principal terms to be met with, and indicate the extent to which their meaning has changed, but before doing so it is desirable to explain one or two technical or semi-technical terms employed in connection with the parts of a flag. The part next the staff or line to which it is attached is called the "hoist" by seamen, or heraldically the head or "chief"; the remainder of the flag is the "fly." The fly may be forked or swallow-tailed. If the end of the fly is divided by a simple incision which does not remove material, it is said to be "slit." The fly may be produced into a number of pointed or round-ended tails, to which the Crusaders gave the name of tongues (*linguae, lingulae*). The British and many other ensigns have

---

[1] I.e. Flag (Danish and Norse), Flagg (Swedish), Flagge (German), Vlag (Dutch).

in the upper part next the staff a rectangular compartment containing a national device. In modern flags this usually occupies one-fourth of the flag, but in early flags it was much smaller. This is called a "canton." The other terms that need explanation at this stage are as follows:

Σημεῖον (Semeion). This word appears to have been first used in the abstract meaning of "sign" or "signal"; to have been then applied to the object by which the signal was made, or which signalised the presence of the commanding officer. In the early period of Greece this was not a flag, but a staff-like object.

Insigne, pl. **Insignia**. The Latin equivalent of the above, denoting a sign, signal, or staff of office.

Signum. A token or sign, especially the distinctive sign of a division of the Roman army. Also used to denote "signal" in the abstract.

Vexillum. A square flag hung from a transverse bar at the head of a staff; the principal form of flag in use in the classical period. In late writers this word is used to cover any form of flag, and from the eighth century onwards will be found applied as well to objects that were not flags, for which the word *insigne* should have been used.

Banner (late Latin *bandum*, *bannum*). A rectangular flag attached laterally to its staff. Originally of much greater depth than length, a "band" of coloured material attached to a lance by one of its longer sides, it gradually became square. The banner was primarily the personal flag of an emperor, king, lord or knight, and served to mark his presence in the army or fleet, and as a rallying point for his retainers. On the introduction of heraldic devices these were inserted upon it. It was also employed by religious or civic bodies for a similar purpose. In modern language this term is usually applied to flags hung from transverse bars, displayed in religious or political processions, but we shall not employ it in this meaning.

Gonfanon, Gonfalon. This word appears in the *Anglo-Saxon Chronicle* as *guðfana*, and in the *Chanson de Roland* as *gunfanun*. It is apparently derived from the Norse *gunn-fane* (war-flag) and in its earlier forms was probably of the shape shown on the Northumbrian coins about 925 A.D.[2] Among the Normans two centuries later it had a square body and ended in three or more long tails, a form handed on to the Italian Communes. Some writers apply this name (inaccurately) to flags of vexillum form, with or without tails at the base.

Standard. This word presents great difficulty, and it has undergone a radical change in meaning which (so far as I am aware) has never been explained. As no historical survey of the development of the flag can fairly ignore the need for such an explanation it will be necessary to treat it at some length. At different periods in history since the eleventh century the word under one or more of its many forms (e.g. estandart, standart, standardum, standarz, standarum, standalem), has had the following meanings:

(i) A tall pole or staff supporting some object that was not a flag.

(ii) A tall pole or mast set in a four-wheeled chariot, supporting various ob-

---

[2] See Plate II, fig. 10.

jects, including one or more flags.

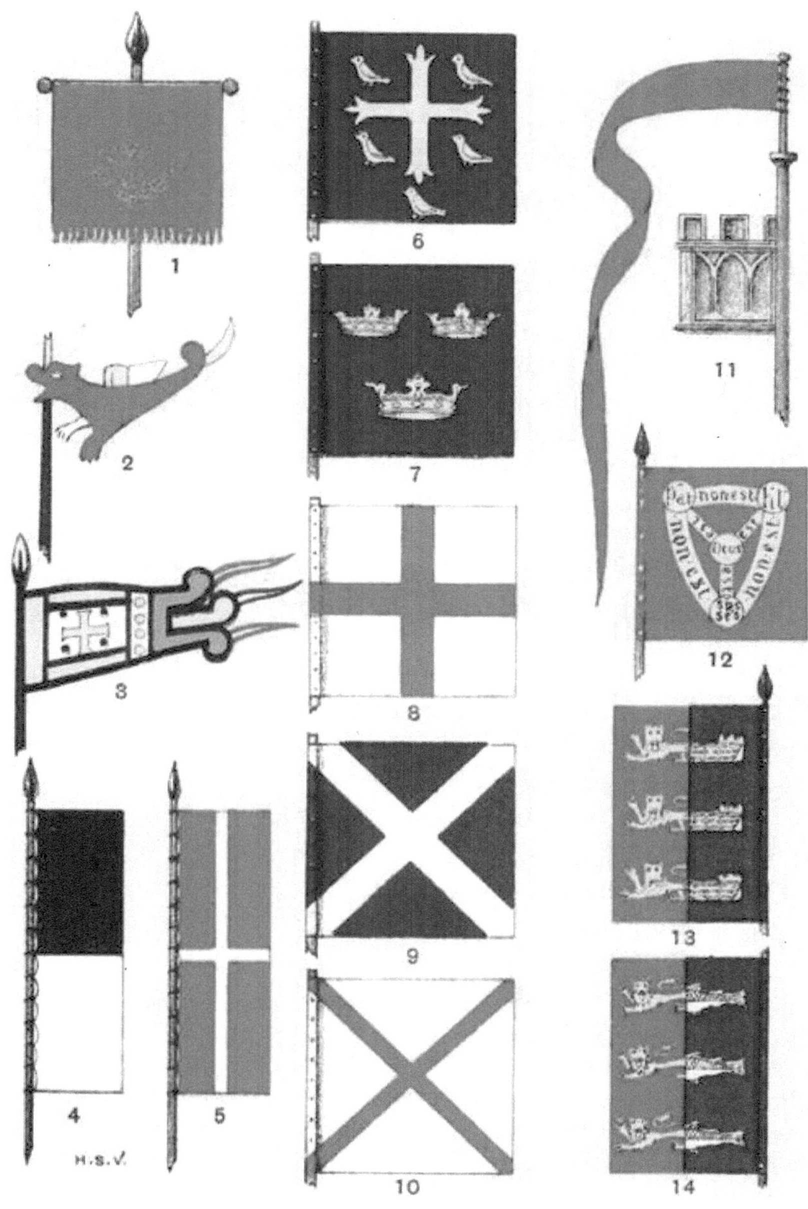

Plate I

Early Flags

1. Vexillum   2. Harold's Dragon   3. William's Gonfanon
4. Knights Templars' Bauçan   5. Knights Hospitallers   6. St Edward

7. St Edmund   8. St George   9. St Andrew

10. Irish Saltire   11. Baucan   12. Holy Trinity

13. Cinque Ports   14. Yarmouth

(ii) A tall pole or mast set in a four-wheeled chariot, supporting various objects, including one or more flags.

(iii) An elongated tapering flag containing the arms or badges of a king or noble.

(iv) A rectangular banner containing the royal arms.

One of the earliest appearances of the word is in the *Chanson de Roland*. The oldest existing MS. of this poem was, it is true, not written before the latter part of the twelfth century, but it is well known that the poem itself is much older. In this long poem of some 4000 lines the word occurs thrice only, and is confined to the episode which relates to Baligant, Emir of Babylon, which M. Gaston Paris considers to be the work of another author. The passages in question are:

> 3265. Li amiralz mult par est riches hum
> Dedavant lui fait porter sun dragun
> E l'estandart Tervagan e Mahum.
>
> [The Emir is a very great man
> Before him he has carried his dragon
> And the standard of Tervagan and Mahomet.]
>
> 3329. Carles li magnes, cum il vit l'amiraill
> E le dragun, l'enseigne, e l'estandart,
>
> [Charlemagne, when he saw the emir
> And the dragon, the flag and the standard,]
>
> 3551. Baliganz veit sun gunfanun cadeir
> E l'estandart Mahumet remaneir.
>
> [Baligant sees his gonfanon fall
> And the standard of Mahomet remain (defenceless).]

In speaking of the flags the poet (or perhaps poets) uses either the words "enseigne" or "gunfanun" or, in one instance, "orie flambe." What then was the "Standard of Mahomet" which the author of this section has in mind? The story he is telling is, of course, purely mythical, so that he, or the original inventor of the myth, must have met the word and the object which it connoted in some other connection. The most likely source of this knowledge is the First Crusade. During the struggle for the possession of Jerusalem in the summer of 1099, Robert of Normandy, in personal combat, seized from one of the Saracen Emirs an object which is described as a very long pole covered over with silver, having at its top a golden ball or apple (*pomum aureum*). This was called a standard, a word which was evidently at that time of recent introduction, for the contemporary historians, some of whom had been eye-witnesses of the events they relate, have various ways of spelling it, and usually refer to it in such a way as to indicate that the word was not in familiar use[3]. According to Albert of Aix[4] this standard was borne in front of the army of the "King of Babylon" and was the centre around which the flower of the army gathered and to which stragglers returned. A few years later Fulcher of Chartres notes the capture of three more "standards," but does not describe them.

The second form of standard (which was apparently imitated from the Italian *carrocio* presently to be described) makes its appearance nearly a hundred years later. In an engagement with the Saracens near Acre at the end of August, 1191, the banner of Richard I was borne aloft on a machine of which the unknown but contemporary author of the *Itinerarium Regis Ricardi* gives the following description:

> The Normans formed a rampart around the Standard, which in order that it may be better known we have not thought it out of the way to describe. It consists, then, of a very long beam, like the mast of a ship, placed upon four wheels in a frame very solidly fastened together and bound with iron, so that it seems incapable of yielding either to sword, axe or fire. Affixed to the very top of this, the royal flag, commonly called banner, flies in the wind. For the protection of this machine, especially in battle in the open, a selected band of soldiers is appointed, so that it may not be broken down by onrush of the enemy or overthrown by any injury, for if by any chance it should be overthrown the army would be dispersed and confounded, because it would not know in what part of the field to rally. Moreover, the hearts of the soldiers would be filled with the fear that their leader had been overcome if they did not see his banner borne aloft. Nor would they in the rear readily come forward to resist the enemy if, from the withdrawal of his banner, they feared that some ill fortune had happened to their king. But while that standard remained erect the people had a sure place of refuge. Hither the sick were brought to be cured, hither were brought the wounded, and even famous or illustrious men tired out in the fighting. Whence, because it stands fast as a sign to all the people, it is called the "Standard."[5] It is placed upon four wheels, not without reason, in order that, according to the state of the battle, it may be either brought forward as the enemy yield or drawn back as they press on.

It is to a machine similar to this, and bearing aloft a pyx and three banners, that the battle near Northallerton in 1138 owes its name of Battle of the Standard.

The use of this form of standard was not confined to the English; indeed it seems to have been in general use in the armies of western Europe in the twelfth

---

[3] E.g. Albert of Aix: longissima hasta quod vocant standart. Baldric of Dol: admiravisi stantarum. Peter Tudebode: Quod stantarum apud nos dicitur vexillum. Robert the Monk: vexillum admiravissi quod standarum vocant.

[4] *Historia*, lib. vi: this with the other authorities quoted will be found in the *Recueil des Historiens des Croisades.*

[5] Unde quia stat fortissime compaginatum in signum populorum a stando standardum vocitatur.

and thirteenth centuries, and the transference of the name from the support to the royal, ducal, or state flag that it bore was a natural consequence. This transference evidently began to take place about the end of the thirteenth century, for in 1282 the State gonfanon of Genoa, hitherto called the "vexillum" of St George, in the *Annales Genoenses*, becomes the "Stantarium B. Georgii." In England the change seems to have taken place a little later. I have not met with it before the year 1323, when the Exchequer Accounts contain references to Standards (Estandartz, estandardes) bearing the royal arms and made of worsted of Aylesham.

But the name was not given in England to every form of flag bearing the royal arms or cross of St George. It was confined to a particular type intermediate in length between the streamer and the banner[6]. This type was evidently the direct descendant of the "gonfanon," which is the only form of flag represented on such of the great seals of our early kings as show flags at all[7]. From the fact that it is this form which is depicted at the masthead of the ships in early seals, as for instance those of Hastings and Lyme Regis (thirteenth century) and of Dover (1305) reproduced in Plate III, we may infer that it was the type most convenient for use at the head of the "standard," and therefore the type to which the name gradually became applied. During the fourteenth century the tails were reduced in number to two and the flag made to taper gradually throughout its length. Finally, the heralds established a form in which the tails were short, blunt and rounded off at the end, which they decided should contain the cross of St George in chief with the motto and badges of the owner, but not his arms, in the fly. This change seems to have taken place about the end of the fifteenth century. By the restriction of the royal arms to flags of banner form the name "standard," when qualified by the adjective "royal" (but only in this connection), became transferred to the royal banner of arms, not only in popular speech which makes no account of such technical niceties, but also in official usage from Tudor times to this day.

Streamer. A long and relatively narrow flag flown at sea from the masthead, top or yardarm, often reaching down to the water. The earlier name of the modern "pendant." The term is also applied to any ribbon-like flag or decoration.

Pennon. Originally a small pointed flag worn at the lance-head by knights; but the word was used at sea in the fourteenth and fifteenth centuries to denote a short streamer.

Pennoncel. A small pennon.

Pennant (in modern official language written "pendant," but pronounced "pennant"). A synonym for "streamer," a name which it has gradually replaced.

Geton, gytton, guidon. A small swallow-tailed flag.

Ensign (corruptly written "ancient" during the sixteenth to eighteenth centuries). This word was borrowed from the land service in the sixteenth century to denote the striped flag then introduced on the poop of ships. In explaining the

---

[6] In 1337 streamers were from 14 to 32 ells long and 3 to 5 cloths wide; standards were 9 ells long and 3 cloths wide; while banners were 1¾ ells long and 2 cloths wide.

[7] E.g. those of William II, Henry I, Stephen and Alexander I of Scotland.

meaning of this word in the Army, Barret[8] remarks: "We Englishmen do call them (Ensigns) of late Colours, by reason of the variety of colours they be made of, whereby they be the better noted and known to the companie."

Colours. Originally applied to an ensign; afterwards extended to mean the flags commonly flown by a ship. At the end of the seventeenth century a "suit of colours" included ensign, jack and pendant.

Jack. A small flag flown on the bowsprit.

Upon the water, as upon the land, the Standard (taking the word in its earliest meaning) seems to have preceded the Flag by many centuries. The earliest knowledge we have of its existence is derived from the pottery of the pre-dynastic Egyptians, to whom, on the most moderate estimate of Egyptologists, a date not later than 4000 B.C. has been assigned. Among the primitive decorations of the earthenware vases and boxes of that period the representation of a boat[9] frequently appears. In these boats, which seem to have been in use only on the Nile, the two cabins amidships are a prominent feature. At the end of the aftermost cabin rises a tall pole with an emblem at the top, which is believed to represent the district or town to which the owner of the boat belonged. There are at least eighteen different forms of this emblem[10], but these standards all agree in having in their upper part two pendent objects which appear to be long ribbons or streamers attached to the pole. These standards were developed into the nome-standards of the Egyptian armies, but they never again appear in Egypt in connection with boats, which from the time of the First Dynasty onwards are invariably represented without standard or flag of any kind, although in rare instances the top of the steering oar is decorated with two long ribbons.

Standards appear to have been in use at a later date among all the Semitic nations, but evidence of their use upon the sea before the fifth century B.C. is not forthcoming. From about the end of that century onwards Sidon and Aradus (Arvad), the two great seaports of Phoenicia, referred to by the prophet Ezekiel in his lamentation for Tyre[11] as supplying the mariners for that city, placed upon their coinage[12] a representation of a war galley. At the stern of this galley, supported against a curved ornament similar to that to which the Greeks gave the name "Aphlaston," is placed a tall staff having at its top a globe within the arms of a crescent, representing the sun and moon. In the earlier examples this is too indistinct for successful photographic representation but it is clearly visible in the coins of the fourth century shown in Plate II[13].

[8] *The Theorike and Practike of moderne warres,* 1598.

[9] The fact that the object represented is really a boat has been disputed, but there seem to be no good grounds for the objections made. The question is discussed by Dr Wallis Budge in his *Egypt in the Neolithic and Archaic Periods* (Books on Egypt and Chaldea, vol. IX), pp. 71 et seq.

[10] They are represented in de Morgan's *Recherches sur les Origines de l'Egypte,* in Dr Wallis Budge's work just cited, p. 78, and in Capart's *Primitive Art in Egypt,* p. 210.

[11] Ezekiel, chap. xxvii.

[12] See the British Museum *Catalogue of Greek coins (Phoenicia),* edited by Mr G. F. Hill, and Mr Hill's remarks in his introduction, p. xxii.

[13] In Figs. 1, 2, 3 and 5.

Plate II

Coins

1. Sidon, *c.* 370 B.C.   2. Sidon *c.* 380 B.C.   3. Sidon *c.* 360 B.C.

4. Sidon *c.* 90 B.C.   5. Sidon *c.* 400 B.C.   6. Aradus, *c.* 350 B.C.

7 and 8. Histiaea, *c.* 300 B.C.   9. Rome (Hadrian)   10. Northumbria, *c.* 925 A.D.

11. Northumbria, *c.* 940 A.D.

After the submission of those cities to Alexander the Great in 333 B.C. the globe and crescent seems to have been exchanged for a cruciform standard similar to that shown in the left hand of the goddess Astarte in the coin of 87 B.C. depicted in Plate II, fig. 4. This cruciform standard was probably adopted by Alexander from the Athenians, the most prominent naval power of Greece, among whom it seems to have been an object of great significance[14]. On two great amphorae awarded to the victors in the Panathenaic games of 336-5 B.C., now in the British Museum, it is represented in a manner which can leave no doubt as to its symbolic importance. On one of them Athene holds in her hand a long cruciform staff, the head of which is expanded in ovoid form. On the other amphora the goddess has by her side a short column which is surmounted by a winged Victory (Nike) holding in her left hand a similar standard, and in her right the aphlaston of a galley. Unfortunately for our purpose, the Athenians did not represent ships upon their coinage, but similar standards are seen in the hand of the nymph Histiaea upon the coins of the Euboean town of that name, dated circa 313-265 B.C., two of which are represented in Plate II, figs. 7 and 8. Many other instances, too numerous to detail, will be found upon later Greek coins. In these the crosses are not all of the same design, and Prof. Babelon has collected examples of thirty-six forms, all more or less different, from the plain cross to a more elaborate form in which the head terminates in a ball and two small winged figures of Victory kneel at the ends of the arms. Some of these forms are decorated with narrow streamers; in many of them the cross-piece is not at right angles to the staff, but it is possible that this may be due to an attempt at perspective. One other instance deserves mention: the excavations on the site of the important city of Pergamum in Asia Minor, once the capital of the kingdom of Pergamus, and afterwards that of the Roman province of Asia, have brought to light the bas-reliefs which decorated the balustrade of the Portico of Athene Polias. On this bas-relief, which, in the opinion of M. Collignon[15], alludes to naval victories under Attalus (241-197 B.C.) or Eumenes II (197-159), the cruciform standard is twice represented in highly ornate forms terminating in pine cones at the head; in each case it is accompanied with the aphlasta and beaks of galleys.

A careful study of all the examples leads to the conclusion that this globe and crescent, or cruciform, standard was the symbol of naval authority, the prototype in fact of the Admiral's flag. The name of this standard is not specifically stated, but there can be no doubt that it is the *semeion* (σημεῖον) frequently referred to by Greek authors in describing naval actions. That the *semeion* was a solid object we know from the fact that it was raised aloft in giving signals[16]. There is evidence that *semeia* were of various forms and that these forms were distinctive of the na-

[14] For a more detailed discussion of these standards see papers by Dr Assmann and Mr Hill in the *Zeitschrift für Numismatik*, vol. xxv, and by Prof. E. Babelon in the *Revue Numismatique* for 1907. Prof. Babelon holds that this cruciform staff is the object which the Greeks called στυλις, a word whose meaning has never been satisfactorily determined, and that its primary object was to support the "aphlaston." The other writers do not concur. His theory that the boards which formed the aphlaston were movable and, supported by the "stylis," served to aid the navigation of the ship will not, I think, command many adherents.

[15] Pontremoli et Collignon: *Pergame, Restauration et description des Monuments de l'Acropole*, Paris, 1900.

[16] See the instances quoted in the chapter on signals, p. 142.

tionality of the ship. Of Artemisia, queen of Halicarnassus, who accompanied Xerxes in his expedition against Greece and fought on the Persian side at the Battle of Salamis (480 B.C.), Polyaenus, in his *Strategemata*, relates that she had two *semeia*, one of "barbarian" form, the other Greek. When she was pursuing a Greek ship she raised aloft the barbarian standard[17], but when fleeing before a Greek ship she raised the Greek standard, so that her pursuer took her ship for Greek and kept off from it. The "barbarian" standard used by Artemisia was probably the globe and crescent above referred to, for Sidon supplied Xerxes with the best of his ships, and it was in Sidonian ships that Xerxes himself was wont to embark[18]. It seems, on the other hand, probable that a cruciform standard was in common use by all the Greek states at an early period, for Polyaenus relates that Chabrias, the Athenian general, just before his action off Naxos in 376 with the Lacedaemonian fleet under Pollis, ordered his subordinate commanders to remove the *semeia* from their ships and to keep in mind, in the ensuing conflict, that all ships bearing such signs were enemies[19].

The flag was evidently unknown to the early Greeks; it is never mentioned by Homer, and indeed there is no equivalent word in the language of the classical period, yet at the time when we first meet with the standard on the Phoenician coins flags were in common use by the Chinese. The Chinese classics on the art of war known as the Sun Tzu and Wu Tzu, written in the fifth century B.C., make frequent reference to them. They played a very important part in marshalling the army and inspiriting the soldiers, and the correct moment to strike the enemy was judged by the disorder of their flags. According to Wu, the Chinese flags contained various animal emblems.

The origin of the flag in European waters may however be dated from the end of the fifth century B.C., when a primitive form was, if later writers[20] are a safe guide, in use in the Athenian navy. This was the "purple garment" or "Phoinikis[21]," used as a signal for combat or as the sign of the Admiral's ship. Possibly the use of this emblem may have been imitated from the Phoenicians. It may, on the other hand, have originated independently, from a necessity of rendering the cruciform standard more conspicuous in action. There is not sufficient evidence to decide this point, but it is significant that the *vexillum* in use among the Romans at a somewhat later date shows traces of a similar origin.

The military standard or *signum* of the Romans consisted of a lance with silver-plated shaft with a cross-piece at the top, from which in some instances a small vexillum was suspended. From the ends of this cross-piece, whether it held a vexillum or not, hung ribbons with silver ivy leaves at the ends. Below were a number

---

[17] τὸ βαρβαρικὸν ἀνέτεινε σημεῖον. *Strategemata*, VIII, 53 (iii). Polyaenus flourished circa 150 A.D. and was therefore writing long after the event he relates, but he appears to have had access to earlier authors whose works have now perished.

[18] Herodotus, VII, 100, 128.

[19] *Strategemata*, III, 11 (xi).

[20] E.g. Diodorus Siculi, XIII, 46, 77; Polyaenus, I, 48 (ii); Polybius, II, 66 (ii).

[21] Φοινικις said to be derived from Φοίνιξ dark red or purple. Φοίνιξ which also denotes a Phoenician is of doubtful etymology and may have been derived from the name of the date palm.

of discs, which are believed to represent the honours conferred upon the Legion to which the *signum* belonged[22]. Below these again was a crescent, as a charm against ill-fortune. In the *signa* of the Praetorian guard the discs were replaced by crowns alternating with medallion portraits of the imperial house. These *signa* were used as company ensigns to facilitate the tactical movements of the Legion. The principal standard of the Legion, answering to the Regimental Colours, was the *aquila* or eagle. Pliny the Elder[23] informs us that

> Caius Marius in his second consulship (B.C. 103) assigned the eagle exclusively to the Roman Legions. Before that period it had only held the first rank, there being four others as well, the wolf, the minotaur, the horse and the wild boar, each of which preceded a single division. Some few years before his time it had begun to be the custom to carry the eagle only into battle, the other standards being left behind in camp. Marius however abolished the rest of them entirely.

The *vexillum* consisted of a square piece of material, usually red or purple but sometimes white or blue, hung by the top edge (or sometimes its two top corners only) from a cross-piece at the head of a lance and heavily fringed along its bottom edge. The peculiar method of attachment at the corners, which caused it to hang in heavy folds instead of straight down, would seem to indicate an origin similar to that of the Greek "Phoinikis." This was the standard appropriated to the cavalry and to the special detachments of infantry, and it is said to be the oldest of the Roman military standards. It hung before the General's tent and was used in giving the signal to prepare for battle[24]. From its use in this connection it naturally became the sign of a commander of a fleet of ships[25] and was used in giving the signal for fleet actions.

Flavius Vegetius[26], writing at the close of the fourth century A.D., distinguishes six kinds of military insignia, viz.: aquila, draco, vexillum, flammula, tufa and pinna. The *Draco* or dragon had been borrowed from the Parthians after the death of Trajan. It took the form of a dragon fixed upon a lance with gaping jaws of silver. The body was of coloured silk, and when the wind blew down the open jaws the body was inflated. The *Flammula* (little flame) was an elongated flag attached to the staff at the side, split throughout its length so as to form two narrow streamers. The *Tufa* seems, from the name, to have been some form of tuft[27] or helmet-crest,

---

[22] *Vide* Stuart Jones, *Companion to Roman History.*

[23] *Natural History*, Book x, 5 (4).

[24] Caesar, *B.G.* ii, 20: vexillum proponendum, quod erat insigne, quum ad arma concurri oporteret.

[25] Tacitus, *Hist.* v, 22: Namque praetoriam navem vexillo insignem, illic ducem rati, abripiunt.

[26] *De Re Militari*, iii, 5: "Muta signa sunt aquilae, dracones, vexilla, flammulae, tufae, pinnae. Quocunque enim haec ferri iusserit ductor, eo necesse est signum suum comitantes milites pergant." He is here using the word *signum* in the sense of signal, and divides these signals into *vocalia* or orders given by word of mouth, *semi-vocalia* or those given by trumpet, and *muta* or those denoted by the movement of the standards.

[27] Du Cange, *Glossarium*: Tufa genus vexilli apud Romanos ex confertis plumarum

but the exact form is not known. It is of interest as having been adopted in Britain under the name *Tuuf*[28]. *Pinnae* was the name given to the side wings of the soldiers' helmets, apparently formed of feathers. The precise form of the *pinna* standard is not known, but it is probable that the fan-shaped feather standards which are displayed at the coronation of the pope are a survival of this, or the preceding form.

Until the end of the Roman Empire the standard was used at sea only for signalling purposes or to mark the ship in which the leader was embarked. Thus in the action off Marseilles in b.c. 49, in which Caesar's fleet under the command of Brutus engaged the Massilian fleet which was fighting on the side of Pompey, the ship in which Brutus was embarked was quickly recognised by the leader's standard, and narrowly escaped being rammed by two triremes from opposite sides[29].

There are frequent references to this standard in classical writers and it is often depicted in reliefs or on coins. From these it is clear that its position was on the starboard quarter of the ship, at the leader's right hand; it was raised there in going into action, and its removal was a sign of disaster or retreat. It would seem that it was also removed if the fleet was about to be engaged by superior forces, presumably in order that the enemy might not concentrate against the leader's ship. Thus in b.c. 36 Octavian, when expecting an attack at sea by Pompey, embarked in a liburnian and sailed round the fleet exhorting his men to have courage. When he had done this he lowered his standard "as is the custom in times of very great danger[30]."

Pompey, whose success at sea had already induced him to exchange the customary purple cloak of the Roman commander for a dark blue one, "as the adopted son of Neptune," inflicted on Octavian the defeat that the latter had anticipated, but was shortly afterwards himself defeated at Naulochus by Agrippa, whom Octavian, a few years later, after the battle of Actium, honoured with a special dark blue flag[31] as a symbol of his naval superiority. From the account given by Appian of the action off Naulochus it is clear that there was no distinguishing flag in the private ships, as he expressly states that the only difference in the ships of Octavian and Pompey lay in the colours of the towers erected on them. From another passage in Appian[32] it appears that it was the rule for the inferior commander to lower his standard on approaching a superior. It is evident that these standards were not "national" in the sense that our modern flags are national.

It is difficult to understand why an invention so apparently simple as the laterally-attached flag should have been so late in making its appearance in Europe (except in the form of small ribbon-like streamers), but the fact remains that it globis.

[28] See p. 29.

[29] *De Bello Civili*, ii, 6: Conspirataeque naves triremes duae navem D. Brut quae ex insigni facile agnosci poterant, duabus ex partibus sese in eam incitaverant.

[30] Appian, v, 111: ἐπὶ δὲ τῇ παρακλήσει τὰ στρατηγικὰ σημεῖα, ὡς ἐν κινδύνῳ μάλιστα ὤν, ἀπέθετο.

[31] Dio, li, 21: σημείῳ κυανοειδεῖ ναυκρατητικῷ. Suetonius ii: caeruleo vexillo donavit.

[32] *Civil Wars*, v, 55.

is not until the close of the eighth century A.D. that we meet with evidence of its existence. About the year 800 Pope Leo III caused a mosaic to be placed on the apse of the Triclinium of the Lateran Palace, in which on the right Christ was represented as handing the keys of the Church to Pope Sylvester and a flag to Constantine, while on the left St Peter was handing a pallium to Leo and a similar flag to Charlemagne. Except for some fragments in the Vatican this mosaic has disappeared, but engravings showing it before and after restoration are to be found in a description of the Lateran published at Rome in 1625[33]. In these the flags are depicted as attached by one side to a staff, whilst the fly is cut into three pointed tails. The field in both flags is charged with six roses, but the reproduction made from early drawings by Benedict XIV in 1743, which is still in existence at Rome in the Tribune against the Santa Scala, shows the flag on the right, which is of a green colour, sprinkled with golden stars, not roses. In the year 800 Charlemagne was crowned emperor at Rome, and received from the Patriarch of Jerusalem the keys of that city together with a flag the form of which is not stated. Evidently these flags were symbols of authority, as we have seen the vexillum to have been centuries before.

There are several instances during the succeeding centuries of this ceremonial presentation of a flag by high ecclesiastical authorities to the leaders of expeditions whose aims received the approval of the Church, the most important, from our point of view, being the presentation made to William the Conqueror before his expedition to England. Beside these there appear to have been other flags in use which symbolised the patronage and protection of some especial saint, as for instance the vexillum of St Maurice borne in the Spanish campaigns of Charlemagne.

It seems probable that the laterally-attached form of flag had its origin in the East, for Ximenes de Rada, Archbishop of Toledo, who died in 1247, mentions this form as one of the special characteristics of the Arabs who overcame Roderic in 711 A.D. and conquered Spain[34].

It is true that, as will be seen in the next chapter, the Danes were using this form in the ninth century, but it is more probable that they had adopted it from the Franks than that they had invented it; certainly the only standards of the Germanic tribes known to the Romans were animal emblems, which were kept in the sacred groves until required in battle[35].

The form of flag that first comes into evidence in the Lateran mosaic, that in which the flag is attached laterally to the staff while the fly is cut into three pointed tails, appears again upon two Carlovingian book-covers of carved ivory, one of the ninth and one of the tenth century, now preserved in South Kensington Museum. Neither of these bears any device upon it, but in another book-cover of the twelfth century in the same collection a small cross saltire appears in the body of the flag, and the tails are proportionately of much greater length. This form, to which the term "gonfanon" became applied, was the principal form in use until the twelfth

---

[33] Alemannus, *De Lateranensibus parietinis*.

[34] *De Rebus Hispaniae*, III, 18: Arabum ... qui sua capita tegunt vittis, ... habentes vestis diversis coloribus variegatas, tenentes gladios et ballistas, et vexilla in altum tensa.

[35] *Germania*, VII: effigiesque et signa quaedam detracta lucis in praelium ferunt.

century, when it began to be replaced by the rectangular banner, which offered a more suitable field for the display of the personal devices that afterwards developed into heraldic charges.

The most important historical monument that has survived to illustrate the use of the gonfanon is the celebrated piece of embroidery known as the Bayeux Tapestry. We need not here enter into the controversy that has so long raged over the question of the exact date to be assigned to this unique work. The weight of evidence inclines strongly toward a date within the last two decades of the eleventh century, but if we admit a date as late as 1150 A.D. it will not materially affect the conclusions we shall draw. In addition to five rather rudimentary forms at the mastheads of the ships, twenty-five gonfanons in all are depicted, two with five tails, one with four, and the remainder with three. Only a small proportion of the hundreds of armed men who appear in the various scenes of military activity portrayed bear gonfanons on their spears. These are the greater leaders—the barons, as the Normans called them. The variation in the number of tails is probably merely an incidental caprice of the designer or embroiderers, but there is one gonfanon which greatly exceeds the rest in size and in the length of its tails, which in this case alone are shown of such length as to curl in the wind[36]. It appears in the representation of that crucial moment in the battle at which the Normans, taken with a sudden panic, and believing that their Duke had fallen, were about to quit the fight, when William, lifting his helmet from his face, turned towards them and called out that he was still alive and by God's help would yet conquer. At the same time, a companion figure, which from the mutilated superscription in the tapestry appears to be Eustace of Boulogne, lifts this gonfanon high in the air with his left hand while with the right he points to the Duke's face; a significant action, calling attention in a twofold manner to William's presence. This gonfanon is probably the one consecrated and sent by Pope Alexander; the principal flag of the Norman army on the day of battle[37]. It cannot be supposed that the most elaborate flag in the whole tapestry is merely the personal gonfanon of Eustace, and indeed the assertion of M. Marignan that the device shown in this gonfanon represents the arms of the Counts of Boulogne has been sufficiently refuted by Dr Round[38]. As a matter of fact this device (which may be described as a cross formy between four roundels) was not an uncommon one at that period. It will be found upon the reverse of many of the coins of the Holy Roman Emperors from Charlemagne onwards and upon those of some of the English monarchs before the Conquest. On the other hand, the gonfanons which appear in earlier scenes in the tapestry either

[36] See Plate I, fig. 3.

[37] "There in the midst of all, the guiding star of the whole army, floated the consecrated banner, the gift of Rome and of Hildebrand.... There rode the chief of all, the immediate leader of that choicest and central division, the mighty Duke himself." Freeman, *Norman Conquest*, 2nd edition, III, 463. It is true that (p. 465) Freeman says "I cannot see the banner in the tapestry," but if he was looking for a "banner" he certainly would not find one at this early date, and Wace (v, 11451) expressly says that it was a "gonfanon": "L'Apostoile...un gonfanon li enveia." Freeman supposes (p. 768) that at this point Eustace is giving advice to which William will not listen, but surely this is a misconception of a striking incident spiritedly portrayed by the designer.

[38] "The Bayeux Tapestry" in *Monthly Review*, Dec. 1904.

in William's hand or in the hand of the gonfanoner in attendance on him, display only a plain Greek cross. It is therefore not unreasonable to assume that this particular device was associated with sovereign power and would consequently be suitable for a banner that was intended to be an outward sign of the Pope's claim to transfer the sovereignty of England from Harold to William. Moreover, according to Wace, William formally adopted the consecrated gonfanon as his own before the battle:

> Li Dus apela un servant
> Son gonfanon fist traire avant
> Ke li Pape li enveia,
> E cil le trait, cil le despleia:
> Li Dus le prist, suz le dreça
> Raol de Conches apela
> Portez dist-il mon gonfanon

> The Duke called a servant
> Caused his gonfanon to be brought forward
> Which the Pope sent him
> And the man brought it, he unfolded it
> The Duke took it, raised it erect
> Called to him Raol de Conches
> Bear, said he, my gonfanon.

Roman de Rou, v, 12713-9.

Thus it appears that William's original gonfanon was not borne in the battle, but was replaced by the consecrated flag, which would thereby become the rallying point for the army and the special sign of the Duke's location in the field.

Raol, who was the hereditary gonfanoner of the Duke of Normandy, asked permission to decline the honour of bearing the consecrated flag on the ground that he wished to take part in the fighting, as did Gautier Giffard, to whom it was subsequently offered, and it was finally handed to Toustain.

Before we deal with the remaining flags we must first examine the square object shown at the masthead of William's ship the 'Mora.' This has been commonly supposed to be the "consecrated banner" in question, but, as pointed out by Freeman[39], it is really a great lantern. The Norman army embarked at St Valery in the estuary of the Somme late in the afternoon of the 27th Sept., and before William had got on board the 'Mora' the sun had set. As he did not wish the fleet to make the English coast before daybreak, he gave orders that on reaching the open sea the ships were to anchor near him until he gave a signal by lighting the lantern at the masthead and sounding the trumpet, when they were to follow him across[40]. The object above the lantern, which resembles a cross, may be intended to repre-

[39] *Op. cit.* p. 400: "the lantern on the Duke's mast is shown plainly in the Tapestry."

[40] William of Poitiers (his chaplain) says: "Verum ne prius luce littus, quo intendunt, attingentes, iniqua et minus nota statione periclitentur; dat praeconis voce edictum, ut cum in altum sint deductae, paululum noctis conquiescant non longe a sua rates cunctae in anchoris fluitantes, donec in ejus mali summo lampade conspecta, extemplo buccinae clangorem cursus accipiant signum."

sent the weather-vane spoken of by Wace:

> Une lanterne fist le Dus
> Metre en sa nef el mast de sus
> Ke les altres nès le veissent
> Et empres li lor cors tenissent
> Une wire-wire dorée
> Out de cuivre en somet levée.

> The Duke caused a lantern
> To be placed in his ship at the masthead
> So that the other ships might see it
> And hold their course near him.
> A gilded weather-vane
> Of copper it had raised on top.

Roman de Rou, v, 11592-7.

The remaining flag of the Norman army is an enigma. In form, the segment of a circle fringed along the circumference, it contains a representation of a bird with closed wings and outstretched claws, placed with its back to the staff, so that when the spear is held inclined forward, as in the Tapestry, it appears to be standing on the ground. The suggestion of Meyrick that this represents an ancestral flag of the men of the Cotentin, the descendants of the Danes of Harold Blaatand, is more ingenious than satisfying, for the Danish raven was never depicted in this tame position. Its attitude resembles that of the hawks seen perched on Guy's hand in the two early scenes in which he leads Harold to William, and indeed in the lower border, which throughout the tapestry contains frequent allusions to the events depicted above it, there appears immediately below this flag a hawk chasing a rabbit. From its unusual—not to say unique—form it would seem to belong to a people of different race from that of the bulk of the army, and the only body of men present in William's army fulfilling this condition were the Celts of Brittany, whose leader Alan had command of the third division of the army, and whose flag therefore must have been one of the most important of those in the field.

On the English side, the most important object is the Dragon Standard (Plate I, fig. 2) which is symbolically shown in two positions: upright in the hand of the standard-bearer, and fallen to the ground with its bearer lying dead across its staff. Immediately behind it Harold himself is likewise represented twice, first upright and drawing the arrow from his eye, and then prone, receiving his final wound. A little before this, in the scene which portrays the death of Harold's brothers Gyrth and Leofwine, there lies on the ground a triangular flag, with fringed tails hanging from the lower edge, a form similar to that found on the tenth century Northumbrian coins[41]. This is the only flag which, like the standard, is lying on the ground; its overthrow must therefore have had a great symbolic importance in the mind of the designer of the tapestry, and the only flag that we know of which would fulfil this condition is that one against which the brothers took their stand (see p. 31). This was the flag upon which the figure of a fighting man was worked

---

[41] See Plate II, fig. 10 and p. 30.

in gold, and although the tapestry does not show this figure (probably because there is not room for it), there can be little doubt that the representation of that flag is intended.

> L'estendart unt à terre mis
> E li Reis Heraut unt occis
> E li meillor de ses amis;
> Li gonfanon à or unt pris.

> They have overthrown the standard
> And slain King Harold
> And the best of his friends;
> They have taken the gold-worked gonfanon.

Roman de Rou, v, 13956-9.

We have, in the preceding pages, traced the development of the flag up to the closing years of the eleventh century without finding any evidence of the existence of a national flag, that is, of a flag flown, not to denote the presence of some particular leader at sea or on the field of battle, or that some especial religious sanction or blessing had been conferred or expected, but to indicate that the ship, town or other strong place upon which it was placed owned allegiance to some particular state or sovereign authority: a flag that might, on suitable occasion, be flown by any subjects of that state, not as their personal ensign but as a symbol of the collective body of which they were members.

While the Roman Empire stood at the height of its power, with the whole civilised world under its dominion, there was no need of any such device; and long after it had in fact passed away the theory of its nominal existence survived and hindered the development of any national consciousness. It is clear that this feeling must have been strong since we find it shared by such a man as Theodoric the Ostrogoth, who, although *de facto* ruler of Italy from 493 to his death in 526, professed his allegiance to the Eastern Empire and showed anxiety to get his position recognised by the Emperor at Constantinople. The history of the next five hundred years is that of a continuous succession of struggles for power and possession of territory between kings, nobles and ecclesiastics, and although the crowning of Charlemagne by the Pope in 800 was a formal repudiation by Rome of the authority of the Eastern Emperor there is no indication that the idea of nationality had yet arisen in the minds of men. The flag which Leo III presented to him was not in any way a national emblem; it was the symbol of his supreme authority and no more. In the ninth and tenth centuries there existed a certain number of religious flags of greater or less reputation for their wonder-working powers, of which the Oriflamme of Saint Denis may be taken as the type, but these were never national in the sense in which we have defined this word above.

The great movement known as the Crusades, which commenced at the end of the eleventh century, and after two hundred years of failure, relieved by a few transient successes, finally exhausted the enthusiasm of western Europe at the end of the thirteenth century, has been claimed as one of the main causes of the growth of national sentiment. In a sense this is no doubt correct, though it is equally true that its failure was primarily due to the national antagonisms of the peoples who took part in the expeditions to the Holy Land, and the partisan jealousies and individual self-seeking of their leaders. But there is no doubt as to the effect it had in widening the mental horizon of all the peoples of western Europe, and it is therefore not surprising to find indications of a development of flag design during the course of the struggle. Nevertheless, if we expect to find traces of any national or popular flags among the early crusaders we shall be disappointed. The kings, nobles, and military orders of the Temple and Hospital had each their own special banner, but the common people had none, and it was not until the year 1188, one hundred years after the first crusaders had entered Syria, that a means was provided for distinguishing the rank and file of different nationalities by a variation in the colour of the crosses upon their shoulders. From the beginning, the cross set upon the clothing of rich and poor alike had been the outward symbol of a common religion and, in theory, of a common aim among all who took part in the conflicts with the followers of Mahomet, but the flags which led the armies into action and crowned the towers of captured castles or the gates of towns were those of the individual leaders. Squabbles over the precedence of such flags were not infrequent. The well-known instance of Richard I and Philip of France at Messina in 1190 was perhaps the most important in its after effects, but it was by no means the first or last of such occurrences. In 1098 the Emir in command of one of the castles in the neighbourhood of Antioch, seeing that the Saracens had been dispersed, and fearful for the result if the Christians assaulted the castle, offered to surrender, and asked for a Christian flag, which he placed on the highest point of the walls. He took that nearest to hand, which happened to be that of Raymond of Toulouse. The followers of Bohemond were very angry at this, and in the end the Emir gave back Raymond's banner and erected that of Bohemond in its place. In August of the following year the Emir of Ascalon, frightened by the fall of Jerusalem, made a similar offer of surrender to Raymond and hoisted his flag over the gate of the city. Godfrey of Bouillon, who had just been elected ruler of Jerusalem, claimed possession for himself, whereupon the Emir sent back Raymond's flag and refused to surrender to either of them.

The placing of the flag of one of the crusading leaders upon castle or town was usually sufficient to protect that place from further assault, but it was not always respected. On the capture of Jerusalem in July, 1099, a remnant of the wretched inhabitants who had escaped torture and massacre at the hands of the Christians, had taken refuge on the roof of the mosque which occupied the site of Solomon's Temple. Tancred, moved by pity, wished to spare them, and he and Gaston de Bearn gave them their gonfanons as a protection. This served them for a few hours, but the Crusaders had not tasted enough blood, and early next morning, ignoring the protection thus formally granted, they shot them down with arrows or put them to the sword—men and women alike. Raymond and Tancred had in a like manner given protection to the defenders of the Tower of David, who received their flags "as a sign of protection and life." Raymond was more successful, perhaps because the Tower of David was not so easily entered, and he succeeded in getting the prisoners away safely, thereby giving rise to the scandalous imputation that he had neglected his duty and sold his protection for gold.

Our last instance of the use of the flag during this (the first) Crusade will concern its employment at sea. In May, 1102, Jaffa was being threatened by the Saracens, and Baldwin, then King of Jerusalem, was anxious to encourage the inhabitants to hold out. The Saracen forces prevented him from getting there by land; he therefore embarked at Arsuf in a buss, together with one Goderic, who is described by Albert of Aix as an English pirate. On approaching Jaffa the flag of Baldwin was fastened to a spear and raised high in the sun, so that the Christians in Jaffa, on seeing it, might be sure that Baldwin was still living. The Saracens also recognised it, and hastily collecting a force of twenty galleys and thirteen other craft, attempted to sink the buss. The king, however, got through in safety.

We have, unfortunately, no exact description of the various flags mentioned, for the contemporary writers do not condescend to give such details, though they occasionally allude to some characteristic feature. Thus the flag of Bohemond is stated to have been of a red colour (*rubicundum, sanguineum*) while that of Robert of Normandy was yellow (*aureum*). That of Baldwin is referred to several times as being white. On one occasion it was torn from his lance through being driven into the body of an Arab whom he slew. The flags[42] borne on lances in battle were evidently of gonfanon form, as there are several references to the tails flying in the faces or over the heads of the enemy, but it seems that there were also a number of larger flags, for several of the greater leaders, including Bishop Adhemar the Papal Legate, had a special flag-bearer (*vexillifer*). These were probably also of gonfanon form during the First Crusade, for the deep rectangular banner does not appear to have been introduced until the Second Crusade.

It seems that crosses were borne in some of the flags, but there is no mention of any personal device, though some flags are stated to have been resplendent with purple and precious stones. It is commonly supposed that the introduction to western Europe of the cross of St George (the red cross on white ground) dates from this first crusade, yet it does not appear at that time to have been associated with him. On the 28th June, 1098, the crusaders besieged in Antioch by Corbogha, finding themselves within measurable distance of destruction by famine, determined to risk all upon a pitched battle. In this forlorn hope they were completely successful. Unable to account for this by any earthly cause, they imagined that they had seen a great army on white horses, clothed in white and bearing white banners in their hands, issue from the neighbouring mountains and come to their assistance. The leaders of this ghostly army, recognised by their names written on their banners, were St George, St Demetrius, and St Mercurius[43]. If at this time the red cross had become the distinctive sign of St George one or other of these writers would surely have mentioned it, but all agree that the banners were white.

We may gather a few more details regarding the flags of the crusading period from some of the earlier *chansons de geste*. The gonfanon, the use of which was confined to the nobility, was fastened to the shaft of the spear before going into action

[42] The chroniclers adopt no technical terms for the flags, but use *vexillum* or *signum* indiscriminately, the former word being no longer restricted to hanging flags, and being occasionally used for a standard or even for a cross.

[43] Thus Albert of Aix; Tudebode substitutes Theodore for Mercurius, and Robert the Monk, Maurice.

by three or five nails[44], and it must have needed a strong fastening if it was to remain on the spear throughout the battle. Indeed, the poets give a realistic touch to their descriptions of the various combats by narrating how their heroes drove the cloth of the gonfanon into the body of the foe. As they sat upright upon their horses the tails of the gonfanon reached down to their hands or even to their feet.

> Dunc met sa main en sa vermeille chalce
> Si traist tut fors une enseigne de palie
> A treis clous d'or en sa lance la lacet
> Ot le braz destre brandist l'espié en haste
> Des i qu'as poinz les lengues d'or li'n batent.

> Then thrust his hand into his scarlet hose
> And drew forth an ensign of rich silk
> With three golden nails fastened it to his lance
> In his right hand brandished the spear with vigor
> Down to his fist the golden tongues beat down.

Guillaume d'Orange, v. 317.

The designs are simple in colour—red, white, yellow—and there is no mention of any charge upon them, though in one instance a red gonfanon is marked by a golden cross:

> L'espié trait en sa main au vermel gonfanon
> Une Crois i ot d'or.

Conquête de Jerusalem, v. 425.

The pennons were carried by knights; they appear to have been of similar colours to the gonfanons, but were much smaller.

> Tos chevaliers, n'i a cel n'ait penon.
> (All knights, there was not one but had a pennon.)

Ogier l'Ardenois, v. 4440.

We have already noticed that the name "Standard" appears first applied to a Saracen ensign. Further corroboration of this is supplied by the *Chanson d'Antioche* and *Le Conquête de Jerusalem*. In the latter poem the author (Richard the Pilgrim) has imagined a wonderful standard carried on an iron chariot and made of ivory and various precious woods, and of an enormous height:

> L. toises longes i puet on brachoier
> Onques nus homs de char ne vit si haut clochier.

The custom of marking the flag with some distinctive heraldic device appears to have been introduced about the middle of the twelfth century, for the seal of Philip of Flanders (A.D. 1161) shows the Flemish lion on his banner. During the Third Crusade, which followed upon the re-capture of Jerusalem by Saladin (October, 1187), the banner[45] of Richard I of England, which flew from the top of the

---

[44] *Ogier l'Ardenois, v.* 1744: A trois claus d'or son gonfanon lacié. *Ibid. v.* 9910: A cinq claus d'or.

[45] *Itin. Regis Ricardi:* regium cum leone vexillum.

"Standard" already described, contained a single lion, while that of his great rival, Philip Augustus of France, was blue powdered with gold fleurs-de-lis. The Knights of the Temple, who first come into view in 1128, adopted a banner half black and half white (drear and black to their foes but fair and favourable to their friends) to which they gave the name *bauçan*[46]. Their rivals, the Knights of the Hospital of St John in Jerusalem, who first enter into military activity in 1136, had a red banner with a white cross upon it. The representation in Plate I (fig. 5) is taken from an early manuscript of Matthew Paris and shows a Latin cross; the eight-pointed cross[47], associated with this order, was rarely used except on the vestments of the order, though it occasionally appears on the banner of the commander-in-chief.

Mention has already been made of the consecrated flags which it was customary for the Pope to present to the leaders of expeditions which had the approbation of the Church. The flag entrusted to the Bishop of Puy, the Papal Legate present at the First Crusade, was of this nature. It is referred to in 1098 as the *signum magni papae*. In 1104 when Paschal sent Bohemond into France to gather support for him against the Emperor, he entrusted him with another of these flags, to which the name *vexillum Sancti Petri* is applied. This change of name would appear to indicate a difference in the device on the flag. That difference was probably the introduction of the two Keys of St Peter beside the cross, a point of some interest to us as it might affect the question of the identity of the gonfanon on the Bayeux Tapestry already discussed, and incidentally the date of that work. We have, however, no certain knowledge of the presence of these keys before the year 1203. In March of that year Innocent III sent to Calojohannes, King of the Bulgars and Wends, one of these flags, together with a letter in which he explained its symbolism at some length. This flag contained a cross and the two keys symbolic of the powers entrusted to Peter according to the tradition of the Church[48]. From the tenor of this letter it may be inferred that the device was not a new one in 1203, so that this was no doubt the device upon the *vexillum S. Petri* met with during the Third Crusade in 1199 and 1201. An interesting instance of the use of a flag to convey authority occurs in 1216, when Rupen, nephew of Leo of Armenia, was formally seised of the lordship of Antioch by the patriarch of that city handing him a flag in the church of St Peter.

Thus far we are still without evidence of the existence of any flag that could be described as "national," and we shall therefore turn our attention to the birthplace of so much that was great in art and literature, the Italian city-states, and since we are primarily seeking evidence as to the early use of the flag at sea (though hitherto without much success) we shall turn first to the maritime states of Genoa and Pisa.

Of these two, Pisa was the first to rise as an important maritime city, and in 980 she was supplying vessels to transport the troops of the Emperor Otho II. By the

[46] Plate I, fig. 4. Vexillum balzanum, so named from "balzan," a piebald horse; the word was subsequently corrupted to "beauseant."

[47] Known as the Maltese Cross—Malta having been handed over to the Knights after their ejection from Rhodes by the Turks in 1522.

[48] Baluzius, *Epistolarum Innocentii III Pontificis lib. undecim.* 1682: Praetendit autem non sine mysterio crucem et claves; quia beatus Petrus Apostolus et crucem in Christo sustinuit et claves a Christo suscepit. Repraesentat itaque signum crucis, etc.

end of the eleventh century a system of government by Consuls had been firmly established, and the city can be looked upon as an independent state. Shortly after this (in 1114) the Pisans proceeded to capture the Balearic Isles from the Saracens. A contemporary metrical account[49] of this struggle gives an indication of the flags then in use in the following words:

> Tunc vexilla gerens Pisanae signifer urbis
> Valandus cuneos in campum ducit apertum.
> Hinc Ildebrandus sanctae vexilla Mariae
> Consul habens dextra saevos incurrit in hostes,
> Sedis Apostolicae vexillum detulit Atho.

Here we have evidence of at least three different flags in the Pisan host: the Standard-bearer of the city carries the communal flag, the nature of which is not indicated (in 1242 and 1350 it was a plain red flag); Hildebrand the Consul carries a flag[50] of the B. V. Mary; and Atho carries the papal flag[51], which had no doubt been presented by the Pope when sending his benediction to the expedition through the Archbishop of Pisa. These flags were fastened to spears (*hastis vexilla micabant*) which were used in the conflict without regard to the sanctity of the emblems borne on them:

> Tunc Ildebrandus consul dirum Niceronta
> Transfodiens ferro per pectus dirigit hastam
> Vexillumque trahit madefactum sanguine Mauri.

This matter-of-fact method of utilising the flag of the B. V. Mary by thrusting its staff through the breast of an enemy and withdrawing it stained with his blood does not accord with modern notions of the sanctity of the flag.

The first important step in the rise of Genoa occurred in 958, when Berengarius and Adalbert guaranteed its communal rights. Some thirty years after this the Cathedral was founded, and as it was dedicated to St Lawrence it is evident that at this early date St George had not yet become the patron saint of the city.

The original manuscript of the *Annales Genuenses*, which narrate (not without partisan bias) the principal events affecting the state and its relations with Pisa and other rivals during the twelfth and thirteenth centuries, was at one time in the Archives of Genoa, but it is now in the Bibliothèque Nationale at Paris. Commenced by Caffaro in 1154 on the basis of a diary of events, which he had kept since early youth, and continued from time to time by later writers under the instructions of the municipal authorities, it presents a contemporary record from the year 1099 to 1293, and, what is even more important for our purpose, it contains in its margin a number of illustrations in which flags appear both ashore and afloat.

Evidently, at some date after 958 the Genoese transferred their spiritual allegiance from St Lawrence to St George in much the same way that the Venetians

---

[49] Laurentius Veronensis, *De Bello majoricano*.

[50] The plural form *vexilla* seems to have been necessitated by the scansion of the verse.

[51] Michael de Vico in his *Breviarium Pisanae Historiae*, written in 1371, says this was red (*vexillum vermileum*) and that thereafter the Pisans always flew a red flag.

had transferred their allegiance from St Theodore to St Mark when the supposed relics of that saint were translated from Alexandria to Venice, or as the English, in the fourteenth century, replaced Edward the Confessor by St George, but it is not until the year 1198 that we meet with a distinct reference by name to the flag of St George as being that of the State. From that year onward it is frequently referred to in terms which leave no doubt that it had been the outward symbol of Genoese power from a much earlier period. Indeed, in an illustration, against the year 1113, of the castle of Porto Venere, then newly built by the Genoese, there flies above the castle a large three-tailed gonfanon bearing a cross that extends to the three sides and to the commencement of the tails. This is a pen-and-ink sketch, so that the colour of the cross is not shown, but there can be little doubt that this was a flag of St George. I say *a* flag of St George because, although the red cross on white was ultimately adopted as the State ensign, *the* State flag of St George in the thirteenth century was not a cross at all; it was an actual representation of St George himself on horseback in the familiar attitude of slaying the dragon with a spear. This is shown clearly in a coloured miniature which accompanies the events of 1227. In that year, at the commencement of the struggle between the papacy and the Emperor, the Genoese laid siege to Savona and the neighbouring town of Albizzola, which were attempting to withdraw from their allegiance to their great neighbour and to take sides with the Emperor Frederick. The artist depicts the siege operations against these two towns, and shows the principal citizens of Savona on their knees before the Podesta of Genoa in his tent, humbly offering their submission[52]. Before the tent floats a large red gonfanon, rectangular in form, and with four square-ended tails, having the above-mentioned device in a light yellow colour, and the word "vexillum" written under it to call attention to the fact that it was the State flag.

The record of the events in 1242 provides a typical example of the use of this flag of St George by the Genoese. Having heard on the 10th July that the Emperor Frederick had sent sixty galleys and two great ships under the command of Ansaldus de Mari to Pisa, and that the Pisans were themselves fitting out fifty-eight galleys and other vessels under Buscarius Pisanus, the Genoese immediately fitted out eighty-three galleys, with thirteen tarids[53] and four great ships, at Genoa. These were all painted white with red crosses in lieu of the sea-green colour in which they had hitherto been accustomed to paint their vessels[54]. Instructions were then sent throughout all the districts owning allegiance to the city that all men should prepare to embark, armed and supplied with victuals. The Podesta[55] then collected the people in the Square of St Lawrence, and after delivering an oration encouraging them for the coming conflict, he, amid general rejoicing, solemnly took possession of the state flag of St George, "to the honour of God and of Holy

[52] Reproduced in colour in the *Monumenta Germaniae Historica. Scriptores*, vol. 18. The MS. itself has also been reproduced in photographic facsimile.

[53] The tarid at this date was shorter and broader than the galley, and therefore able to carry a heavier burden, but it was on this account less mobile, and therefore defensive rather than offensive in action. These tarids were fitted out with fighting castles (*hediffitia* (aedificia) *mirabilia ad proelium*) to increase their defensive qualities.

[54] Depictae colore albo cum crucibus per totum, dimisso tunc glauco colore quo depingi solebant.

[55] Chief Magistrate or "President" of the Republic.

Church and the confusion of their enemies," and constituted himself Admiral of the fleet. His next step was to superintend the election of eight Protentini and ninety-six Comiti according to districts[56]. He then handed to each Protentinus, who became the Squadron Commander of one of the eight squadrons into which the fleet was divided, a splendidly worked flag embodying the device of his district (*vexillum unum juxta formam cuiuslibet compagnae mirabiliter designatum*) and to each Comitus two flags; one of the State device (*vexillum ad signum communis*), evidently the red cross of St George, which he was to place on the starboard quarter of his ship, and the other containing the lion of St Mark (*vexillum ad signum Venetorum Sancti Marchi*), which was to be placed on the port quarter. This is an extraordinary instance of the use of dual national flags in a fleet, and was the consequence of a treaty made between Genoa and Venice in 1238 whereby the two great rival sea powers agreed that their war vessels should bear the flags of both States as a token of amity and alliance between them. The Admiral's flag was then erected in one of the best galleys, and the Protentini (Squadron Commanders) and Comiti (Captains) proceeded to hoist theirs in the galleys and tarids assigned to them, which were then apportioned off to the various squadrons. No officers were appointed to the four great ships (*naves magnae*), which were evidently victualling and store ships, relying almost entirely upon sail power for propulsion and therefore of little use in fighting at that period. As there were 96 comiti and 96 fighting ships, it is clear that the galleys of the Admiral and of the eight Protentini had each three flags, the State flag and the district flags being probably placed in the bows. This appears to be the first recorded instance of the division of a fleet into squadrons by means of flags. The most striking detail of the interesting events in 1227 and 1242—one that has hitherto escaped attention—is the fact that in the Republic of Genoa, one of the earliest States to adopt a national flag, two forms of that flag existed side by side; one containing a representation of the patron saint (*vexillum Beati Georgii*) flown only in the presence of the chief of the State or the Commander-in-chief, the other containing merely the red cross emblematic of that saint, the general device of the community (*signum communis*), in other words the flag of the common people. Thus the supreme power and the common source of that power are represented distinctly, and in such a way as to indicate that fundamentally they were one and the same thing.

There are other instances in these Annals from which it is clear that the flag of St George was erected only in the galley of the Admiral. Indeed in 1282 it was expressly ordained by the *Sapientes Credentiae* (Council of XV) that no leader should have the title of Admiral, but only of Captain, unless he had at least ten galleys under his command, and that the flag of St George should not be borne at sea unless the fleet comprised ten or more galleys.

---

[56] The term "Protentinus" was adopted from the Normans then ruling in Sicily, who had acquired it from the Byzantines. As in Sicily, the Protentinus appears to have been primarily the chief magistrate of one of the districts (compagnae) into which the state territory was divided for administrative purposes, the "comitus" being one of his subordinate officers. Thus the fleet was organised on a territorial basis. The term "comitus" was afterwards applied to the officer occupying the position of boatswain in a galley, but it has not that meaning at this date.

On the farther side of Italy another great maritime power had sprung into existence at Venice. Owing to its remoteness from the lines of military communication and the protection of its surrounding lagoons, Venice enjoyed a comparative immunity from outside interference that enabled her to form a settled government at a much earlier date than had been possible at Genoa or Pisa, although the city was of much later origin. In such circumstances one might suppose that the Venetians would choose a national symbol at an early period, and that the famous Lion of St Mark was adopted for this purpose shortly after the translation of the relics of that saint to Venice in 828 A.D.[57] I have, however, not met with any reference to this celebrated flag earlier than the passage in which Villehardouin describes the attack of the Crusaders on Constantinople in July, 1203. As the fleet approached the walls of the city the aged and blind Doge Dandolo stood at the prow of his galley with the Gonfanon of St Mark displayed before him. When he landed the Gonfanon was carried before him,

> And when the Venetians saw the Gonfanon of St Mark on land and the galley of their leader which had been beached in front of them, then each man felt himself shamed, and all approached the land, and those in the huissiers (horse transports) leapt out and went on shore, and those in the great ships got into barges and got to the shore as quickly as each one could.

It will be noted that there was but one gonfanon of St Mark, that borne before the leader, although there were evidently many other flags, for in describing the preparation of the fleet for action a little earlier Villehardouin states that banners and gonfanons were erected on the castles of the ships, and that shields were placed along the sides[58].

Here we have evidently an arrangement of flags somewhat similar to that already described as prevailing in the Genoese fleet. The State flag is confided to the commander-in-chief, while other ships display the banners of the subordinate leaders.

But it is doubtful whether the idea of a national ensign originated in the maritime states. The first of the Italian cities to adopt a democratic form of government was Milan, where the people, under the leadership of their Archbishop, Aribert, successfully resisted the Emperor Conrad himself. In the course of the struggle, about the year 1038, Aribert introduced as a rallying point for his people in battle a movable standard, which is described by Arnulf as a lofty beam, like the mast of a ship, fixed on a strong wagon and bearing a golden apple at the summit, from which hung two white streamers (*pendentibus duobus candissimi veli limbis*). Midway on this pole was placed a crucifix, to which the eyes of the citizens might turn for comfort whatever the fortunes of the fight might be. This device was afterwards adopted by most of the city-states of Italy, and under the name of *carroccio* (chariot) will be met with frequently in their annals. In its later development an

---

[57] A medal of Doge Pietro Candiano, 887 A.D., has on the reverse a war vessel with a flag at the mast, too small to show any distinctive marks.

[58] LXVI: furent drecies les banieres et li gonfanon es chastiaus des nés, et les houces ostées des escuz et portendu li bort des nés.

altar was placed at the base of the mast, while the wagon, drawn by white oxen, was hung with scarlet cloth and the city flag floated at the masthead.

Among the cities that adopted this form of standard were Cremona, where it was named "Berta," Brescia, Bologna, Florence and Parma. In the case of Parma, where the standard was called "Blancardo," an interesting instance of its symbolic importance other than in battle is recorded. In 1303, when Ghiberto of Correggio obtained possession of that city, he got himself confirmed as "lord, defender, and protector of that city, and was invested by the resignation into his hands of the standard of the Virgin and the flag of the Carroccio[59]."

This investiture by flag, already illustrated in the case of Charlemagne and Rupen, is worthy of two further illustrations. In 1329 Padua recognised Alberto della Scala as its lord by presenting him with the flag of the people (*vexillum populi*) in public assembly, and in 1406 acknowledged its overthrow by Venice by presenting the same symbol to the Doge Steno. In this year also Verona acknowledged its defeat by surrendering to the Venetians its communal flag (a white cross on red ground) and its *vexillum populi* (a golden cross on azure field).

As a final example of the use of flags in the mediaeval Italian republics we may take the case of Florence. In October, 1250, in the course of a sanguinary struggle between the Guelphs and Ghibellines, the popular party (then Guelph)

> marched in military array to San Lorenzo, and there elected thirty leaders, annulled a portion of the functions of the Podestà, and appointed as guardian of the new government a captain of the people, Messer Uberto da Lucca, with whom were to be associated twelve elders (two for each division of the town) as councillors for him and advisers of the people.
>
> The captain was to be a foreigner; but the elders were to be Florentines.
>
> The fighting population was divided into twenty companies each with a standard of its own, and the force thus created was intended, under the leadership of the captain, to defend the liberties of the people within the town. Outside Florence the army was still to be commanded by the Podestà. The captain's standard showed a red cross on a white field: to this day the ensign of the town of Florence. The nobles and the powerful burghers (popolani) formed a separate force—that of the knights. Each sesto or division of the town had a separate ensign for its troop of cavalry, and these banners, with many others, were given solemnly by the Podestà on every Whitsunday.
>
> The contado was also divided into companies under respective standards, and when called into the town, fell naturally into line with the city bands.

---

[59] Sismondi, *History of the Italian Republics in the Middle Ages*, ed. by Wm. Boulting, p. 252.

All these changes were intended to check the power of the Ghibellines, who soon came to be so hated by the majority of Florentines that a common banner even was felt as an intolerable evil, and the Guelph party adopted a red lily on a white field, leaving the white lily on a red field (the old arms of the commune) to the opposite faction[60].

Here again we have two national flags as at Genoa, but with a marked difference in the underlying meaning. One, the red flag with white lily, the ensign of the aristocratic classes: the other, the red cross, that of the common people.

From the facts set forth in the preceding pages (and they are supported by a number of less important details with which we shall not weary the readers' attention) it may be inferred that national flags came into being during the course of the twelfth century and had a twofold origin. In the case of the smaller states organised on a popular basis under continually changing Consuls or magistrates, they arose from the necessity of having some clearly recognisable rallying point in action that was not personal and therefore subject to frequent change. This was supplied either by a common devotion to a particular saint, as at Genoa and Venice, or by the adoption of one particular colour, as at Pisa, or in the solitary case of Rome, the greatest of all in wealth of historic memories, by the re-adoption of an ancient classic device, the S.P.Q.R. of the Senatus Populusque Romanus. In the larger states, which from their very size were at that period necessarily organised on a feudal basis, the banner of the sovereign lord became the national flag. This was what happened in France and (as will appear in the next chapter) also happened in England.

In this, the most memorable advance in the use of flags, it was the city-states of Italy that led the way; and it was the great development during the Crusades of the activity of the maritime states of Genoa, Venice and Pisa that spread the example throughout Europe.

By the end of the thirteenth century the maritime city-states of northern Europe, which had arisen to prominence in consequence of the development of their shipping under the influence of the Crusades, had begun to make regulations governing the use of their flags at sea. Thus the maritime laws of Hamburg, to which Pardessus[61] assigns a date prior to 1270, contained a provision to the effect that every burgher of that town should fly at sea a red flag[62], under penalty of three silver marks, unless the flag had been lowered in time of danger, and a like penalty was to be inflicted on any stranger who flew this flag, on plaint being made against him. A similar provision appears in the Maritime Law of Riga of the same date, with the difference that the flag is to bear a white cross, the colour of the field not being stated, though at a later date it is given as black. The Laws of Lubeck contain a like provision in 1299, the "Lubeschen Vloghel[63]" being presumably the flag, white and red in two horizontal bands, flown by that town until its absorption into

[60] Bella Duffy, *The Tuscan Republics,* pp. 78-80.
[61] *Collection de Lois Maritimes,* ii, 337.
[62] In the seventeenth century this red flag was charged with a white castle.
[63] Pardessus, ii, 411.

the German Empire.

Two years earlier, in 1297, appeared the first recorded provision for the bearing of an English flag at sea, and we may therefore, with the close of the thirteenth century, quit the wide field of research that we have been attempting to survey for a more detailed investigation of the history of British national flags.

CHAPTER II

EARLY ENGLISH, SCOTTISH, AND IRISH FLAGS

(I) ENGLAND

So far as may be judged from the scanty records that remain, the ancient inhabitants of these islands do not seem to have known the use of flags until the Romans made them acquainted with their military *signa*. Adopted by the Saxons either directly from the Romans before they left their homes on the continent or from the Britons whom they subdued, flags formed, from the seventh century onwards, an important part of the regalia. Speaking of Eadwin King of Northumbria, under date 628 A.D., the Venerable Bede says:

> his dignity was so great throughout his dominions that banners (vexilla) were not only borne before him in battle, but even in time of peace when he rode about his cities and towns or provinces the standard bearer was wont to go before him. And when he walked about the streets that sort of standard which the Romans call Tufa, and the English Tuuf, was borne before him[64].

A few years later, on the translation of the bones of King Oswald, the royal vexillum of purple and gold (*auro et purpura compositum*) was placed above the tomb, a practice that was followed through many centuries.

The Saxons of Wessex adopted as their principal war standard the dragon, which in various forms was destined to appear at many crucial moments in English history. At the battle of Burford in 752, according to Henry of Huntingdon, the Wessex standard was a golden dragon, while the Mercians used the vexillum[65].

The Danish vikings, who commenced their descents upon the southern coasts of England in the middle of the ninth century, had as their ensign a raven embroidered in a flag, which appears to have been used for divination. In the year 878 Hubba

> the brother of Hingwar and Halfdene, with 23 ships ... sailed to Devon, where with 1200 others he met with a miserable death, being slain before the castle of Cynuit[66]. There (the Christians[67])

---

[64] Beda, *Historia Ecclesiastica*, ii, 137. For *Tufa*, see *ante*, p. 11.

[65] *Historia Anglorum*: "Aciebus igitur dispositis, cum in directum tendentes appropinquarent, Edelhun praecedens West sexenses, regis insigne draconem scilicet aureum gerens, transforavit vexilliferum hostem."

[66] Probably Combwich, *vide* Major, *Early Wars of Wessex*, 1913.

[67] Under the Devon earldorman Odda, Alfred being then in hiding at Athelney.

gained a very large booty, and amongst other things the flag called Raven[68], for they say that the three sisters of Hingwar and Hubba, daughters of Lodobroch, wove that flag and got it ready in one day. They say moreover that in every battle wherever that flag went before them, if they were to gain the victory a live raven would appear flying in the middle of the flag, but if they were doomed to be defeated it would hang down motionless, and this often proved to be so[69].

From this description it is clear that the raven flag was attached by one side to a staff, instead of by the top to a crosspiece like the Roman vexillum. We meet with it next at the beginning of the eleventh century, when the Danish hordes again invaded England under Sweyn and Cnut and conquered it. The anonymous author of the *Encomium* of Queen Emma, the wife of Cnut, gives a description of the flag and attributes to it magical properties, in which he is good enough not to expect his readers to believe. He says:

For they had a flag of wondrous portent, which, though I may well believe this to be incredible to the reader, yet because it is true I will mention it in this truthful account. Of a truth, although it was woven of quite plain white silk and there was no image of any kind in it, yet in time of war there always appeared in it a raven, as though it were woven thereon, which when its own party was victorious appeared with open beak, shaking its wings and moving its legs, but when that party was defeated, very quiet and with its whole body hanging down (toto corpore demissus)[70].

Possibly this flag was triangular, for in the early years of the tenth century the viking kings of Northumbria introduced into the reverse of their coins a triangular flag affixed laterally to a staff[71]. The top edge of this was horizontal and the lower, which was inclined upward from the staff, was heavily fringed. In the field was a small cross, which had—possibly under the influence of a nominal christianity— replaced the raven, although that bird is found on the obverse of some of the later coins[72]. These coins are of especial interest to us as they contain the earliest representation of a flag of any of the northern nations. This triangular flag appears first in a coin of Sihtric, who, after being driven from Dublin by the Irish in 920, reigned at York and died about 927, and later in a coin of Regnald (King of Northumbria in 943) and upon coins of Anlaf (949-952)[73].

It is about this period that flags first become associated with particular saints.

[68] "Vexillum quod Reafun nominant." Cf. the *A. S. Chronicle*, "þær wæs se guðfana genumen þe hie Hraefn."

[69] Asser, *Life of King Alfred*.

[70] *Emmae Reginae Anglorum Encomium*, lib. II.

[71] Plate II, fig. 10.

[72] Plate II, fig. 11.

[73] Anlaf seems to have lived alternately in Ireland, Scotland, and Northumbria, and to have been King of Dublin in 945. On his final expulsion from Northumbria in 952 he returned to Ireland, and after the battle of Tara in 980 became a monk at Iona. See Todd, *War of the Gaedhil with the Gaill* (Rolls Series).

Among the treasures sent by Hugh the Great, Duke of the Franks, to King Æthelstan in 927 was a banner of St Maurice, which is said to have been of especial assistance to Charlemagne in his Spanish wars[74]. We do not know what form this banner took, presumably it was a representation of the saint, but it is of especial significance to us that this saint had been a soldier, for it enables us in some measure to understand why St George had such an extraordinary vogue a few centuries later.

At the battle of Assandune (1016) in which the English under Eadmund Ironside were defeated by the Danes under Sweyn and Cnut, the Raven was opposed to the Dragon and to another ensign described as a "Standard." This is the first occasion on which an English king appears in the field with two different "standards," and it is of interest to note that his place in battle was between them[75].

It is to be regretted that Henry of Huntingdon did not explain what this royal "Standard," for which he has no exact Latin equivalent, was like. He tells us that Harold also had a "Standard" (*signum regium quod vocatur Standard*) at the Battle of Hastings, and that a band of Norman knights bound themselves by oath to seize it: an effort in which they were successful, although many were slain. This Standard was apparently the "Dragon" seen in the Bayeux Tapestry in the hands of Harold's standard-bearer[76]. According to William of Malmesbury[77], Harold, who was fighting on foot, placed himself with his brothers near his *vexillum*, which was in the likeness of a man fighting, and was sumptuously adorned with gold and precious stones. After the battle William presented it to the Pope. Probably this fighting man was the emblem of the South-Saxons, for on the Sussex Downs above Wilmington—once the home of Earl Godwin, Harold's father—may be seen the outline of a gigantic figure armed with a staff or lance in either hand[78]. Evidently Harold's position was between the Dragon standard, and his personal ensign, a position similar to that occupied "according to custom" by Eadmund fifty years before.

Of these two the "signum regium," or principal "standard" appears to have been fixed in a central position or rallying point, while the other, the Dragon, was carried in the hands of a standard-bearer chosen for his personal strength and prowess. In September of the year 1191 when Richard was fighting in the Holy

[74] William of Malmesbury, *De Gestis Regum Anglorum*: "Vexillum Mauricii beatissimi martyris Thebae legionis principis, quo idem rex in bello Hispano quamlibet infestos et confertos inimicorum cuneos derumpere et in fugam solitus erat cogere."

[75] Henry of Huntingdon, *Historia Anglorum*: "Cum enim Dacos solito acrius pugnare videret (Edmund) loco regio relicto, quod erat ex more inter draconem et insigne quod vocatur 'Standard,' cucurrit terribilis in aciem primam."

[76] Plate I, fig. 2; see p. 16.

[77] *Gesta Regum Anglorum*: "Rex ipse pedes juxta vexillum stabat cum fratribus...vexillum illud post victoriam papae misit Willelmus, quod erat in hominis pugnantis figura, auro et lapidibus arte sumptuosa intextum."

[78] There is a smaller figure of a man in the act of striking with a club on the downs near Cerne Abbas in Dorset. Possibly both these figures are pre-Saxon. The horse, a favourite subject for treatment in this manner, is almost certainly pre-Saxon; yet it was adopted by the Saxons of Kent.

Land in company with the French under the Duke of Burgundy, and the crusading army was drawn up for battle, Richard fixed his standard in the midst of the forces and handed the Dragon to Peter des Preaux to carry, despite the claim of Robert Trussebut to bear it by hereditary right[79]. By this time the royal "standard" supported an heraldic banner that displayed the lion which Richard placed upon his first great seal and which on his return to England he multiplied by three; but why did a symbol so obviously pagan as the Dragon survive the Conquest and that greater attention to religion—or at any rate to its outward observance—that the Conquest had brought in its train? William of Normandy had conquered England beneath the aegis of the gonfanon with golden cross that the Pope had blessed for him, yet we hear no more of it. The battle of the Standard in 1138 was fought around a ship's mast bearing aloft the banners of St Peter, St John of Beverley and St Wilfred of Ripon. The very crusade in which Richard was engaged had been inaugurated with the solemn assumption of coloured crosses by the combatants at the hands of the Archbishop of Tyre, white for the English, red for the French, and green for the men of Flanders[80]. Yet the standard under which the English crusaders were led to the attack was none of these, but the same Dragon under which the Parthians had fought the Romans and the men of Wessex had beaten the men of Mercia. And the chronicler who records this fact was an eye-witness.

When, in the twenty-eighth year of his reign, Henry III was about to visit the Abbey at Westminster, which he was rebuilding,

> he commanded Edward FitzOdo to make a Dragon in the manner of a Standard or Ensign of red Samit, to be embroidered with gold, and his tongue to appear as though continually moving and his eyes of Saphires or other stones agreeable to him[81]

which was to be placed in the Abbey Church against the King's coming thither. What then was its religious significance?

But we must leave this question to the student of folklore[82]. Suffice it to say that the Dragon was borne in the English army at Lewes in 1216, at Creçy in 1346, and finally at Bosworth Field in 1485, whence, in company with two banners, one containing the image of St George and the other a Dun Cow, it was carried in state to St Paul's Cathedral. Under all the Tudor sovereigns the Dragon formed one of the supporters of the Royal Arms, it appeared on the streamers of the *Henri Grace à Dieu*, and to this day it supports the Arms of the City of London and gives a name to one of the Officers of Arms—Rouge Dragon.

Before we turn aside to retrace the steps by which St George became the patron saint of England and the red cross on white ground England's national flag, we must first briefly notice the other saintly banners with which, for a time, it contested the pre-eminence. Mention has already been made of the "Standard"

---

[79] Roger de Hoveden, *Chronica* "cum ... rex Angliae fixisset signum suum in medio, et tradisset draconem suum Petro de Pratellis ad portandum contra calumniam Roberti Trussebut, qui illum portare calumniatus fuit de jure praedecessorem suorum."

[80] See p. 35.

[81] Dart, *Westmonasterium*, 1742.

[82] See especially Elliot Smith, *The Evolution of the Dragon*, 1919.

from which the battle of 1138 took its name. This standard consisted of the mast of a ship fixed on a four-wheeled frame. At the top was placed a silver pyx containing a consecrated wafer, and beneath this were suspended the banners of St Peter (of York), St John (of Beverley), and St Wilfred (of Ripon). The entirely religious nature of this standard is no doubt due to the fact that the English levies had been gathered under the direction of Thurstan, the aged Archbishop of York[83].

The banner of St John of Beverley was again in evidence during the Scottish wars of Edward I, and during these same wars there appears for the first time the banner of another north of England saint, St Cuthbert of Durham. Both these banners were carried by ecclesiastics, who were paid by the king for their services. In addition to these, which seem to have been carried only in the Northern wars, there were in use, as appears from the Wardrobe Accounts for 1299-1300[84], five other banners: two of the Arms of England, one of the arms of St George, one of the arms of St Edmund, and one of the arms of St Edward.

A description of the banner of St Cuthbert has been preserved for us in a MS. of the sixteenth century[85]:

> There was also a Baner ... called Sanct Cuthbertes Baner which was five yards in length. All the pippes of it were of sylver to be sleaven on a long speire staffe, and on the overmost pype on the hight of yt was a ffyne lytle silver crosse, and a goodly Banner cloth perteyned to yt. And in the mydes of the banner cloth was all of white velvett, halfe a yerd squayre every way, and a faire crose of Read velvett over yt, and within ye said white velvett was ye holy Relique, ye Corporax that ye holy man Sancte Cuthbert did cover the chalyce withall when he sayd mess. And the Resydewe of ye Banner clothe was all of Read velvett, imbrodered all with grene sylke and goulde most sumtuousle.

The arms of England were at this period the three leopards (or lions): those of St George the well-known red cross. St Edmund's arms are believed to have been three golden crowns on a blue field[86], those of St Edward (Edward the Confessor) were, also on a blue field, a cross flory between five martlets, gold[87]. Some of Edward's coins show on the reverse a cross between four small birds that may be taken to be martlets, the heraldic swallow without feet or beak. These alone of all the saintly "arms" appear to have had any direct connection with the man with whose name they are associated.

Under Henry V there was added to these a banner emblematic of the Holy Trinity[88], which was carried at Agincourt. In addition to these we hear of a banner of St William, carried in the Earl of Surrey's army in the north in 1513.

---

[83] In this same battle the Scots were led under the Dragon standard. See p. 47.

[84] *Liber quotidianus Contrarotulationis Garderobae* 29 Edward I. This was printed by the Society of Antiquaries in 1787.

[85] *Rites of Durham* (Surtees Society), 1903.

[86] Plate I, fig. 7.

[87] Plate I, fig. 6.

[88] Plate I, fig. 12.

It will have been noticed that, with the exception of the two apostles, only one of these saints, St George, is of foreign extraction. How did it come to pass that this foreign saint completely eclipsed those who, in the literal sense of the word, were strictly national?

Few saints have been so universally honoured as St George, and yet there is not a saint in the calendar about whose life so little that is authentic is known. He was a soldier who attained the crown of martyrdom during the reign of Diocletian. That is the extent of our knowledge, and on this meagre foundation the wildest, the most incredible legends have been embroidered. Even the date of his death is not certain[89], yet from an early age he was one of the most popular of saints, especially in the East, where he was revered by Mahometan and Christian alike. And here it is to be noted that he is not the George of Cappadocia, the Arian Bishop of Alexandria who met with the death his acts had amply merited at the hands of the populace in the year 361, although so eminent an authority as Gibbon[90] has declared them one and the same.

The cult of St George spread from East to West. In the fifth century he was honoured in Gaul. The monastery at Thetford, founded in the reign of Canute, was dedicated to him[91], and the churches of St George at Fordington (now a part of Dorchester) and Southwark were founded before the Norman Conquest. But although his feast day (23rd April) had been included by the Venerable Bede in his *Martyrologium* it does not appear to have been generally observed in England till a later date. One of the payments in the Misae roll of 14 John (1213)[92] is dated as the day before the feast of St George, and this feast was included among the minor festivals by the Council at Oxford in 1222[93], yet it is not mentioned in the Constitutions of the Bishop of Worcester in 1240[94]. It is included in the list of saints' days drawn up by the Synod of Exeter in 1287, but it is not included in lists drawn up by Archbishops of Canterbury in 1332 and 1400, nor in one drawn up by the Bishop of Bath and Wells in 1342[95].

The explanation of this lies in the fact that St George was not a churchman's but a soldier's saint. It is to our crusading kings, Richard and Edward I, and to their followers that he owes a popularity that extends to numbers that do not reverence saints and would be hard put to it to name offhand half a dozen others.

St George became especially popular among the crusaders, and his miraculous intervention was believed to have decided victory in their favour on several occasions. The early sculptured tympanum over the south door of St George's Church at Fordington is supposed to represent the saint intervening in behalf of the Christians at the battle of Antioch in 1098. The same subject occurs in a mural

---

[89] It is usually taken as 303 but the Rev. Baring Gould in his *Lives of the Saints* shows good reason for believing the actual date to be 285.

[90] *Decline and Fall of the Roman Empire*, chap. XXIII.

[91] Baring Gould, *Curious Myths*, 1872.

[92] *Exchequer Accounts*, 349½.

[93] Bail, *Summa Conciliorum*.

[94] Wilkins, *Concilia Magnae Britanniae et Hiberniae*.

[95] *Ibid.*

painting in the church at Hardham in Sussex[96]. Both painting and sculpture are assigned to the twelfth century. In both instances the saint is on horseback and carries a lance; with the butt end he strikes down the foe. Near the head of the lance is a gonfanon the fly of which is split into long tails. No sign of the cross now remains in the painting, but in the sculpture it is plainly visible at the head of this gonfanon. As the earliest representation in England of St George's flag, this sculpture is of especial interest.

As already remarked in the previous chapter, the date at which the red cross on a white field first became associated with St George is not known. Jacobus de Voragine, the thirteenth century author of the *Legenda Aurea*, quotes an earlier history of Antioch as his authority for the statement that at the Siege of Jerusalem (1099) the Christians hesitated to ascend the scaling ladders until St George, clad in white armour marked with the red cross, appeared and beckoned them on.

The date at which St George's cross became accepted as the English national flag has also yet to be ascertained. It does not appear to have been used as such at the time of the Third Crusade. In January, 1188, when Henry II and his followers enrolled themselves in response to the preaching of William of Tyre, they received white crosses, while the French took red and the Flemings green ones[97]. At first sight it may seem that there is some error in this statement. We know that at a later period the English had adopted the red cross on white ground while the French made use of a white one on a blue ground. Cleirac[98], writing in 1661 and knowing of no other authority for the statement than Matthew Paris, attempted to solve this difficulty by "restoring" the text and interchanging "red" and "white," but this simple expedient is not allowed to the modern student. The statement occurs not only in Matthew Paris, who had probably taken it from the Abbot Benedict's *Gesta Regis Henrici Secundi*, but also in the works of John de Oxenedes, Bartholomew de Cotton, Roger de Wendover and Ralph de Diceto. It is not probable that so many contemporary, or nearly contemporary, writers would make or repeat such a statement if it were erroneous.

Time and circumstances have not permitted of an absolutely exhaustive examination of the public records, but after a lengthy search in all likely places the author has not been able to find any mention of the "arms" or flag of St George in English earlier than the year 1277. In the roll of accounts[99] relating to the Welsh

---

[96] Keyser, *Norman Tympana and Lintels*, 1904; *Sussex Archeological Collections*, xliv.

[97] Benedict Abbas, *Gesta Regis Henrici Secundi*: "Praedicti vero reges in susceptione crucis ad distinguendam gentem suam signum evidens providerunt. Nam rex Franciae et gens sua cruces rubeas susceperunt, et rex Angliae et gens sua cruces albas susceperunt, et comes Flandriae cum gente sua cruces virides suscepit."

[98] *Les Us et Coutumes de la Mer.*

[99] *Exchequer Accounts*, ³⁄₁₅. Rotulus forinsecus de guerra Walliae anno *regni regis Edwardi* quinto.

"Flind. D*ie* mart*is* in Festo S*an*c*ti* Laur*en*tii [*pro* tribus peci*is* de Buckeram et t*ri*bus peci*is* tel*ae* de Aylesham empt*is* *per* man*us* Admeti cissoris ad faciend*um* C Braceria et $\overset{xx}{xj}$ penuncella de Armis s*an*c*ti* Georgii et *pro* emendend*um* et sudend*um* eor*un*dem Braceri*um* et penuncell*orum*. ci s vi d. Item *pro* sex peci*is* tel*ae* de Aylesham empt*is* ad faciend*um* Braceria et penunc*ella* *pro* peditib*us* Regis *per* manus eiusdem A. xx s. It*em* *pro* cl uln*is* tel*ae* tinct*ae*

War of that year (the fifth of Edward I) occur payments to Admetus, the king's tailor, for the purchase of white and coloured cloth, buckram, etc., for the manufacture of pennoncels and bracers "of the arms of St George." In the original these entries have all been struck through, probably because they were accounted for elsewhere in some roll now perished. While this account only mentions three streamers of the king's arms, it includes the comparatively large number of 340 pennoncels of St George's arms. It is probable that banners of the king's arms and of the arms of St Edward and St Edmund were also in use, together with banners of the feudal lords taking the field, just as we find them in use twenty-three years later at the siege of Carlaverock[100], but it is evident from the entries above referred to that the arms of St George were in great, if not exclusive, demand for the smaller flags, which in some cases are expressly stated to be for the king's foot soldiers (*pro peditibus regis*).

We have, therefore, in determining the probable date of the introduction of St George's cross as an English national flag to take into account the following facts.

In the year 1188 the red cross was not a mark of English nationality, although it was certainly in use in the East and by the Genoese as a religious emblem associated with St George.

In 1213 the feast of St George was recognised by the Court officials and used in dating payments, but was not yet generally observed by the people.

In 1222 this feast was included among the minor festivals to be observed in the English Church, but its omission in later lists shows that it was not universally observed and that no special importance was attached to it.

The cross of St George is definitely referred to in 1277 in circumstances that leave no doubt that it was then in use in England as a national emblem.

We must now briefly recall the state of affairs in England during those ninety years. After Henry II assumed the cross in 1188 his quarrel with Philip of France and with his own son prevented him from proceeding to the Holy Land. Richard, who succeeded him in 1189, spent only six months of his ten years' reign in England. On his return in 1194 after his long absence at the Crusades and in captivity, he spent only two months in this country and then went to France, where the remainder of his life was spent. The whole of John's reign was spent in quarrels with his subjects. Henry III, throughout his long reign of fifty-six years, took up an attitude which was decidedly un-English. On the other hand, Edward I is generally recognised by historians as the first king of "English" nationality. At the date of his succession to the throne he was absent at the Crusades, and as the country was enjoying peace at the hands of those entrusted with the administration of the government he did not return to England until 1274. This peace was not broken until the attempt of Llewellyn to secure the absolute independence of Wales brought on the Welsh War of 1277.

---

emptis pro eodem c s. Item pro custura cxx penuncellorum de Armis sancti Georgii per manus eiusdem A. xxiij s] (*other similar entries for material for Bracers*) ... pro tribus Stemeris emptis ad fracandum intus arma Regis vij s. vj d.

[100] *Vide* Nicolas, *Siege of Carlaverock*.

Having all these circumstances in view, it seems on the whole probable that the cross of St George, although more or less familiar to the English, was first erected by Edward I into a national symbol for a people that, by the incorporation of the foreign elements introduced at the Norman Conquest (assisted by the loss of the greater part of the continental possessions of its kings) had at length become a homogeneous nation. From the entries in the roll above referred to and from similar entries in later rolls of Edward I it appears that the cross of St George was almost entirely confined to the pennoncels on the spears of the foot-soldiers and to the "bracers" which the archers bore on their left forearms. Why the bracer should be singled out for this distinction is not clear, but it will be remembered that little over a hundred years later the bracer of Chaucer's "Yeoman" was a conspicuous part of his dress.

> And in his hond he bar a mighty bowe
> *   *   *   *   *
>
> Upon his arme he bar a gay bracer
> And by his side a swerd and a bokeler[101].

We may suppose that the cross of St George, the simplest and most conspicuous of all the saintly devices, was chosen as the distinctive badge of all those not entitled to armorial bearings and not clothed in the livery of the feudal lords. Indeed, from the expression "for the King's footsoldiers" (*pro peditibus regis*), which occurs in more than one of the rolls, it would seem that the St George's cross was used instead of the royal arms for the soldiery raised directly by the king and not brought into the field under the banner of any of the nobles. It is not until the reign of Richard II that we meet with an order for the whole of the army to be ensigned with the St George's cross.

Among the greater banners that of St George was not as yet supreme; it was indeed only one of four, for when the Castle of Carlaverock was taken in the year 1300:

> Puis fist le roy porter amont
> Sa baniere et la Seint Eymont
> La Seint George et la Seint Edwart
> Et o celes par droit eswart
> La Segrave et la Herefort
> Et cele au Seignour de Clifford
> A ki li chasteaus fut donnes[102].

> Then the king caused his banner
> and that of St Edmund, St George,
> and St Edward to be displayed on
> high, and with them, by established
> right, those of Segrave and Hereford
> and that of the Lord of Clifford
> to whom the castle was entrusted.

---

[101] *Prologue to the Canterbury Tales,* II. 108 et seq.
[102] Nicolas, *Roll of Carlaverock.*

The first step towards the promotion of St George to a position of predominance seems to be due to Edward III, who in gratitude for his supposed help at the Battle of Creçy founded the Chapel of St George at Windsor in 1348. It is from this time that we may date the actual dethronement of Edward the Confessor from the position of "patron saint" of England and the definite substitution of St George in his place. This process was completed under Henry V after the Battle of Agincourt. A Convocation of the province of Canterbury held at St Paul's towards the end of 1415 raised the festival of St George to the position of a "double major feast" and ordered it to be observed throughout the province (which includes England and Wales south of Cheshire and Yorkshire) with as much solemnity as Christmas Day. The Archbishop[103], in his formal communication to the Bishop of London of the decision arrived at, refers to St George as being "as it were the patron and special protector" of the nation, "For by his intervention, as we unhesitatingly believe, not only is the armed force of the English people directed in time of war against hostile incursions, but by the help of such a patron the struggles of the unarmed clergy[104] in time of peace are frequently strengthened[105]."

When the Prayer Book was revised under Edward VI, the festival of St George was abolished, with many others. Under the influence of the Reformation the banners of his former rivals, St Edward and St Edmund, together with all other religious flags in public use, except that of St George, entirely disappeared, and their place was taken by banners containing the royal badges.

We have seen that the appearance of the red cross on the clothing of the soldiery can be traced back to the "bracer" of the archers of 1277. The Ordinances of War made by Richard II at Durham in 1385, when on his way to repel a threatened invasion from Scotland, required every man in the king's army to bear a large cross of St George on his clothing before and behind. Richard appears to have adopted this expedient from the Scots, though they were of course not the first people to make use of it. On the 1st of July in that year orders had been issued for the soldiers of the Scottish army to be marked with a white St Andrew's cross (see p. 45). At that date Richard was at Westminster; he left there about the 4th of July, was at Leicester on the 7th, and at York from the 17th to 22nd. On the 26th he had reached Durham; he remained there till the 28th, and arrived at Morpeth by the 31st. The ordinances which he issued at Durham must therefore be dated at the end of July[106], and as there is no evidence that the English were at this time

[103] Henry Chicheley.

[104] I.e. fighting against ghostly enemies.

[105] Wilkins, *Concilia*, iii, 375: "Hujus itaque dispositionis ex clementissima et benignissima Dei Salvatoris nostri misericordia procedentis consideratione, nationis Anglicanae plebs fidelis, etsi Deum in sanctis suis omnibus laudare ex debito teneatur, ipsum tamen, ut orbis affatus, ipsaque gratiae desuper concessae experientia, rerum cunctarum interpres optima, attestantur, in suo martyre gloriosissimo, beato Georgio, tanquam patrone et protectore dictae nationis speciali, summis tenentur attollere vocibus, laudibus personare praecipuis et specialibus honoribus venerari. Hujus namque, ut indubitanter credimus, interventu, nedum gentis Angligenae armata militia contra incursus hostiles bellorum tempore regitur, sed et pugna cleri militaris inermis in sacrae pacis otio sub tanti patroni suffragio celebriter roboratur."

[106] In the MS. they are dated xvii July, but this is apparently an error for xxvii.

in the habit of marking their coats with the red cross before and behind, we may reasonably infer that it was then done for the first time in direct imitation of the Scots. This provision is also found in the similar ordinances made by Henry V at Mantes in 1419, the only difference between them being that while under the older orders no prisoner was allowed to wear this cross, under the later ones prisoners in the custody of their captors might do so.

Ordinances of War made by King Richard II at Durham Ao 1385. Cott. MS. Nero D. vi, f. 89.

Item que chescun, de quel estat condicion on nacion qil soit, issint qil soit de nostre partie, porte un signe des armes de Seint George large devant et autre aderer, sur peril qe sil soit naufre ou mort en defaute dycel, cely qe le naufra ou tue, ne portera nul juesse pur li, et que nul enemy ne porte le dit signe de Seint George, coment qil soit prisoner ou autrement sur peyne destre mort[107].

Ordinances of War made by Henry V at Mawnt (Mantes, prob. July, 1419). *Lansdowne MS. 285.*

Also, that every man of what estate, condicion or nacion that he be, of oure partie, bere a band of Seint George suffisant large, upon the perile, if he be wounded or dede in the fawte thereof, he that hym wounded or sleeth shall bere no peyn for hym: and that none enemy bere the said signe of Seint George, but if he be prisoner & in the warde of his maister, upon peyn of deth therefore[108].

There is no record of the flags flown on English ships earlier than the thirteenth century, but there can be little doubt that in the eleventh and twelfth centuries they were of the rudimentary form (little more than wind vanes) depicted on the ships of the Bayeux Tapestry. The invention of the banner of arms about the middle of the thirteenth century provided a ready means of distinguishing the nationality, port of origin, or ownership of a ship at sea, and its use for that purpose is indicated in a number of seals of seaport towns which may be dated from the latter half of that century. Thus the seal of Lyme Regis (Plate III, fig. 1), incorporated in the reign of Edward I, shows in addition to the early type of gonfanon simply charged with a cross, displayed from the masthead, banners of arms on spears amidships, the arms being those of England and of Castile and Leon, the latter in compliment to Eleanor of Castile, Queen of Edward I. The seal of Sandwich (Plate III, fig. 4), somewhat earlier in design if not in actual date, shows in addition to a small pendant at the masthead, a banner on the forecastle and two banners on the aftercastle. The ship in the seal of Faversham (Plate III, fig. 5) displays a pendant at the masthead, the banner of St George on the forecastle, and a banner charged with three chevronels on the aftercastle, while the ship of Hastings (Plate III, fig. 6) displays the banner of the Cinque Ports (Plate I, fig. 13) at the bow and the banner of England on the aftercastle, in addition to a gonfanon at the masthead. From the closing years of this century onwards a number of documents have survived in the Public Records which give indications of the nature of the flags displayed at sea. Thus the accounts[109] of the ship sent from Yarmouth to fetch the "Maid of Nor-

[107] Twiss, *The Black Book of the Admiralty*, ɪ, 456.
[108] *Ibid.* ɪ, 464.
[109] *Exchequer Accounts*, 4/26.

way" in 1290 show that this ship was provided with banners of the Royal Arms and silken streamers, and in the year 1294 sum of 5s. 6d. was expended in the purchase of a streamer, and 20d. for a banner containing the figure of St George, for a galley building at York, while for one building at Southampton in the same year no less than 40s. (relatively a large sum) was expended in purchasing two streamers and twenty-five banners of the Royal Arms. The most interesting documents of that period are, however, first an ordinance made at Bruges on 8th March, 1297, between Edward I and the Count of Flanders[110] which provided that all ships of England, Bayonne and other places under the English crown going to Flanders should display a banner of the Royal Arms (*le signal des armes du Roy d'Engleterre*) and that the ships of Flanders should display the arms of the Count and be provided with letters patent sealed with the seal of their port of origin confirming their right to do so—probably the earliest instance of the existence of "ships' papers" upon record. The second document[111] is a long recital of disputes at sea between the mariners of England and Bayonne on the one side and the Normans on the other, during the years from 1292 to 1298. From this it appears that in a pitched battle which took place off the coast of Brittany the Normans had flown at the mastheads streamers of red sendal 30 yards long and 2 yards broad called "baucans," and "signifying death without quarter and mortal war in all parts where mariners are to be found."

When we enter upon the fourteenth century the sources of information become more ample and the flags show greater diversity of device. The ship in the seal of Dover of 1305 (Plate III, fig. 3) displays the banner of the Cinque Ports on the stern castle and a gonfanon at the masthead. The accounts of the king's armourer in 1322 contain entries of eighty penoncels for galleys with the royal arms in chief, a large number of banners of the arms of St Edmund (Plate I, fig. 7) and of the arms of St Edward (Plate I, fig. 6), standards of the royal arms, penoncels of St George for lances, and three banners of St George, but it is not clear whether any of the above, except the 80 penoncels, were for the king's ships. The material used, in addition to sendal, was worsted, sindon and cloth of Aylsham.

A roll of the expenses of John de Bukyngham, clerk of the great wardrobe, shows the following flags to have been manufactured under his directions for the king's ships in 1350:

> 2 penoncels of sindon, 7¼ yards long and 2 cloths wide, red with a white pale charged with 3 blue garters,
>
> 2 penoncels 3¼ yards long and 3 cloths wide, charged with a shield of the royal arms surrounded by a blue garter,
>
> 2 streamers for the "Jerusalem," one 32 yards long and 5 cloths wide with the royal arms in chief and striped red and white fly; the other 30 yards long, of red worsted, charged with white dragons, green lozenges and leopards' heads,

---

[110] Rymer, *Foedera*, II, 759 and Marsden, *Law and Custom of the Sea* (N.R.S.), I, 46.

[111] Printed in *Lettres des Rois, etc.* (Documents inédits sur l'histoire de France) I, 392, and in part by Mr Marsden (*op. cit.* I, 50). See also p. 163.

2 standards for the same ship, 8 yards square,

A streamer for the "Marye," 32 yards long with figure of St Mary in chief, and the royal arms quarterly in the fly,

A streamer for the "Edward" 33 yards long with an "E" in chief and the royal arms in the fly,

Streamers for the "John," "Edmund" and several other ships with figures of the saint appropriate to the name painted upon linen cloth in chief,

3 streamers 5, 10, and 30 yards long with the royal arms in chief and fly chequered green and white powdered with green and red roses,

A streamer 24 yards long and 4 cloths wide for the ship assigned to the King's Wardrobe, charged with the royal arms, with a black key in chief, and 6 standards for the same ship with a leopard at the head followed by a black key and the royal arms.

A few years later we have an indenture dated in the forty-third year of Edward III whereby John de Haytfeld, clerk of the armour and artillery of the king's ships, acknowledges the receipt from Thomas de Carleton, the king's armourer[112], of a number of flags of the following types:

Streamers with the royal arms in chief varying in length from 8 to 38 yards

Standards with the royal arms in chief varying in length from 7 to 12 yards

Banners of the royal arms

Banners of St George

A Gonfanon of council of red tartaryn worked with nine golden angels supporting a shield of the royal arms, each angel having on his head a chaplet of the Order of the Garter (*Un gonfanon de conseil de tartaryn rouge batuz od ix angelis dor tenantz un escu des armes du Roy eiant suz les testes chapeles de garetters des conflarie de saint Georg*e)

A gonfanon blue and white with a shield of the royal arms surrounded by a garter powdered with a golden fleurs de lis.

A similar indenture made with John of Sleaford, Clerk of the Privy Wardrobe, mentions 18 standards of worsted of the royal arms, and 234 standards of linen of the arms of St George with leopards of worsted in chief.

The flags of the fifteenth century were of similar type. A roll of the tenth year of Henry V[113], containing a long list of articles supplied for the royal ships, mentions the following flags:

[112] *Exchequer Accounts*, ³⁰⁄₁₆.
[113] *Exchequer Accounts*, ⁴⁹⁄₂₉.

For the "Trinity Royal"
> A banner of council of the royal arms and St George,
> Gittons of the Holy Trinity, St Mary, St Edward, royal arms,
> St George, the ostrich feather, and swan,
> Standards of St Mary, St George, the ostrich feather and royal arms.

For the "Holy Ghost"
> A streamer of the "Holy Ghost,"
> Gittons of the Holy Ghost, antelope, royal arms, swan and
> St Edward,
> Standards of the Holy Ghost, St George, antelope and swan.

For the "Gabriel"
> A streamer of St Katherine,
> A gitton of St Edward.

For the "Nicholas"
> A streamer of St Nicholas,
> Gittons of St Edward, royal arms and ostrich feather,
> Standards of St Edward and St George.

For the "Grace Dieu"
> A streamer of St Nicholas,
> A gitton of St Edward.

This exuberance of design persisted until the Reformation in England put the saints out of favour. While in the early years of Henry VIII the 'Henri Grace à Dieu' was provided with banners of England, England and Spain, Castile, Guienne, Wales, Cornwall, the pomegranate and rose, the rose of white and green, and St Edward streamers "with a dragon" 45 and 42 yards long, one with a lion 36 yards long, one with a greyhound 18 yards long and two "litell streamers with crosse of saint George" 15 and 12 yards in length respectively, and other ships had banners of St Peter, St Katherine, St Edward, St Anne, the dragon, greyhound, portcullis and red lion, towards the end of his reign the saintly flags had disappeared for ever, except for the red cross of St George, and the royal arms and royal badges alone remain. Thus the ship reproduced in the frontispiece from a plan of Calais harbour[114] made about the year 1545 displays, in addition to the huge streamer of St George, only the royal arms and the royal badges of the fleur-de-lis and crown, ostrich feather, portcullis and crown, and rose and crown.

The rolls of Anthony Anthony, prepared in the last year of Henry VIII, show streamers party green and white (the Tudor colours) with St George's cross in chief; banners of St George and of the Tudor colours in horizontal stripes, and a few banners of the royal arms, and of the fleur-de-lis badge.

The accounts for the year 1574, when ensigns appear for the first time among sea stores, give the following details as to their construction. There were twenty-four of them made "for her Ma[ts] newe shippes," the material being "bolonia sarcenett of diverse coulors." Staves were provided, one with a gilt and the others with steel heads, with a pair of tassels to each. The flags were provided with can-

[114] B. M. *Cott. Aug.* ɪ, ii, 57[b.]

vas sockets. For the banners red and blue say was provided, with buckram for the socket, and "mockadoe fringe." Streamers and banners were primed, painted and coloured in oil colours by Wm Herne, the queen's serjeant painter, and the streamers were of the following lengths:

> 84 feet long and 9 feet broad at the head
> 60 feet long and 7 feet broad at the head
> 54 feet long and 8 feet broad at the head
> 45 feet long and 6 feet broad at the head
> 36 feet long and 6 feet broad at the head

There were besides four banners of fine linen cloth, fringed, and quartered with the royal arms, each being 15 feet long and 13 feet 6 inches deep. "And more twoe banners of damask thone of crymson with a lyon of gold, thother of purple with affaulcon of silver fringed with silke."

When Drake and Hawkins set out for their last voyage in 1594 they were provided with

> 4 flags gilt with her Majesty's arms costing 60s. each
> 30 flags of St George costing 16s. and 8d. a piece
> 3 streamers with the Queen's badges in silver and gold that cost £8 each.
> 80 other streamers costing 25s. each, and
> 26 ensigns;

the total cost of these flags reaching the large amount (for those days) of £221.

Very little record remains of the flags flown by British merchant ships during this period. It has been already remarked that those going to Flanders at the end of the thirteenth century were ordered to fly the royal arms, and banners of these arms appear on the ships in the early seals of Lyme Regis, Hastings and Bristol. The fifteenth century seal of Yarmouth (Plate III, fig. 2) shows the banner of St George on the forecastle, a pendant with cross of St George in chief at the masthead, and a banner of the arms of Yarmouth[115] (closely resembling the Cinque Ports flag but with herrings' tails substituted for the dimidiated hulks) upon the stern castle. In the seal of Tenterden (Plate III, fig. 7) and of Rye, also of the fifteenth century, the banner of St George is prominent. It seems probable that from the fourteenth century onwards ships not belonging to the king or the nobility flew the flag of St George when they flew any flag at all. In ships belonging to the greater nobles the custom appears to have been to display a streamer of the owner's badges; thus the ships in the "Warwick Pageant[116]," drawn circa 1490, display streamers containing the badges of the bear and ragged staff with St George's cross in chief. Ships of lesser owners, belonging to an important seaport such as the Cinque Ports or Yarmouth, appear to have flown the recognised flag of that port in addition to a flag or streamer of St George.

By the end of the sixteenth century the use of the royal arms had become confined to the Admiral of the Fleet; the royal badges had nearly disappeared from the sea, though they are occasionally to be met with during the next century, and

[115] Plate I, fig. 14.
[116] *Cott. Julius* E. iv.

the flag of St George had taken the lead as the distinguishing characteristic of English ships, both men-of-war and merchantmen.

Plate III

Seals

1. Lyme Regis, 13th cent.

2. Yarmouth, 15th cent.

3. Dover, 1305

4. Sandwich, 13th cent.

5. Faversham, 13th cent.

6. Hastings, 13th cent.

7. Tenterden, 15th cent.

8. King's Lynn, late 16th cent.

(II) SCOTLAND

The history of the national flags of Scotland is much less complicated than that of the flags of England, for the northern nation had decided upon their patron saint at a much earlier date than their neighbours south of the Tweed. There was a similar struggle for supremacy among competing saints, but the issue was decided in the eighth century and appears to have remained unchallenged ever since. In the words of Wm Forbes Skene, the Scottish historian,

> With the departure of the Columban Clergy, the veneration of St Columba as the apostle of the northern Picts seems to have been given up, at least by the southern portion of that people, and St Peter now became the patron saint of the kingdom and continued to be so till the year 736, when Angus the son of Fergus established his power by the defeat of Nectan himself, and the other competitors for the throne. As the king rapidly brought the territories of the other Pictish families under his sway, and even added Dalriada to his kingdom, he seemed desirous to connect a new ecclesiastical influence with his reign, for in the same year that he completed the conquest of Dalriada he founded a church at St Andrews, in which he placed a new body of clergy, who had brought the relics of St Andrew with them, and this apostle soon became the more popular patron saint of the kingdom, while the previous patronage of St Peter disappeared from the annals[117].

It is probable that the cross-saltire was adopted by the Scots as a national ensign at a very early period, but there seems no direct evidence of this before the fourteenth century. The earliest Scottish records were unfortunately lost at sea in the ship that was sent to return them to that country, whence they had been carried off, with the Stone of Destiny, by Edward I.

In the summer of the year 1385 the Scots planned a raid into England, in which they were assisted by a considerable contingent of French. The Ordinances for the allied army drawn up by the Council for this occasion and promulgated on the 1st July contained the following proviso:

> Item every man French and Scots shall have a sign before and behind, namely a white St Andrew's Cross, and if his jack is white or his coat white he shall bear the said white cross in a piece of black cloth round or square[118].

It will be noted that the field on which the cross-saltire was to be placed was immaterial, but if the coat happened to be white the field was to be black. There is other evidence that the ground colour was not an essential part of the design,

---

[117] *Chronicles of the Picts, Chronicles of the Scots and other early Memorials of Scottish History* (Rolls Series), Preface, clix.

[118] *The Acts of the Parliaments of Scotland*, ɪ, 191: "Item que tout homme francois et escot ait un signe devant et derrere cest assauoir une croiz blanche saint andrieu et se son Jacque soit blanc ou sa cote blanche il portera la dicte croiz blanche en une piece de drap noir ronde ou quarree."

although the prevailing colour at a later date seems to have been blue. In the Accounts of the Lord High Treasurer of Scotland[119] for the year 1512 there is recorded a payment for a roll of blue say for the banner of a ship "with Sanct Androis cors in the myddis." In 1513 the ground colour was also blue. In 1523, however, when orders were again issued for each man to bear the white saltire before and behind, no ground was mentioned, while in 1540 and 1542 the ground colour of the ensigns was yellow and red (the Stuart livery colours) or red, as the following entries show:

1540

Item, the x day of Junii deliverit to Thomas Arthur to be iii anse3eis[120] to the schippis xvj elnis reid and 3allow taffites of cord, price of the elne xviij s.   Summa xiiij li. viij s.

Item, deliverit to him to be the croces thairof iiij elnes half elne quhyte taffites of Janis[121] price the elne xv s.

Summa iij li. vij s. vj d.[122]

1542

Item, the vij day of August, deliverit to Charles Murray to be and ansen3e, x elnis raid and 3allow taffitis of cord, price of the elne xviij s. and twa elnis quhite taffites of Janis to be croces thairto, price of the elne xiiij s.   Summa x li. viij s.[123]

There is a similar entry on the 12th for 8 ells red, and 2½ ells white for the cross.

Cleirac, in his *Explication des Termes de Marine, etc.*[124], gives for the Scotch flag a ground of red or blue, and also a ground of red, yellow and green, with the saltire in a canton or overall[125]. It is probable, however, that he was relying on obsolete information, for there seems no other evidence of a parti-coloured field so late as 1670[126], though a red ensign for ships, with white saltire in a blue canton[127], was in use until the Legislative Union of 1707.

It remains to say a few words about the royal banner, which may be considered in a sense national although it is the personal heraldic flag of the sovereign and ought not to be used by any subject. The rampant lion with a tressure fleur-

---

[119] *Accounts of the Lord High Treasurer of Scotland* (Rolls Series), edited by Sir Jas. B. Paul, III, 90.

[120] Ensigns.

[121] White taffety of Genoa (jean).

[122] *Op. cit.* VII, 189.

[123] *Ibid.* IX, iii.

[124] Rouen 1670, bound with his Les Us et Coutumes de la Mer.

[125] Escosse le Sauteur d'argent qui est la Croix des Chevaliers Saint Andre, au drap de gueles ou d'azur: portent aussi face de gueles d'or et de Synope qui est verd, le Sauteur au quanton ou sur le tout.

[126] The work appears, however, to have been written in 1634.

[127] Plate X, fig. 1.

de-lisé first appears in a seal of Alexander II appended to a Charter dated 1222[128]. Except for the period during which Mary Queen of Scots, after her marriage with the Dauphin, impaled the French Arms with her own it has remained unaltered, in the form in which we now see it quartered in the Royal Standard, since the thirteenth century.

The Raven and the Dragon Standards found their way into Scotland, but are not met with after the twelfth century. In the early years of the eleventh century Sigurd, Earl of Orkney, who afterwards carried the Raven standard against the Irish at Clontarf, was challenged by Finleic, Earl of the Scots, to battle at Skedmire.

> Sigrod sought his mother that she might divine unto him upon the matter, for she was a wise woman. The earl told her that the odds in number between his foeman and his own men would not be less than seven to one. She answered, "I would have brought thee up all thy life in my wool-basket, if I had known that thou wert bent upon living for ever; but 'tis Fate that settles a man's days whatever he is. It is better to die with honour than to live with shame. Now take this banner, which I have wrought for thee with all my skill! And I say, by my knowledge, that the victory shall be to them before whom it is borne, but deadly shall it be to them that bear it." The banner was made with much fine needle-work, and with exceeding art. It was wrought in the likeness of a raven, and when the wind blew upon the banner it was as if the raven flapped his wings in flight. Earl Sigrod was very angry at his mother's words; and gave the Orkneymen their ethel-holdings free to raise a levy for him; and went to Skedmire to meet Earl Finleic, and each of them set his host in array. And as soon as the battle was joined, Earl Sigrod's standard-bearer was shot to death. The Earl called upon another man to carry the standard, and he bore it for a short while and then fell also. Three of the Earl's standard-bearers fell indeed, but he won the victory[129].

The Dragon appeared as the Scottish Royal Standard at the Battle of the Standard (1138). According to the contemporary "Relatio de Standardo[130]," written by St Aelred, Abbot of Rielvaulx Abbey in Yorkshire, when the Scots broke and fled those in flight saw from the position of the royal standard, which was in the likeness of a dragon[131], that their king was not slain, and gathering themselves to him they renewed the fight. On this occasion the Scottish king's son made use of the following ruse. Finding himself cut off with a few companions, he told them to throw away the banners by which they were to be recognised from the English and then, mixing with the latter as though fighting on their side, they reached his father in safety.

Except for a short period during the reign of James IV (1473-1513) a Scots navy

---

[128] Dunbar, *Scottish Kings*, p. 89.
[129] *Orkney Saga*, xi.
[130] *Chronicles of the Reigns of Stephen, etc.* (Rolls Series), iii, 181.
[131] Regale vexillum, quod ad similitudinem draconis figuratam facile agnoscebatur.

was either non-existent or of little importance, and it is therefore not to be expected that any great development took place in its flags; nevertheless, from the Lord High Treasurer's accounts it appears that no less a sum than £72. 7s. 6d. was expended upon the "mayn standert" of the "Great Michael" in 1513. This flag appears to have had a St Andrew's cross on a blue ground at the head, and a fly of red and yellow on which the royal badges of the red lion and white unicorn appeared. Other flags of this period were the banners of St Andrew and St Margaret, and a banner and standards with the red lion upon a yellow field.

(III) IRELAND

In St Patrick the Irish possess a patron saint who is in the truest sense national. Although a native of Scotland, the best of his life and work was devoted to the people among whom in early youth the fortune of war placed him. He seems, moreover, never to have had a serious competitor for their favour[132], and they have been unwavering in their allegiance to him. Nevertheless, there is no ancient flag, and no symbol except the shamrock, associated with his name.

Flags do not seem to have been in use at a very early period among the celtic nations, and when we meet with them in Irish literature in the eleventh century the terms used for them are not native Irish words but had apparently been borrowed from the Danish invaders who wrought such havoc to the ancient Irish civilisation from the ninth to the eleventh centuries. The word used by the author of the *Cogadh Gaedhel re Gallaibh* is "mergi[133]," which is believed to be borrowed from the Scandinavian "merke" (mark), while the other word met with, "confingi," seems to be derived from the Norse "gunfana."

At the great battle of Clontarf fought in the year 1014 between the Irish under their king Brian Borumha and the Danish invaders of Ireland under the Earl Sigurd, assisted by the revolted king of Leinster, the Irish under Brian had many banners, but these banners were known by their colours rather than by any particular device in them.

> Brian looked out behind him and beheld the battle phalanx ...
> and three score and ten banners over them, of red, and of yellow,
> and of green, and of all kinds of colours; together with the ever-
> lasting, variegated, lucky, fortunate banner that had gained the
> victory in every battle and in every conflict, and in every combat
> ... namely the gold-spangled banner of Fergal Ua Ruairc[134].

These banners appear to have been personal to the chiefs and to have been taken down when they were slain, even if their forces still remained undefeated. During the conflict Brian, who on account of his age took no part in the battle and was engaged in prayer at a little distance, enquired repeatedly of his attendant whether the banner of his eldest son, Murchadh, still remained aloft. Towards the end he asked once more, and the attendant reported that it was far from Murchadh

[132] Except possibly in St Brigit and St Columcille.
[133] Elsewhere "meirge."
[134] *War of the Gaedhill with the Gaill (Cogadh Gaedhel re Gallaibh)*. Ed. with translation by J. H. Todd (Rolls Series), p. 156.

but still standing. Brian said "The men of Erinn shall be well while that banner remains standing because their courage and valour shall remain in them all, as long as they can see that banner." At length Murchadh was mortally wounded, and although the enemy were defeated his banner was taken down. When his father asked again, the attendant answered, "... the foreigners are now defeated and Murchadh's banner has fallen." "That is sad news," said Brian, "... the honour and valour of Erinn fell when that banner fell and Erinn has fallen now indeed."

It may be concluded from this narrative that the Irish of the eleventh century had no national flag common to the whole people. This, together with the fact that after the death of Brian no Irish king arose great enough to secure the allegiance of the whole nation, may explain why the Irish never developed a national flag as did the English and Scots.

The red saltire on white ground which represents Ireland in the Union flag had only an ephemeral existence as a separate flag. Originating as the arms of the powerful Geraldines, who from the time of Henry II held the predominant position among those whose presence in Ireland was due to the efforts of the English sovereigns to subjugate that country, it is not to be expected that the native Irish should ever have taken kindly to a badge that could only remind them of their servitude to a race with whom they had little in common, and the attempt to father this emblem upon St Patrick (who, it may be remarked, is not entitled to a cross—since he was not a martyr) has evoked no response from the Irish themselves.

The earliest evidence of the existence of the red saltire flag[135] known to the author occurs in a map of "Hirlandia" by John Goghe dated 1567 and now exhibited in the museum of the Public Record Office. The arms at the head of this map are the St George's cross impaled with the crowned harp, but the red saltire is prominent in the arms of the Earl of Kildare and the other Geraldine families placed over their respective spheres of influence. The red saltire flag is flown at the masthead of a ship, possibly an Irish pirate, which is engaged in action in the St George's Channel with another ship flying the St George's cross. The St George's flag flies upon Cornwall, Wales and Man, but the red saltire flag does not appear upon Ireland itself, though it is placed upon the adjacent Mulls of Galloway and Kintyre in Scotland. It is, however, to be found in the arms of Trinity College, Dublin (1591), in which the banners of St George and of this saltire surmount the turrets that flank the castle gateway.

The Graydon MS. Flag Book of 1686 which belonged to Pepys does not contain this flag, but gives as the flag of Ireland (which, it may be noted, appears as an afterthought right at the end of the book) the green flag with St George's cross and the harp, illustrated in Plate X, fig. 3. The saltire flag is nevertheless given as "Pavillon d'Ierne" in the flag plates at the commencement of the *Neptune François* of 1693, whence it was copied into later flag collections.

Under the Commonwealth and Protectorate, when England and Scotland were represented in the Great and other Seals by their crosses, Ireland was invariably represented by the harp, and in the Union flag of 1658, as will be seen

---

[135] Plate I, fig. 10.

later, it was the harp that was added to the English and Scottish crosses to form a flag representative of the three kingdoms. At the funeral of Cromwell the Great Standards of England and Scotland had the St George's and St Andrew's crosses in chief respectively, but the Great Standard of Ireland had in chief a red cross (not saltire) on a yellow field[136].

When the Order of St Patrick was instituted in 1783 the red saltire was taken for the badge of the Order, and since this emblem was of convenient form for introduction into the Union flag of England and Scotland it was chosen in forming the combined flag of England, Scotland and Ireland in 1801.

Ireland has been represented in the royal standard since 1603 by the golden harp on a blue field, but it would seem that this is not the original arms of that country, for the augmentation of arms granted by Richard II to his favourite Robert de Vere, Earl of Oxford, whom he created Duke of Ireland in 1386, was *azure, three crowns, or,* and these are said to have been confirmed as the true arms of Ireland by a commission of enquiry under Edward IV. The harp, which appears to have been an ancient badge of Ireland, was formally adopted as the arms of that country by Henry VIII in the year when he changed the royal style from "Dominus Hiberniae" to "Rex Hiberniae." The change in the colour of the field from blue to green, as is commonly seen in the flags of Irishmen in rebellion against English rule, is believed to have originated with Owen Roe O'Neill in 1642.

There is very little information as to the flags flown in Irish ships. From a date at least as early as the thirteenth century certain of the Irish ports were accustomed to supply ships for the king's service[137]. Such ships would have flown the English or Cinque Ports flag. There is indeed a mention in the State Papers of 1586[138] of an Irish ship attacking an English merchantman under the Scots flag, "showing forth a Skottish ensigne," and a passage in Dudley's voyage in 1594[139] from which it may be inferred that there was no recognised Irish flag at that date. In Feb. 1785, a brig from Dublin hoisted at Antigua a green ensign with the harp and crown in the centre, which was seized by Collingwood's orders, and later in the same year another ship from Belfast, flying a similar ensign, was detained until the master had gone ashore and bought proper colours for the vessel[140].

---

[136] Prestwich, *Respublica*.

[137] E.g. Nicholas quotes an example in 1233, when the inhabitants of Dublin were directed to prepare their new great galley for the king's service, and ships from Waterford, Dublin, Youghal, Ross and Drogheda were supplied for the Flanders expedition in 1304. Some, perhaps all, of these ports were affiliated to the Cinque Ports, as, for instance, Youghal, which became "one of the Petylymmes of the Cinque Ports in Ireland" in 1462. (*Cal. Pat. Rolls.*)

[138] *S. P. D. Eliz.* CLXXXVII, 13.

[139] See p. 201.

[140] It may be pointed out, however, that under the present Merchant Shipping Act the flying of such a flag, if it did not imitate the British or other national colours, would not be illegal, but the ship must show the red ensign when required under Art. 74 of that Act.

CHAPTER III
THE UNION FLAGS AND JACKS

In the preceding sketch of the early history of the British flags we have, so far as evidence is available, followed the steps by which the red cross on a white ground came to represent the people of England, and we have seen, though less clearly, how the white saltire on a blue ground became the chosen flag of the Scottish nation. It now remains to trace the process by which these two flags became united in one, and finally, by the addition of a red saltire to represent Ireland, developed into the present Union flag.

On the death of Queen Elizabeth in March, 1603, the succession to the crown lay open.

> There had been no repeal of the stipulation made by Henry VIII, both in Act of Parliament and in his will, that after the death without heirs of his three children, Edward, Mary and Elizabeth, the crown should descend to the heirs of his younger sister, Mary.... Consequently, the rightful heir when Elizabeth lay dying was no scion of the Scottish House, but the eldest representative of the Suffolk line—Princess Mary's great-grandson, Edward Seymour, Lord Beauchamp. But Elizabeth's ministers were not the slaves of legal niceties. The Queen's neutrality left their choice unfettered; and though expectation of personal profit largely moved them, their action proved politic. Lord Beauchamp was a man of insignificant position and character; James VI, however contemptible in many respects, had experience as a ruler, and a contiguous kingdom to add to the endowments of the English Crown[141].

---

[141] *Cambridge Modern History,* iii, 360.

Plate IV

Union Flag

1. Union of 1606 and 1707   2. Union of 1801

But the union of crowns brought about by Elizabeth's ministers with the tacit approval of the two nations did not directly lead to the union of peoples. The Parliaments remained separate; national jealousies ran high, especially in England, and James was foiled in his efforts to bring about the closer union he sought. Nevertheless, he was determined[142] that the union of the two nations should have some other outward expression than the change in the royal standard, and in the beginning of the fourth year of his reign he issued a proclamation in the following words:

> A Proclamation declaring what Flags South
> and North Britains shall bear at Sea.
>
> Whereas some difference has arisen between our Subjects of South and North Britain, Travelling by Sea, about the bearing of their flags, for the avoiding of all such contentions hereafter, We have with the advice of our Council ordered That from henceforth all our subjects of this Isle and Kingdom of Great Britain and the Members thereof shall bear in their maintop the Red Cross, commonly called St George's Cross, and the White Cross, commonly called St Andrew's Cross, joined together, according to a form made by our Heralds and sent by Us to our Admiral to be published to our said Subjects[143]. And in their foretop Our Subjects of South Britain shall wear the Red Cross only as they were wont, and our Subjects of North Britain in their Foretop the White Cross only as they were accustomed. Wherefore We will and command all our Subjects to be conformable and obedient to this Our Order, and that from henceforth they do not use to bear their flags in any other Sort, as they will answer the contrary at their Peril.
>
> Given at our Palace of Westminster the 12th. day of April in the 4th. year of our Reign of Great Britain France and Ireland Annoq. Domini 1606.

Unfortunately the naval records of the early years of the seventeenth century have almost entirely disappeared from the State archives; the "State Papers" themselves are but fragmentary remains; and the English Privy Council Registers from 1602 to 1613 were destroyed by the fire at Whitehall in 1618, so that it is impossible to say what were the points of contention referred to in the Proclamation.

[142] Mr Oppenheim suggests that this was partly due to James's natural vanity and his jealousy of anything that could remind the English seamen of their late Queen.

[143] This was sent to the Lord High Admiral to be communicated to the Navy and Mercantile Marine, *vide* draft letter *S. P. D. Jas I*, App. xxxviii, 16. An earlier draft altered from a signet warrant of James I, and now in part illegible, is to be found in *S. P. D. Jas I*, App. xxxv, 23, misplaced among the papers of 1603. The deleted ninth and tenth lines, however, read: "Given under [our signet?] at our Pallace of Westm[r] the first day of April in the fourth year of o[r] raigne of Great Britaine ffrance and Ireland."

A writer on the Union flag in the *Archeological Journal*, 1891, misled by the date at the top of the page containing the entry of the above Proclamation in the Syllabus to Rymer's *Foedera*, has stated that there was an earlier proclamation issued in 1605; an error that has been repeated by several subsequent writers.

The birth of the flag that is now the pride of so many millions was indeed obscure. Intended at first for use only at sea, it appears to have excited no attention except from those directly concerned with shipping. The royal and merchant navies were alike dwindling away, and the sea did not fill that place in the minds of James' subjects that it had filled in the greater days of Elizabeth.

The only strictly contemporary evidence of the actual design chosen in 1606 is to be found in the following appeal from the shipmasters of Scotland, whom it did not by any means please.

Edinburgh
7 Aug. 1606

> Most sacred Soverayne. A greate nomber of the maisteris and awnaris of the schippis of this your Majesteis kingdome hes verie havelie compleint to your Majesteis Counsell that the form and patrone of the flaggis of schippis, send doun heir and commandit to be ressavit and used be the subjectis of boith kingdomes, is very prejudiciall to the fredome and dignitie of this Estate and will gif occasioun of reprotche to this natioun quhairevir the said flage sal happin to be worne beyond sea becaus, as your sacred Majestie may persave, the Scottis Croce, callit Sanctandrois Croce is twyse divydit, and the Inglishe Croce, callit Sanct George, haldin haill and drawne through the Scottis Croce, whiche is thairby obscurit and no takin nor merk to be seene of the Scottis Armes. This will breid some heit and miscontentment betwix your Majesteis subjectis, and it is to be feirit that some inconvenientis sall fall oute betwix thame, for oure seyfairing men cannot be induceit to ressave that flag as it is set doun. They haif drawne two new drauchtis and patronis as most indifferent for boith kingdomes which they presented to the Counsell, and craved our approbatioun of the same; bot we haif reserved that to your Majesteis princelie determination,—as moir particularlie the Erll of Mar, who wes present and hard thair complaynt, and to whome we haif remittit the discourse and delyverie of that mater, will inform your Majestie, and latt Your Heynes see the errour of the first patrone and the indifferencie of the two new drauchtis. And sua, most humelie beseiking your Majestie, as your Heynes has evir had a speciall regaird of the honnour, fredome and libertie of this your Heynes antient and native kingdome that it wuld pleis your sacres Majestie in this particulair to gif unto your Heynes subjectis some satisfactioun and contentment, we pray God to blisse your sacred Majestie with a lang and prosperous reignne and eternall felicitie[144].

There is nothing to show that this appeal met with any response, but the Scots never took kindly to the new flag and rarely used it until after the Legislative Union of 1707. Sir Edward Nicholas in 1634 was doubtful "whether the Scots have

---

[144] *The Register of the Privy Council of Scotland*, vii, 498.

used to carry that Flag of the Union."

It is unfortunate that these "drafts and patterns" have disappeared, perhaps in the same fire that consumed the "form" made by the heralds. There is no doubt about the main outline, but the absence of precise detail has led several writers — purists in heraldic matters — to contend that the white border of the red cross was simply a narrow fimbriation[145]. I think, however, that examination of the available evidence will show that this border did not originate as a mere "fimbriation," that it was in fact part of the field of the English flag, and that the new flag was, as described by Sir James Balfour[146], "the flagis of St Andrew and St George interlaced," not merely the red cross surmounting the Scots flag. Material proof that it was so regarded sixty years later is in existence in Amsterdam in the shape of actual flags captured during the Second and Third Dutch Wars, and belonging therefore to the second half of the seventeenth century. These show a very wide border to the red cross, and in two instances[147] the red cross, the white border and the white saltire are each of the same width.

The heralds had been faced by a dilemma. It was impossible to combine the two flags so as to form a new one without giving precedence to one of them. If quartered, the upper canton next the staff was the place of honour, and both could not occupy it at the same time. In the reign of James II this difficulty was solved, in the case of the Royal Arms, by placing the Scots' Lion in the first quarter in the Great Seal of Scotland. Possibly a similar solution was suggested by the Scottish shipmasters. But there was a precedent for a closer union than this quartered form, which no doubt the heralds had in mind. Elizabeth had granted the Levant Company, by her charters of 1581 and 1592, the right to wear as a flag "the Armes of England with the redde crosse in white over the same[148]." We may be quite sure that in consenting to such an arrangement Elizabeth had no thought of giving the national flag precedence over the royal standard, but merely wished to signify their intimate union and the extension of the royal protection to the company. The method adopted in 1606 was exactly the same, the "red cross in white" being placed over the Scots flag.

The quarterly arrangement of the crosses appears to have been used on one occasion; the dispatch of a fleet in 1623 to bring back Prince Charles and the Duke of Buckingham from Spain. Mr Serjeant Knight, in a "discourse" on the St George's flag written in 1678 at the request of Pepys[149], stated that he had in his possession the Order from the Great Wardrobe directed to his father, Mr Thomas Knight, Arms Painter, who was to paint the banners and streamers required for the Prince. The principal flag was to be that shown in Plate V, fig. 1: "Imprimis in ye Prince's

[145] The object of a fimbriation is to prevent colour touching colour or metal touching metal, and, according to modern heraldic rules, it should be as narrow as possible consistent with this result. White is of course a metal: "argent."

[146] *Annales of Scotland* (s.v. 1606), written about 1640.

[147] In the Rijks Museum. There are many illustrations of the Union flag in late seventeenth century MSS., one of the most important of these being the Flag Book of Lieut. Graydon (1686) in the Pepysian Library. They all show a broad border.

[148] See p. 136.

[149] *Pepys MSS.*, Miscellanea, IX.

ship wherein he goes, on ye top ye Crosses of St. Andrew and St. George." Mr Knight assured Pepys that he could not be mistaken about this "cobled Banner," as he scornfully called it, "ye severall arms being trickt in ye margin of ye Order," and he proceeded to give a sketch of it. Indeed, he was disposed to believe this to be the original form of the Union flag:

> having seen severall Flaggs with St. George and St. Andrew quar-
> terly and may every Lord Mayor's Day be seen born by some of ye
> Companies Barges, these flags being made much about that time,
> all men being willing to flatter their new king.

The evidence of the Privy Council Register of Scotland is, however, sufficient to prove that this inference was incorrect.

The documents of 1606 do not give any name to the flag they describe. It appears first to have been called the "Britain" or "British" flag[150], and I have not found the name "Union" earlier than 1625, when it appears in the list of the flags and banners used at the funeral of James I[151]. Three years later it appears in the Sailing Instructions of the Earl of Lindsey[152], but the older name still persisted at sea and is found in inventories of stores and in sailing and fighting instructions until 1639[153].

Hitherto this "British" or "Union" flag had, like the old English flag of St George, been flown equally by merchantman and man-of-war, strangers being expected to distinguish the latter by their more warlike appearance.

Towards the year 1633, however, the old question of the salute in the Narrow Seas was becoming more and more acute, "because," in the words of Sir Wm Monson, "both the French and Hollanders seek to usurp upon his Majesties right[154]." Sir John Pennington, the "Admiral of the Narrow Seas," seized on this as an excuse to advocate a difference in the flags of the king's and the merchants' ships. In a letter dated 7th April, 1634, asking for instructions on various points relative to his duties as Admiral of the Narrow Seas he writes:

> For alteringe of the Coulers whereby his Mats owne Shippes
> may be knowne from his Subiects I leave to yor Lopps more deepe
> consideration. But under correction I conceive it to bee very ma-
> teryall and much for his Mats Honor, and besides will free dis-
> putes with Strangers, for when they omitt doinge their Respectes

---

[150] *S. P. D. Jas I*, ci, 8: A Survey of the present rigging of all His Maj[s] Ships 1618.

    1 Imperiall fflag w[h] the kings armes of taffaty guilded.

    1 Brittish fflag of 15 clothes of taffaty.

    1 of St George of 12 breadths of taffaty.

[151] *S. P. D. Chas I*, i, 98: "the Banner of the Union with the Crosses of both kingdoms."

[152] *Ibid.* cxvi, 50: "When you shall heare a piece of ordnance from ye Adm[ll] of the fleete and see ye Union fflagg in ye misne shrowds y[t] shalbe a signe for ye Counsell of Warre to come aboard."

[153] *Ibid.* ccccxv, 49: Instructions given by Sir John Pennington, 26th March, 1639. "And when you see ye British Flagg spread upon my Mizen Shrowds...."

[154] Really because the English navy had become so weak that other nations saw no longer any reason to yield those marks of respect formerly exacted of them.

to his Mats Shippes till they bee shott at they alleadge they did not know it to be the kinges Shippe[155].

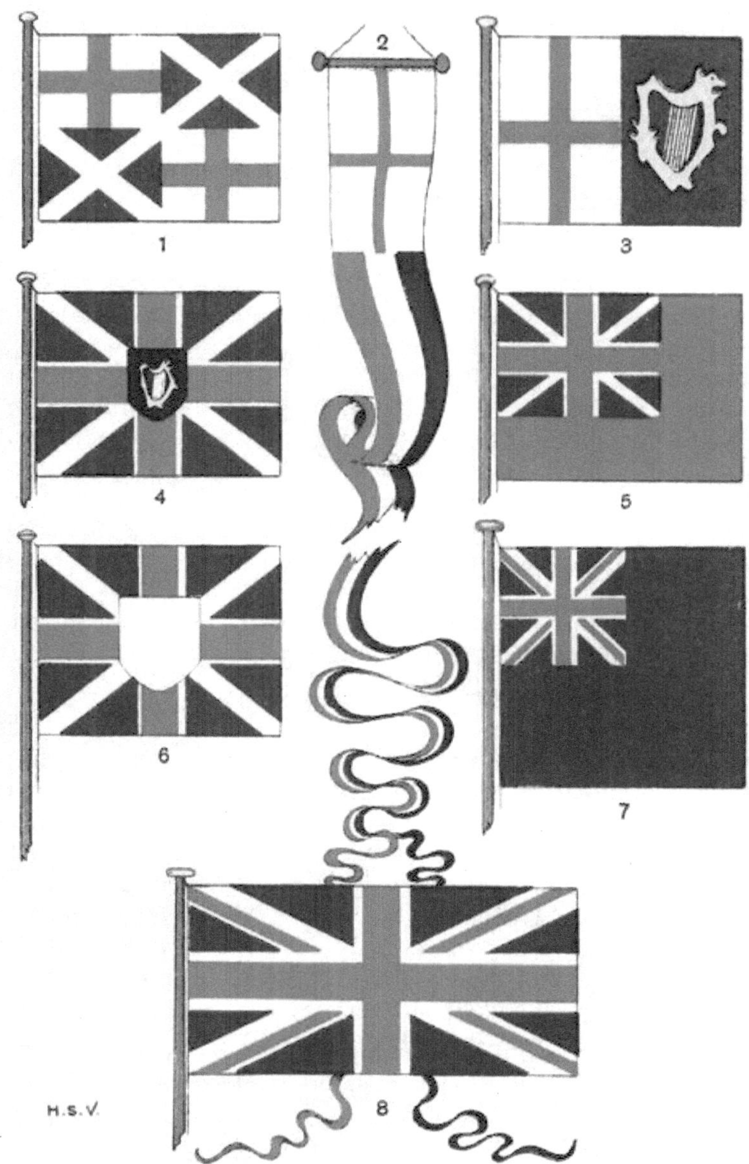

Plate V

Union Flags and Jacks

1. Quartered Union   2. Union Pendant

[155] *S. P. D. Chas I*, CCLXV, 23.

3. Commonwealth Jack   4. Protectorate Jack

5. Budgee Jack   6. Privateer Jack

7. Public Office Jack   8. Admiralty Pattern (modern)

The plea that the existing arrangement caused confusion in the minds of foreigners was quite justified, but it is probable that there was a deeper underlying cause, jealousy of the mercantile marine. Be this as it may, Pennington's suggestion was favourably received, and the approval of the king was obtained to the issue of the following Proclamation:

> A Proclamation appointing the Flags, as well for our Navie Royall as for the Ships of our Subjects of South and North Britaine.
>
> Wee taking into Our Royall consideration that it is meete for the Honour of Our owne Ships in Our Navie Royall and of such other Ships as are or shall be employed in Our immediate Service, that the same bee by their Flags distinguished from the ships of any other of Our Subjects, doe hereby straitly prohibite and forbid that none of Our Subjects, of any of Our Nations and Kingdomes, shall from hencefoorth presume to carry the Union Flagge in the Maine toppe, or other part of any of their Ships (that is) S. Georges Crosse and S. Andrews Crosse joyned together upon paine of Our high displeasure, but that the same Union Flagge bee still reserved as an ornament proper for Our owne Ships and Ships in Our immediate Service and Pay, and none other.
>
> And likewise Our further will and pleasure is, that all the other Ships of Our Subjects of England or South Britaine bearing flags shall from hencefoorth carry the Red-Crosse, commonly called S. George his Crosse, as of olde time hath beene used; And also that all the other ships of Our Subjects of Scotland or North Britaine shall from hencefoorth carry the White Crosse commonly called S. Andrews Crosse, Whereby the severall Shipping may thereby bee distinguished and We thereby the better discerne the number and goodnesse of the same. Wherefore Wee will and straitly command all Our Subjects foorthwith to bee conformable and obedient to this Our Order, as they will answer the contrary at their perills.
>
> Given at Our Court at Greenwich this fifth day of May in the tenth yeere of Our Reigne of England Scotland France and Ireland, Defender of the Faith &c.

The ostensible reason for this distinction in flags—to enable the "number and goodnesse" of the ships of the two nations to be more readily discerned—is obviously an afterthought[156]; a sugar coating to the pill. The customs officers of the various ports could, of course, have provided any information desired relative to the shipping, and were not dependent on the flags for their knowledge of the

---

[156] It is not mentioned in the Council's warrant to the Attorney General directing him to prepare the proclamation.

ships' nationalities. The point is of some interest as it marks a distinct step in the exaltation of the Navy Royal and its officers into a position of superiority over the mercantile marine.

It will also be observed that the proclamation of 1634 does not require the flags to be hoisted at the masthead as did that of 1606. Probably this was no accidental omission but was the outcome of the general introduction of the "Jack" on the bowsprit a year or two before. Flags had no doubt been occasionally carried on the bowsprit from the time when that spar was first invented, but the practice had been exceptional, at any rate in the English navy. An early instance was depicted in a contemporary picture in Cowdray Castle, since destroyed by fire, which represented "the encampment of the English forces near Portsmouth, together with a view of the English and French fleets at the commencement of the action between them on the 19th of July, 1545." In this picture, which fortunately was reproduced in an engraving by the Society of Antiquaries in 1780, the Lord Admiral's ship, the 'Henri Grace à Dieu,' was seen flying a royal standard on the bowsprit. Drake, also, had flown a striped flag in this position in that last voyage which ended for him in his death at sea in January, 1596[157]. Yet when Captain Young submitted his "Noates for Sea Service" to the Earl of Essex[158] he wrote as though the idea were unusual:

> and that the cullers maye bee the better knowne from those of the enemies and yf they chance to have the like it shalbe then convenient that upon o^r misson flagge-staves or th ende of o^r bowlesprits and that theare bee but a smawle litle flagge with a red Crosse yt being but a litle bigger than a vaine of a great Catche[159].

As remarked by Admiral Sir Massie Blomfield[160], this "jack" is not shown in the "illustrations of the flagships of the Expedition of 1596 reproduced in the 'Naval Miscellany,'[161]" so that the suggestion was probably not received with favour.

There is no mention of, or provision for, "jacks" in the inventories which accompanied the report of the committee that inquired into the state of the navy in 1618. Sir Julian Corbett has pointed out[162] that the earliest instance of the use of the word "jack" to denote a flag occurs in the orders issued by Sir John Pennington to one of his captains on 3rd July, 1633. The original has not survived, but the copy[163] is in a contemporary hand and is corroborated by Pennington's Journal, now among the MSS. of Lord Muncaster.

In the summers of the years 1631, 1633 and 1634 Pennington was in command

---

[157] See "An Atlas of Drake's last voyage," by Dr Jules Sottas, *Mariner's Mirror*, May, 1912.

[158] Probably about June, 1596.

[159] *S. P. D. Eliz.* cclix, 48. For full transcript of the second section of these notes see *The Naval Tracts of Sir Wm Monson*, edited by Mr Oppenheim (Navy Records Society), iv, 202. The first part has never been published.

[160] *Mariner's Mirror*, April, 1911.

[161] Navy Records Society, vol. xx, 1902.

[162] *Fighting Instructions* 1530-1816 (N.R.S.), 1905, p. 108.

[163] *B. M. Sloane MS.* 2682. The copy was probably made in 1638.

of a small squadron as Admiral of the Narrow Seas, charged especially with the duty of freeing the coast from pirates. He tells us in his journal[164], under the above date (3rd July, 1633):

> In the morninge it blew very hard at SW by W. Aboute noone we weyed—leavinge the 8th Whelpe in Catt Water and stoode of to sea with the rest of our Fleete, knowinge it to bee a very hard matter for any small vessels to keepe the sea in such fowle weather, and the likelyest place for them to shelter in with these winds was Torbaye, for which place we stoode, causinge the 10th Whelpe to goe a head of us and close aboard the shore, with her coullers and ordynance in, that shee might not bee suspected to bee one of our Fleete, the better to intrap any Pyrates.

The order, which is dated the same day on board the 'Vanguard,' Pennington's flagship, is evidently the one given to the 10th Whelp[165]. It contains instructions as to rendezvous in case the ships lost company, and continues as follows:

> you are to looke out carefully for these pirates night and day; that if it be possible wee maie intrapp them. You are alsoe for this present service to keepe in yo[r] Jack at yo[r] Boultsprit end and yo[r] Pendant and yo[r] Ordinance[166].

The fact that the position of the "Jack" is defined in this order tends to show that the term had not yet become common, and this is fully confirmed by a passage added by Sir Nathaniel Boteler to one[167] of the manuscript copies of his well-known *Six Dialogues about Sea Services*, written about the year 1634.

Boteler, who last served at sea in the Ile de Ré Expedition of 1627, says:

> but of late ther hathe bin invented an order that none of our Englishe shypps should be allowed to carry the king's flagge (that is the English Crosse quartered[168] w[h] the Scottish, and called the Brittish flagge or Colours) save only such shyps as are either of his Ma[ties] owne or serve under his paye, and every such vessel, though but a Catche, is permitted and enjoined to weare one of thes in a smale volume in her Boltsprites Topp. And the flaggs thus worne are tearmed Jacks.

The "Order" referred to is evidently the Proclamation of 1634, which, as already remarked, was the outcome of Pennington's request for instructions. It seems highly probable that it is to the same outstanding personality[169] that we

[164] See *Hist. MSS. Com.* Report x, App. iv, p. 280.

[165] The 'Lion's Whelps,' ten in number, were built in 1628. They were small craft, of the "Pinnace" type, ship-rigged, with spritsail-topmasts.

[166] On a later occasion the two Whelps were ordered to take down their topgallant masts as well, to complete the disguise.

[167] B. M. *Sloane MS.* 2449, a holograph copy: the page is headed "of the Flagge called the Jacke." It does not occur in *Sloane* 758 or *Harleian* 1341, or in the Bodleian MS. *Rawlinson* A 463.

[168] He is using this word incorrectly.

[169] Pennington was the principal figure at sea on the royalist side until the Parliament

owe the institution of the "Jack" on the bowsprit.

From 1634 until the death of Charles I the royal ships continued to be distinguished from the merchant ships by this difference in their flags, although, as a distinct favour, merchant ships were, in a few special cases, granted permission to carry the Union flag.

The execution of Charles I on 30th January, 1649, dissolved the dynastic union between England and Scotland. The two nations, which only a few years before had been united in a "Solemn League and Covenant" against Charles, had been gradually drifting apart, and on the proclamation by the Scots of Charles' son as king the two governments fell into open enmity. In these circumstances the Union flag had become meaningless. On the 22nd of February the Parliament decreed that the "Admiralty" should be settled in the Council of State[170], and the "Navy Committee," that is, the Committee of the Council, who were managing those affairs of the navy that had formerly been within the jurisdiction of the "Principal Officers of the Navy," immediately applied to the Council to know what they were to do about flags.

> This Committee taking notice of the arms yt are engraven upon ye sternes of ye shipps belonging to ye Comonwealth & intended for this Summers fleet doe think fit to inform the Comtee of State therewith that so directions may be given what arms shalbe placed in their steed & likewise what characters shalbe given to the flaggs that are to be worne in this service[171].

The Council of State promptly decided "That the Ships at Sea in service of the State shall onely beare the red Crosse in a white flag[172]," thus bringing the navy back to the old English flag and once more into line with the merchant shipping. The royal arms were ordered to be removed from the sterns and replaced by "the Armes of England and Ireland in two Scutcheons[173]."

Two days later the Generals at Sea were informed, in answer to a further inquiry, that if Scots ships were found "bearing either the red cross or the Armes heretofore called the King's Armes" they were to admonish them to "forbeare the carrying of them for the future[174]."

It is probable that the order of 22nd Feb. was not altogether welcome to the navy officers, for on 5th March, only a few days after the above order had been issued, the Council of State decided upon a new union flag for naval use. The union now to be symbolised was that of England and Ireland. Although Ireland had been more or less under the rule of the kings of England from the time of

drove him from the navy in 1642.

[170] *S. P. D. Inter.* i, 62, p. 7: the Act was, however, dated 23rd. See *Acts and Ordinances of the Interregnum,* ii, 13.

[171] Bodl. *Rawlinson MS.* A 224. The entry is dated 22nd Feb.

[172] *S. P. D. Inter.* i, 62, p. 8. In the letter to the Navy Commissioners the words "quite through the flagg" were added.

[173] *Ibid.* The order about the Arms does not appear to have been immediately acted upon, for it was repeated on 6th June.

[174] *Ibid.* p. 24.

Henry II, it was not until the accession of James I in 1603 that she had found recognition in the royal standard, and it remained for the Commonwealth to give her due recognition in the national flag. The entry in the Council Minute Book runs: "That the fflagg that is to be borne by the Admirall be that now presented, viz: the Armes of England and Ireland in two severall Escotchons in a red flagg wth in a Compartiment (or)[175]."

At the same time two other variants of this design were introduced, a standard and a jack. The order for these cannot be found, but they are referred to in the following letter to the Committee of the Navy signed by Deane and Blake (two of the Generals at Sea[176]) and dated 21st April, 1649:

> Gentlemen
>
> Touching the flaggs &c. It seems strange you referre the proportions to bee ascertained by us, yorselves knowing best the former allowaunces, which wee suppose are alike in number in every expedition, but since the Issue depends on or resolution wee think needfull that you make up what you have allready sent, for orselves three Standards, or viceadmll and Rereadmll with the Admll Viceadmll & Rereadmll of Ireland three flaggs apiece, with two Jackes for every Shipp in the ffleet. ffor the Ensignes and pendants you best know how many are wanting, which (whatsoever they are) with the flaggs &c. we desire may bee noe longer delayed[177].

In the standard, intended to replace the royal standard, and to be used by the Generals at Sea, the yellow "compartment" was omitted and the two escutcheons were surrounded by green branches of laurel and bay. Fortunately, an actual specimen[178] has survived of this interesting flag, which was destined to wave over Blake's ship at the heroic battle of Santa Cruz and to see the rise of the English navy to an eminence unequalled even in the days of Elizabeth.

The jack contained only the cross and harp on their white and blue fields, corresponding with the centre part of the Admirals' flags. It is to be seen in several pictures of battles of the First Dutch War[179]. Apparently this jack was also used

[175] *Ibid.* i, 62, p. 53. See Plate VIII, fig. 3.

[176] The Commissioners (Blake, Deane, and Popham) for exercising the office of "Admiral and General of the Fleet" created by Act of Parliament 24th Feb. 1649, usually known as the "Generals at Sea." They stood in much the same position as that formerly occupied by the late Lord High Admiral, the Earl of Warwick, so far as the management of the fleet was concerned, though without the Lord Admiral's full legal powers, which were vested in the Council of State.

[177] *S. P. D. Inter.* i, 65.

[178] See Plate VI, fig. 5. This flag, which tradition connects with Blake himself, has been preserved at Chatham Dockyard from time immemorial, but was recently loaned by the Admiralty to the Royal United Service Institution, where it may now be seen. Mr Fraser has discussed its connection with Blake in his book *The Fighting Fame of the King's Ships*, 1910, p. 110.

[179] E.g. R. Nooms (Zeeman), *Zeegevecht voor Livorno* (1653), and J. A. Beerstraten, *Zeeslag by ter Heide* 1653, in the Rijks Museum at Amsterdam. Also in etchings by Zeeman.

by ships having letters of marque; "privateers" as we should now call them. In December, 1652, the captain of a small frigate, called the 'Helena,' fought with two armed ships from Brest, "putting out the Parliament Jack on the bowsprit end and the English ensign on the poop, the enemy having hung out the disunion flag or late King's colours[180]."

Early in 1653 the junior Admiral's flag with the red border and yellow compartment seems to have been abandoned, and a flag like the jack, with the harp and cross only, substituted for it[181], probably because the red border would cause confusion when flown in the white and blue squadrons.

Scotland was formally re-united to England by an Ordinance of the Commonwealth Parliament dated 12th April, 1654, and the cross of St Andrew was ordered to be brought once more into conjunction with that of St George:

> And that this Union may take its more full effect and intent Be it further ordained by the Authority aforesaid That the Arms of Scotland viz: a Cross commonly called Saint Andrews Cross be received into and borne from henceforth in the Arms of this Commonwealth as a Badge of this Union.

In the new great seal which was prepared in 1655 the St Andrew's cross was quartered with St George's cross and the Irish harp, but it was not at once introduced into the naval flags, although placed on the obverse of naval medals struck in 1654.

The cross of St Andrew was re-introduced into the naval flags by the following order of the Council of State dated 18th May, 1658[182]:

> That the Standard for the Generall of his Highness ffleete be altered, and doe beare the Armes of England, Scotland, and Ireland, with his Highness Escutcheon of pretence, according to the impression of the Great Seale of England; and that the Jack fflaggs for the fflagg officers of the ffleete and for the severall Shipps of Warre of his Highness be the Armes of England and Scotland united, according to the auncient forme, With the addition of the Harpe, according to a Modell now showd; and that the Comrs of the Admty and Navy to take order That the standard and Jacke fflaggs be prepared accordingly.

In the standard the two crosses and the harp were borne "quarterly" surmounted by an inescutcheon (sable, a lion rampant argent), the personal arms of <u>Cromwell[183], but in the other Admirals' flags and the jack the</u> crosses were super-

See Plate V, fig. 3.

[180] *Letters and Papers relating to the First Dutch War* (N. R. S.), iii, 189.

[181] Bodl. *Rawlinson* A 227. Order of Navy Commissioners hastening supply of flags for the fleet, dated 2nd March, 1653: "3 Standards of ye usuall colo[rs] wth ye field Red, 4 fflags of ye Jack colo[rs]." Cf. also Instructions of Vice Adm. Goodson to Penn 21 June, 1655: "You shall wear the jack-flag upon the maintop masthead during your continuance in the service aforesaid" (*Memorials of the Professional Life and Times of Sir Wm Penn*, ii, 116.)

[182] *S. P. D. Inter.* i, 78, p. 627.

[183] See Plate VI, fig. 6. The quarterly form was best adapted to admit of this surcharge, as the harp was to occupy the centre of the Union flag.

posed, as in the Union flag of 1606, with the addition of a harp in the centre. The "model" has disappeared, like all its predecessors, and nothing remains to show for certain whether this harp was placed in a blue escutcheon as in the earlier Commonwealth flags or not, but since a request was received from Chatham in the following November for 200 yards of blue bewper "for ye altering of all y⁰ fflaggs and Jacks here yᵗ are of yᵉ former fashion into yᵉ new forme[184]" it seems on the whole probable that the harp was in an escutcheon with a blue field.

This return towards the flag of 1606, prophetic of the coming restoration, lasted for a few months only. In September Cromwell died, and his son, the shadow of a great name, after being tolerated as a mere figurehead for a few months, was in the following May forced to abdicate. The remnant of the Long Parliament, which had just re-assembled, passed an "Act for the Great Seal of England" which restored the seal of 1651 with its map of England and Ireland and shields with the St George's cross and the Irish harp. The cross of Scotland vanished and the Commonwealth "Cross and Harp" jack supplanted Cromwell's Union Jack.

In March, 1660, the Navy Commissioners were told to furnish General Mountagu, then in command of the Fleet[185], "with Standards for the Naseby suitable to the Jacks now worne in the ffleete[186]." This was the standard which Mountagu was flying when ordered to cross to the Hague and bring back the king.

On 1st May, 1660, the newly assembled Houses of Parliament passed a joint vote for the restoration of the ancient government, and a few days later, before Charles was publicly proclaimed, the Commissioners of the Admiralty and Navy, at the instance of the Council of State, issued the following order to their subordinate Board:

> In pursuance of an order of the Councell of State of the 5th of this instant May It is ordered that it be referred to the Comrs for the Navy forthwith to take care that such Standards, fflags and Jacke Colours for the ffleete be forthwith prepared as were in use before 1648 and that they be sent downe with all speed to Generall Mountagu as alsoe that Carvers and Painters be appointed to goe down for the altering of the Carved workes according to such directions as they shall receive from Comr Pett, who is ordered by ye Councell forthwth to goe to ye Generall. And the said Comrs are to give order for the sending downe to the Generall One silke Standard and one silke Ensigne and Jacke and such other silke fflags as may compleate a suite for the Naseby[187].

Instructions to this effect must have reached the fleet before it left England, but the flag-makers had evidently not had sufficient time to prepare the new royal standard, for on the 13th May, on the way over, (so Pepys, then secretary to Moun-

---

[184] *S. P. D. Inter.* cxcv, 162. Presumably "ye former fashion" refers to the pre-Commonwealth flags still in store, as the Parliament jack and flag would not lend itself to conversion into the new form.

[185] Nominally in joint commission with Monk as General at Sea.

[186] *S. P. D. Inter.* cciii, 69. This standard was the same as that in use from 1649 to 1658.

[187] *Ibid.* cci, 15.

tagu, tells us[188])

> the tailors and painters were at work cutting out some pieces
> of yellow cloth into the fashion of a crown and C.R. and put it
> upon a fine sheet and that into the flag instead of the State's arms[189]
> which after dinner was finished and set up.... In the afternoon a
> Council of War only to acquaint them that the Harp must be taken
> out of all their flags, it being very offensive to the King.

The Union flag, like the Government, now reverted to its original form, but the right to fly it remained the special prerogative of the State's ships, a prerogative much sought after by merchant ships, and often assumed by them without warrant. For the next half century a long-drawn struggle was waged by the merchant shipping for the possession of this right. It begins with a special instruction sent by the Lord High Admiral, James Duke of York, to the Corporation of Trinity House on 9th March, 1661:

> I desire you will give notice unto all Commanders and Masters of Shipping belonging to the Subjects of the King, my Sovereign Lord and Brother, that from henceforward they forbear to wear the Flag of Union; and also acquaint them, that such as presume to wear the said Flag contrary hereunto, the King's Ships will have orders to take it from them[190].

The Trinity House issued orders to this effect, but although the prohibition had been stiffened with a threat that the flag would be taken by force from those displaying it, the notices seem to have had so little effect that, on 19th Nov., when a royal proclamation was issued "For prohibiting the Imbezlement of His Majesties Stores," the opportunity was taken to make the further threat that the Commander of the ship would be seized also:

> And for preventing the abuse which hath been of late practised concerning Flags, Pendents and other Ornaments His Majesty doth hereby strictly prohibit & forbid the use of His Majesties Colours in Merchant Ships, and doth Authorize and Command all Commanders and Officers of any His Majesties Ships of War not only to take from Merchants Ships all such Colours but likewise to seize the Commander of such Merchant Ships, wherein after the first day of April next they shall be used, and to bring them to condign punishment[191].

It is interesting to find here, as in 1634, an excuse made for the order which is not the main reason for it. No doubt a certain number of colours were embezzled and sold by the boatswains of the king's ships, just as the gunners embezzled and sold the powder, but the desire of the merchant shipping to fly the Union flag was not due to the fact that they might occasionally pick that flag up cheap, it was due

---

[188] *Diary*, 13th May, 1660.
[189] I.e. covering over the escutcheons containing the cross and harp.
[190] *Memoirs of the English Affairs, chiefly Naval...*, 1729.
[191] B. M. 1851, c, 8 (129).

rather to the privileges, especially freedom from pilotage and port dues in foreign ports, which the flag assured them.

Probably the further threat of imprisonment checked the practice for a time, but not entirely, for the Lord High Admiral was again taking action in 1666.

Warrant for taking into custody such Ma[rs] of Merch[t] Ships as
shall presume to Wear the Kings Jack.

> Whereas I am informed yt the Mars of severall Merchant Shipps outward bound from the River of Thames have presumed to Wear the Kings Jack without having leave from myself or the Prinle Officers & Commrs of His Matys Navy or any other just pretence for so doing These are therefore to will and require you forthwith to goe down the River of Thames and examine and enquire what Merchant Ships either do or have lately Wore the Kings Jack not being hired nor carrying goods for His Matys Service and yt you apprehend the Mars of them ... (except the Ship Tryall whereof Hope for Bendall is Mar, which is bound for New England & is to carry some Goods for me) and keep them in safe custody that they may be punished for their presumption.
>
>
>
> And all May[rs] Sheriffs &c.
> Dated 11th May 1666.
> James[192].
>
>

Deterred by these measures from a direct attempt to make use of the Union flag, the merchant shipping hit upon the device of flying a flag which was a sufficiently close imitation of the forbidden colours to deceive foreign powers[193] without falling within the strict letter of the law. In 1674 this practice had evidently become common, for Pepys acquainted the Trinity House, in June, of the King's intention to put a stop to it[194]. Three months later the following proclamation was issued:

> Whereas by ancient usage no merchant's ship ought to bear the Jack, which is for distinction appointed for his Majesty's ships; nevertheless his Majesty is informed that divers of his Majesty's subjects have of late presumed to wear his Majesty's Jack on board their ships employed in merchants' affairs, and thinking to evade the Punishment due for the same, bear Jacks in shape and mixture of colours so little different from those of his Majesty as not to be without difficulty distinguisht therefrom, which practice is found attended with manifold Inconveniences; for prevention whereof for the future his Majesty hath thought fit, with the advice of his Privy Council, by this his Royal Proclamation, strictly to charge and command all his subjects whatsoever, that from henceforth

---

[192] Adm. Lib. *D'Eon MS.* p. 367.

[193] Not a difficult matter, to judge from some of the "union flags" flown by foreign men-of-war at the Naval Review at Spithead in 1911.

[194] Mayo, *The Trinity House of London*, 1905, p. 44.

they do not presume to wear his Majesty's Jack (commonly called The Union Jack) in any of their ships or vessels, without particular warrant for their so doing from his Majesty, or the Lord High Admiral of England, or the Commissioners for executing the office of Lord High Admiral for the time being; and his Majesty doth hereby further command all his loving subjects, that without such warrant as aforesaid, they presume not to wear on board their ships or vessels, any Jacks made in imitation of his Majesty's, or any other flags, Jacks, or Ensigns whatsoever, than those usually heretofore worn on merchants' ships, viz., the Flag and Jack White, with a Red Cross (commonly called Saint George's Cross) passing right through the same; and the Ensign Red, with a like Cross in a Canton White, at the upper corner thereof next to the staff.

And his Majesty doth hereby require the principal officers and Commissioners of his navy, Governors of his Forts and Castles, the Officers of his Customs, and Commanders or officers of any of his Majesty's ships, upon their meeting with, or otherwise observing any merchants' ships or vessels of his Majesty's subjects wearing such a flag, jack, or ensign, contrary hereunto, whether at Sea or in Port, not only to cause such flag, jack or ensign to be forthwith seized, but to return the names of the said ships and vessels, together with the names of their respective masters, unto the Lord High Admiral, Lords Commissioners of the Admiralty, or the Judge of the High Court of Admiralty for the time being, to the end the Persons offending may be duly punished for the same.

And his Majesty doth hereby command and enjoyn the Judge and Judges of the High Court of Admiralty for the time being, that at the several Sessions to be hereafter held by his Majesty's Commission of Oyer and Terminer for the Admiralty, they give in charge, that strict enquiry be made of all offences in the premises, and that they cause all offenders therein to be duly punished. And all Vice Admirals and Judges of Vice Admiralties, are also to do the same, and to attend the due observation hereof, within the several Ports and Places of their respective Precincts.

Given at our Court at Whitehall the Eighteenth Day of September 1674, in the Six and Twentieth Year of our Reign. By his Majesty's Command.

A new competitor for the privilege now appeared in the yacht—a type of pleasure-boat introduced from the Netherlands at the Restoration. In 1676 the request of the Governor of Dover "to have the liberty of wearing his Maj[ts] Jack upon his private yacht" was refused by the king in Council[195], but the practice of hoisting the Union Jack upon yachts without warrant had become sufficiently widespread by 1686 to attract the notice of the navy authorities, as shown by the following

[195] *Pepys MSS*. Miscellanea, ix.

memorandum of Pepys:

> Notes about the Jack taken by S. P. at the Navy Board the 20th of Septr 1686 upon occasion of the liberty taken by Private Yachts to wear the Kings Jack without License.

> Memorandum. That the temptations to this Liberty (besides the pride of it) are

> 1st. That in Holland they are freed by it from taking a Pilot.

> 2dly. As to France they are by the Jack excused from paying the Duty of 50 Sous by Tun paid by every Mercht Man coming into a French Port.

> 3dly. All our Merchant Men lower their Topsails below Gravesend to any ship or vessel carrying the King's Jack, be it but a Victualling Hoy[196].

About this time another form of jack had come into use in the Mediterranean. Its origin is obscure: we first meet with it in some notes of matters to be looked into jotted down by Pepys about 1687: "Quaere, the Practice of wearing Colours in Boats? And the Budgee[197] Jack now familiarly used abroad (as lately by St Loe[198]) being the Union Jack in a Canton upon a Red Flag." It will be seen from this note that it was of similar design to the red ensign instituted in 1707, and from the juxtaposition of "Colours in Boats" it may be inferred that it was a combination of the jack and red ensign for use in boats only. It was afterwards made the distinctive jack of a privateer[199].

For the next few years more serious matters than the misuse of the Union Jack occupied the attention of the authorities, but in 1694[200], when William III was safely seated on the throne, another Proclamation, similar to that of 1674, was issued forbidding merchant ships, except those having letters of marque, to wear other colours than the "Flag and Jack white with a Red Cross commonly called St George's Cross passing quite through the same and the Ensign Red with the like Cross in a Canton White at the upper corner thereof next the staff." The privateers were to wear the same ensign as other merchant ships, but were to have the red (Budgee) jack.

Another Proclamation in identical terms was issued in the first year of Queen

---

[196] *Ibid.*

[197] The name "Budgee," in flag-books of the early eighteenth century, is derived from Bugia (Bougie) in Algeria. In the tenth century this was one of the most important seaports in North Africa, but in the seventeenth century it was fast falling into decay, and beyond the fact that the Algerine pirates lying there were successfully attacked by Sir Edward Spragge in 1673 there was nothing to connect the name with the English navy.

[198] George St Lo.

[199] By the Proclamation of 1694. "All such ships as shall have Commissions of Letters of Mart or Reprisals shall, besides the colours which may be worn by Merchants' ships, wear a Red Jack, with the Union Jack described in a Canton of the upper corner thereof next the staff." It retained this use until privateering was abolished in 1856.

[200] 17 July, 1694. B. M. 21 *h*, 3 (157).

Anne's reign[201].

Meanwhile yet another variant of the Union Jack had been created for the use of ships commissioned by the Governors of the North American Colonies. In July, 1701, the Admiralty complained to the Council of "the inconvenience by Merchant Ships wearing the King's Colours in and among the Plantations abroad, under colour of Commissions from the Governors of the said Plantations," and obtained the Council's approval to the use by such vessels of a distinctive Jack which is thus described in the Instructions to the Governors.

> Whereas great inconveniences do happen by Merchant Ships and other Vessels in the Plantations wearing the Colours born by our Ships of War under pretence of Commissions granted to them by the Governors of the said Plantations, and that by trading under those Colours, not only amongst our own Subjects, but also those of other Princes and States, and Committing divers Irregularities, they do very much dishonour our Service—For prevention whereof you are to oblige the Commanders of all such Ships, to which you shall grant Commissions, to wear no other Jack than according to the Sample here described, that is to say, such as is worn by our Ships of War, with the distinction of a White Escutchion in the middle thereof and that the said mark of distinction may extend itself to one half of the depth of the Jack and one third of the Fly thereof[202].

In 1707 was brought about that complete union of England and Scotland that James had worked for a hundred years before. The first article in the Treaty of Union provided that the crosses of St George and St Andrew should be conjoined in such manner as the queen thought fit. After due consideration of various designs suggested by a Committee of the Privy Council in conjunction with the Heralds College, it was finally decided by an Order in Council of 17th April, 1707, "That the Union Flag continue as at present." Coloured drawings of the Royal Standard, Union Flag, and Red Ensign were formally communicated to the Admiralty by a further Order in Council with instructions that these designs were to be adhered to in the flags flown at sea[203].

But although no change was made in the Union flag an important alteration was made in the Ensign; the English and Scots navies being now united, the Union was introduced into its canton in place of the St George.

In promulgating[204] this change of ensign opportunity was taken to repeat the thunders of the former proclamations against the offending merchant service, but with the inclusion of the Union in the ensign the fight practically came to an end.

---

[201] 18 Dec. 1702. *London Gazette*, 3872.

[202] See Plate V, fig. 6, and page 129.

[203] 21st July, 1707, *Adm. Sec. In. Lrs.* 5151. The illustration in Plate IV, fig. 1, is a reduced facsimile of the Union flag as therein depicted. It will be seen that the St George's cross has a comparatively wide white border, and that the blue was of a lighter colour than that which afterwards became customary.

[204] Proclamation 28th July, 1707, *London Gazette*, 4356.

Before long the general introduction of fore and aft headsails led to the disappearance of the sprit topmast on which the jack had been displayed, and as the flagstaff
on the bowsprit, which took its place, was in the way of the jib when headsails
were set, it became the common practice to fly a jack only when the ship was in
harbour.

With the opening of the nineteenth century came the final change in the design
of the Union flag. By the Act of 1800 the union of Great Britain and Ireland was
to take effect from the first day of the new century, and by the first of the Articles
of Union the "Ensigns, Armorial Flags and Banners" were to be such as the king
by "Royal Proclamation under the Great Seal of the said United Kingdom should
appoint."

The Privy Council, after consulting the Heralds, recommended to the king
"that the Union Flag should be altered according to the Draft thereof marked (C)
in which the Cross of St George is conjoined with the Crosses of St Andrew and St
Patrick." This proposal was approved by Order in Council of the 5th November,
1800.

The Proclamation[205] was issued on the 1st January, 1801. It decreed

> that the Union Flag shall be azure, the Crosses Saltires of St An-
> drew and St Patrick Quarterly per Saltire, counterchanged Argent
> and Gules; the latter fimbriated of the Second[206] surmounted by
> the Cross of St George of the Third[207], fimbriated as the Saltire.

In his desire to adhere to those pedantic formulae which came into being
during the decadence of heraldic art, the draftsman of this clause was unfortunately obscure in a matter that called for the clearest precision. The "Draft marked
C" showed a fimbriation or border for the St George's cross nearly as wide as the
counterchanged saltires[208]. This drawing and the verbal blason of it above recited,
were supplied to the Council by Sir Isaac Heard, the Garter King-at-Arms, and
since in so important a matter he is not likely to have been guilty of carelessness,
while there is no question of incompetence, it is clear that "fimbriated as the saltire" was not intended to denote that the border was to be of the same width as for
the saltire, but simply that this border was to be of the same colour. In other words,
a fimbriation was not so strictly defined as to width in 1800 as some persons at the
present day would have us believe.

There would be no need to dwell upon this point were it not for the importance of this flag and the confusion into which the details of its construction have
fallen.

It may seem an extraordinary statement to make, but it is a fact that the Union
flag is never made in strict accordance with the original design.

---

[205] *London Gazette*, No. 15324.
[206] I.e. the second colour named: argent, or white.
[207] I.e. gules, or red.
[208] See the flag in Plate IV, fig. 2, which is a reproduction of the original drawing
preserved in the Privy Council Register.

In the pattern approved for the navy[209], which is also that flown on the Houses of Parliament and on the Government Offices, and is that adopted almost universally by private individuals of British nationality, the Irish saltire is reduced in width by having its fimbriation taken from itself instead of from the blue ground. Apparently this has been done to bring the outer boundaries in line across the flag, but it seems neither heraldically nor historically correct, for the saltire representing Ireland[210] should be of equal width with that of Scotland.

The other pattern in use is that established in 1900 by the War Office, in an attempt to comply with the literal terms of the Proclamation of 1st January, 1801, as interpreted by modern heraldic definitions[211]. In this pattern the two saltires are of equal breadth, but the "fimbriation" of the St George's cross has been reduced to the same width as that of St Patrick's saltire.

However, these differences are of no serious importance, and indeed this flag seems doomed to misrepresentation, which extends even to its name. A "Union Jack" is, correctly speaking, a small Union flag intended to be flown in one particular place, the bows of one of H.M. ships: yet for many years past this technical distinction has been lost sight of[212] and the misapplication of the term "Jack" has become almost universal, so much so that we have the Government solemnly announcing that "The Union *Jack* should be regarded as the national flag[213]."

The Union Pendant, that is a pendant with St George's Cross at the head and with the fly striped longitudinally red, white and blue (see Plate V, fig. 2) appears to have been first instituted in 1661 as a pendant which combined the colours of the Union flag and which, like that flag, was to be flown only by H.M. ships. It was afterwards known as the "Ordinary" or "Common" Pendant[214]. It went out of use when the squadronal colours were abandoned in 1864, though it survives in a smaller form (in which the fly is not slit) to this day as a signal that the ship's company is engaged in divine service.

---

[209] See Plate V, fig. 8.

[210] For discussion of the question how this came to represent Ireland see Chapter II.

[211] The Union flag flown by the War Office on ceremonial days is, however, of naval pattern.

[212] Probably because after the seventeenth century the Union flag was rarely seen at sea in any other position.

[213] The Earl of Crewe, on behalf of His Majesty's Government, in the House of Lords 14th July, 1908.

[214] Pepys calls it "the Ordinary or Union Pendant used by the King's ships only."

CHAPTER IV

FLAGS OF COMMAND

(I) THE ROYAL STANDARD

Highest in dignity among the flags which have been used to denote the leader of a British fleet comes the Royal Banner commonly spoken of as the Royal Standard.

Its use in this connection has for very many years been obsolete, but before noting the occasions on which it has been flown for this purpose it will be convenient to sketch its history down to our own times.

The royal arms make their first[215] appearance in 1189 in the Great Seal of Richard I as a single lion rampant contourné upon the king's shield. In Richard's second seal, made in 1198 to replace the first one which was lost during his captivity, the single lion became the three lions[216] passant guardant in pale which have remained in the arms of England until the present day. In 1339 Edward III, angered at the assistance given by Philip of France to the King of Scotland, took steps to assert a claim to the throne of France, and, in earnest of this, in January, 1340, he formally assumed the title and arms of King of France, quartering the arms of France (azure semé of fleurs-de-lis) with those of England in the royal banner and on the great seal. In doing this he, somewhat unpatriotically, placed the arms of France in the first and third quarters, thereby giving them precedence over those of England.

---

[215] The art of Heraldry was not established until the thirteenth century, and the armorial bearings associated with the names of our kings before Richard I are the inventions of the mediaeval heralds, who, in their anxiety to give their art a foundation in the past, did not hesitate to assign arms even to the psalmist David.

[216] Or leopards. See *Ency. Brit.* s.v. "Heraldry."

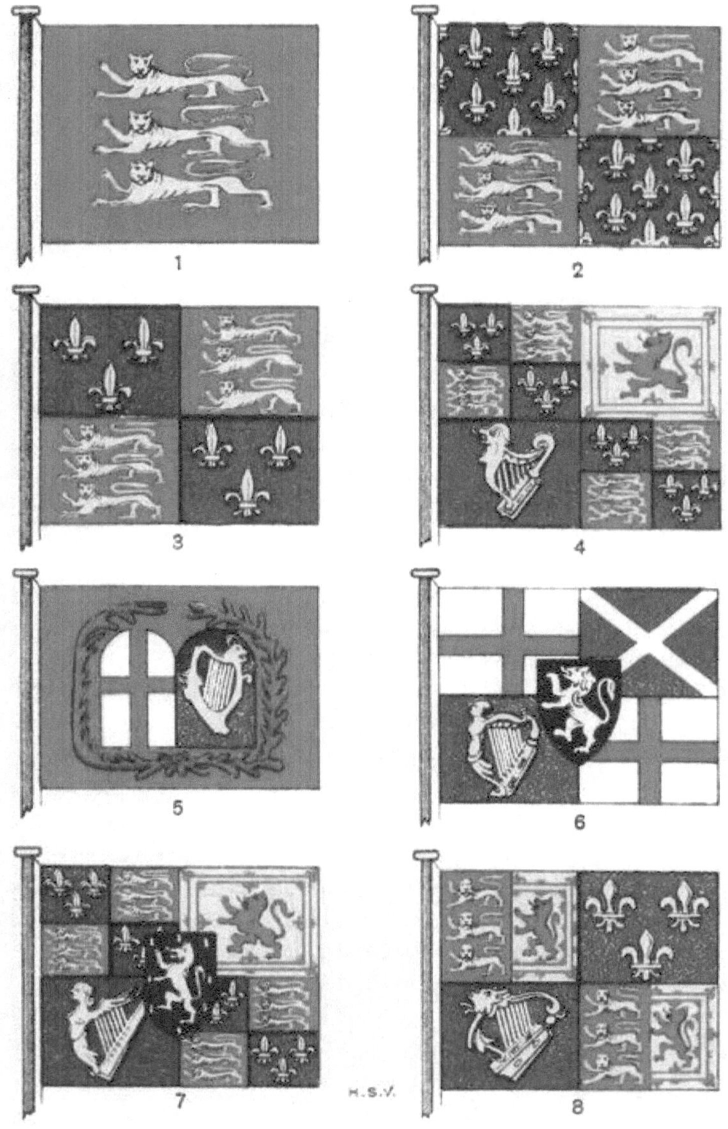

Plate VI

Royal Standards

1. Royal Standard, early
2. Royal Standard, 1340
3. Royal Standard, 1411
4. Royal Standard, Stuart
5. Commonwealth Standard
6. Cromwell's Standard
7. Royal Standard, 1689
8. Royal Standard, 1707

From this date[217] until the death of Elizabeth these were the royal arms of England, but during the reign of Richard II (1377-99) the legendary arms of Edward the Confessor (or, a cross patoncé between five martlets on a field azure) were impaled with them, and Queen Mary, after her marriage with Philip of Spain, impaled the arms of Spain. About the year 1411 Henry IV, in imitation of the change made by Charles V in his arms, reduced the fleurs-de-lis to three in number. On the accession of James I it became necessary to add the arms of Scotland (or, a lion rampant within a double tressure flory and counterflory, gules) and in doing this James took the opportunity to add arms representing Ireland. For these he took the badge chosen for Ireland by Henry VIII (a harp or, stringed argent). Mr Serjeant Knight, in the memorandum referred to on p. 55 becomes very indignant over this harp, and gives vent to his feelings in the following words:

> At the same time (upon what consideration I am ignorant) something was to be added for ye Kingdome of Ireland or something that might signify so much and ye Harpe (as at present borne) it seems resolv'd on. But for what reasons am as ignorant as for ye former, ye Harpe being no more the Armes of that Kingdome or of any one from whence that King was lineally descended than any other Constellation or any of ye Signes of the Zodiack. Having often contemplated this, ye only satisfaction I could forme to myselfe was from ye temper of ye times & doe suspect ye Leaven of Puritanisme in it by soe readily foysting this to ye exclusion of that of his Maty had (as has all his Posterity) an indisputable Hereditary Right unto, equal to that of England, ... viz the Arms of Ulster: or, a cross gules.

This harp was not the ancient arms of Ireland. Those arms are supposed to have been three crowns in pale in a blue field, but as there was never a native king of the whole of Ireland it is clear that there could never have been a native coat of arms representative of the whole country. Placing the arms quarterly of France and England in the first and fourth quarters of his shield, James put those of Scotland in the second quarter and those of Ireland in the third. This arrangement was, however, not invariable. In some of the Irish seals[218] Ireland is found in the second place and Scotland in the third, while in the Great Seal of Scotland made in James II's reign the arms of Scotland occupy the first and fourth quarters, with England second and Ireland third.

After the execution of Charles I, the royal standard was replaced by the Commonwealth standard, with the cross and harp[219]. During the Protectorate (1653-9) the standard consisted of: 1 and 4 the cross of St George, 2 the cross of St Andrew, and 3 the Irish harp, with an inescutcheon of the arms of Cromwell (sable a lion rampant, argent)[220]. The Commonwealth standard came back for a few months

[217] The claim was renounced by the Treaty of Bretigny in 1360, to be renewed again at the suggestion of Parliament in 1369: presumably the French Arms were not used between these years.

[218] E.g. seal of the Exchequer of Ireland (Commonwealth).

[219] See p. 62 and Plate VI, fig. 5.

[220] See p. 63 and Plate VI, fig. 6.

in 1659-60, to be replaced by the royal standard of James I; the makeshift used by Mountagu while on his way to fetch Charles II back to the throne has already been described.

The remaining changes have been succinctly described by Mr Fox-Davies[221] as follows:

> When William III and Mary came to the throne an inescutcheon of the arms of Nassau (Azure, billetty and a lion rampant or) was superimposed upon the Royal Arms as previously borne, for William III, and he impaled the same coat without the inescutcheon for his wife. At her death the impalement was dropped. After the Union with Scotland in 1707 the arms of England (Gules, three lions, etc.) were impaled with those of Scotland (the tressure not being continued down the palar line), and the impaled coat of England and Scotland was placed in the first and fourth quarters, France in the second, Ireland in the third.

> At the accession of George I. the arms of Hanover were introduced in the fourth quarter. These were: Tierced in pairle reversed, 1. Brunswick, gules, two lions passant guardant in pale or; 2. Luneberg, or, semé of hearts gules, a lion rampant azure; 3. (in point), Westphalia, gules a horse courant argent, and on an inescutcheon (over the fourth quarter) gules, the crown of Charlemagne (as Arch Treasurer of the Holy Roman Empire).

> At the union with Ireland in 1801 the opportunity was taken to revise the Royal Arms, and those of France were then discontinued. The escutcheon decided upon at that date was: Quarterly, 1 and 4, England; 2. Scotland; 3. Ireland, and the arms of Hanover were placed upon an inescutcheon. This inescutcheon was surmounted by the Electoral cap, for which a crown was substituted later when Hanover became a kingdom.

> At the death of William IV., by the operation of the Salic Law, the crowns of England and Hanover were separated, and the inescutcheon of Hanover disappeared from the Royal Arms of this country, and by Royal Warrant issued at the beginning of the reign of Queen Victoria the Royal Arms and badges were declared to be: 1 and 4, England; 2. Scotland; 3. Ireland.

---

[221] Fox-Davies, *Complete Guide to Heraldry*, 1909, p. 607.

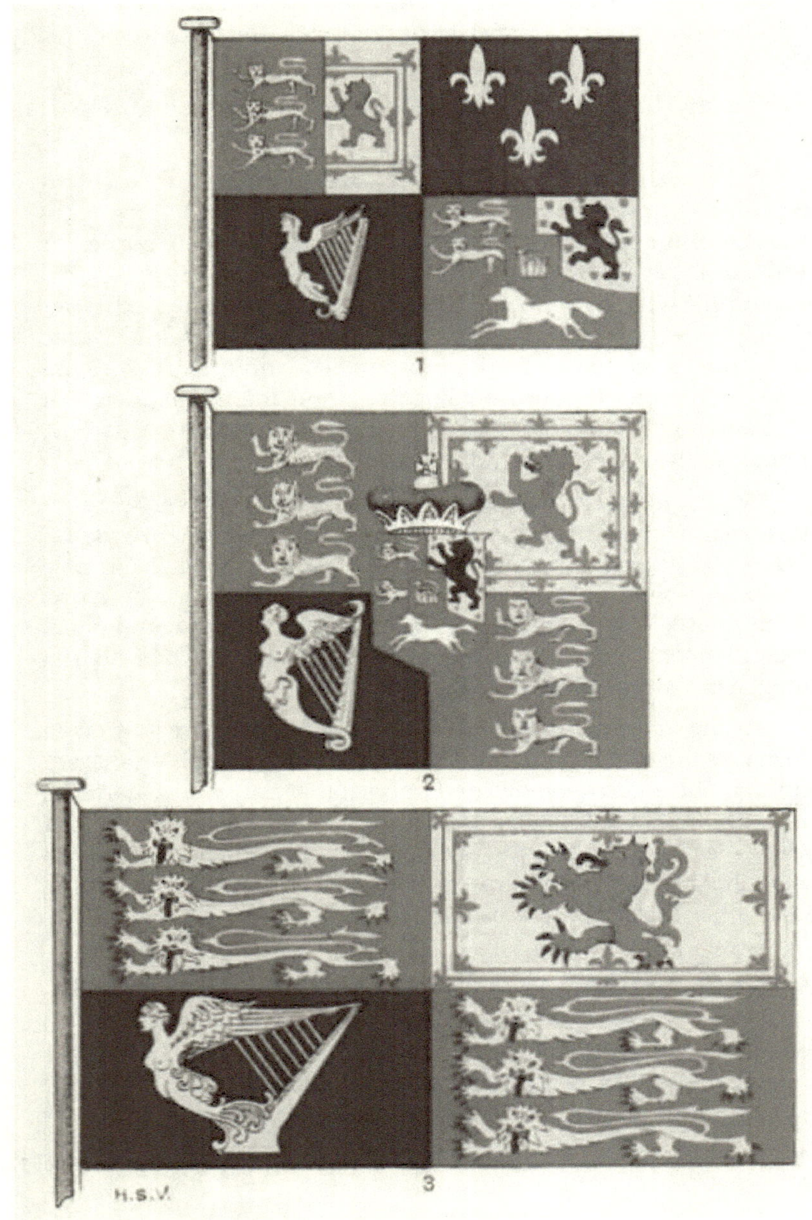

Plate VII

Royal Standards

1. Royal Standard, 1714 2. Royal Standard, 1801

3. Royal Standard, 1837

The principles which governed the use of the royal standard at sea prior to the sixteenth century are somewhat obscure. In the thirteenth century and early part of the fourteenth the three lions (or leopards) of England appear to have been regarded not only as the personal arms of the Sovereign but also as the English national emblem, and to have been used as such by all ships, royal and merchant. By the addition, in January, 1340, of the arms of France, Edward III adopted a royal standard that could no longer be regarded in this light. Yet although the royal standard now became more peculiarly the personal ensign of the king it is clear, from the frequency with which this flag occurs in inventories of ships' stores, that its use was not confined to ships in which the king or his admiral were embarked. It seems, however, to have been flown only on ships temporarily or permanently in the king's service, and to have been displayed by such ships from the deck, in company with the flag of St George and other flags containing royal badges, or emblems representative of the saints after whom the ships were named.

There was, however, some distinction by which the presence of the king could be denoted, and this difference lay most probably in the position of the standard. We know that the "banner of council" placed in the shrouds as a signal to call the council to the flagship, which is the earliest signal recorded as used in the English fleet, dates from this period, and that it contained the royal arms, with angelic supporters, or impaled with the cross of St George, and that from the sixteenth to the eighteenth century this "banner" was the royal standard[222]. But the most prominent position for a flag worn in a ship is at the masthead, and it would seem that it was this position of the standard that was reserved for the king or his deputy, the Lord Admiral. When Edward III led the English fleet to the attack on the French fleet at Sluys in June, 1340, his ship was decorated with banners and streamers containing the new royal arms, and had a silver-gilt crown at the masthead.

> Li rois estoit en un vassiel moult fort et moult biel qui avoit esté fais, ouvrés et carpentés a Zandwich et estoit armés et parés de banières et d'estramières très rices, ouvrées et armoiies des armes de France et d'Engleterre esquartelées; et sus le mast amont avoit une grande couronne d'argent dorée d'or qui resplondisoit et flambioit contre le soleil[223].

It was, however, not the gilt crown but the flags that denoted the king's presence, for Froissart explains that it was by these flags that the French knew the king was himself present. "Bien veoient entre yaus[224] li Normant par les banières que li rois d'Engleterre y estoit personelment[225]."

In 1495, when Henry VII was encouraging John Cabot and his sons in their voyages of discovery, he granted them the right to fly the royal banners and flags: "plenam ac liberam authoritatem, facultatem et potestatem navigandi ad omnes partes ... sub banneris, vexillis, et insigniis nostris[226]," presumably in the same

---

[222] Its use was discontinued on the official adoption of Howe's Signal Book in 1790.
[223] Froissart, i (*MS. de Rome*).
[224] eux.
[225] Froissart, i.
[226] *Hakl. Voy.* vii, 141.

way as they were flown on the royal ships.

The earliest surviving orders directing the Lord High Admiral to fly the royal standard at the masthead are those of 1545, at the end of Henry VIII's reign. "Item the Lord Admiral shall beare one banner of the Kings Maj[ts] Arms in his mayne topp and one flag of saint George crosse in his foretopp[227]."

The royal standard was flown at the main, with the St George at the fore, by Howard during the Armada fights in 1588 and during the Cadiz Expedition of 1596. In 1618, by arrangement with the Marquis (afterwards Duke) of Buckingham, Howard (then Earl of Nottingham) resigned the office, which was transferred to the Marquis. Buckingham made his first appearance at sea as Lord High Admiral when he accompanied Prince Charles on his return from Spain in 1623. For this voyage, a not inconsiderable sum of money was expended in flags, which included:

> Ye great silke flagg wth ye Kings Armes for ye Prince
> the great fflag wth ye Princes Armes & ye armes of Spaine empaled
> a fflag for ye foretop wth the Prince of Wales armes
> a fflag of Bewpers of 24 breadthes wth the Kings Armes
> a fflag of 18 breadthes wth the Kings Armes
> an Ensigne of 16 breadthes wth ye Lord Admiralls armes
> an Ensigne wth ye L[d] Admiralls Badge and Motto[228]

with a number of other flags, ensigns and pendants. As the Prince had a special silk standard, it would seem that one of the other standards was for Buckingham[229]. The Earl of Rutland was in command of this fleet on its outward voyage to Santander, and apparently he was given permission to fly the standard while in supreme command.

The following year Sir R. Bingley was instructed to put his lieutenant, with the king's standard, in a ship to transport the Spanish Ambassador across the Channel[230]. This was a somewhat extraordinary use of the standard, for, with the disuse of flags placed along the bulwarks, it had ceased to be generally flown on ships-of-war. The standard was, however, flown on special occasions by high officers other than the Lord High Admiral when in command of fleets. Wimbledon wore it in the Cadiz Expedition of 1625, and no less than £36 (equivalent to about £400 to-day) was spent on "the great silke fflagg wth his Ma[ts] Armes guilded wth fyne gould and wrought wth oyle Coll[rs]," and it was worn by the Earl of Denbigh in 1628: but when the Earl of Lindsey, who had been appointed one of the Commissioners for the Admiralty after the murder of Buckingham, moved heaven and earth for permission to wear it while in command of the fleet in 1635, alleging among other reasons that it had been flown by the Earls of Arundel and Rutland

[227] *S. P. Henry VIII*, ccv, 160. Instructions drawn up by Sir John Hawkins in the latter part of Elizabeth's reign contain the same provision. "Item the Ld. Admirall shall beare a flagg of the Armes of England upon the Top of his Mayne-mast. And a flagg of St. George one the foretopmast."

[228] *Rawlinson MS.* A 192.

[229] Buckingham flew the standard during the Ile de Ré expedition of 1627.

[230] *Cal. S. P. D.* 15th June, 1624.

and by Sir Robert Mansell, and that he himself had had the honour previously, his repeated applications were in vain; and so "a little maimed" he had to content himself with the Union flag at the mainmasthead.

During the Civil War the Lord High Admiral's standard held a very anomalous position. In 1642 the Parliament had appointed the Earl of Warwick to the office in defiance of the king's wishes, and, although in active opposition to the king, he flew the royal standard. In the summer of 1648 the fleet he commanded lay off the Dutch coast, watching the royalist fleet under the command of Prince Charles. When the Prince summoned Warwick to take down his standard the Earl replied: "I am appointed by both Houses of the Parliament of England to be Lord High Admiral of England, by which right I bear the Standard[231]." The fleets never came to blows or the two standards might have got a little mixed. Warwick had, however, provided against this eventuality just before leaving England by supplying his fleet with pendants of his personal colours[232].

Shortly after this, the command of the royalist ships was handed over to Prince Rupert, and in order that the Parliamentary Naval forces might not have the monopoly of the standard he was given permission to fly one when he thought fit.

Sir Edward Hyde to Prince Rupert.

Hague 27 Jan. 1649.

> Your order for wearing the Standard.... I promised the Prince to give your Highness advertisement of the debate concerning this wearing the standard; in which I learned many things, which I never heard before. It is agreed by all that the standard is properly and of right to be worn only by the Lord High Admiral of England; & when I enquired of the order granted for the Lord Willoughby or Sir William Batten's wearing it, it is said, that it was thought then necessary, since the Earl of Warwick wore a standard, that whosoever commanded the fleet that was to fight against him, should wear one, lest the seamen should be discouraged, and look upon the Earl as the greater person; so that it is the opinion of all, that, when you are like to engage with the Rebel's fleet, your men may expect you should wear that ensign. It is therefore wholly referred to your Highness to wear it upon any occasions you think fit[233].

At the request of the Council of State, the office of Lord High Admiral was abolished in 1649 and its powers transferred to the Council, but as the high authority exercised by the new "Generals at Sea" was in many respects like that formerly exercised by the Lord High Admiral they were empowered to wear at the main masthead the special "standard" referred to above (p. 62) which now

---

[231] Penn, *Memorials of Penn*, I, 262.

[232] *S. P. D. Chas. I*, DXVIII, 120: "I desire you to provide and send downe twenty Pendents of my Colours viz. Yellowe and Tawny for the ships that accompany mee to sea. And I shall n(ee)d a newe Standard for the St George."

[233] *Clarendon S. P.* II, 468, 9.

took the place of the standard with the royal arms. In this "standard," which was really only a modification of the "union" flag, the English lions were replaced by the St George's cross, the Scottish and French arms disappeared, and only those of Ireland remained. This upstart flag soon acquired an honour in battle that had been sadly lacking to the old one since 1588, for it waved over the heroic fights of the First Dutch War and the action at Santa Cruz. In May, 1658, it was superseded at sea by the standard that had been assigned to the Protector in 1653 (see p. 63), but this flag saw no great deeds and disappeared early in 1659, to be replaced by the Commonwealth standard. When Mountagu went over in May, 1660, to fetch back Charles to the throne no royal standard was forthcoming, so he improvised one as already related (see p. 64).

With the restoration of the Stuarts in 1660 the royal standard resumed its place as the Lord Admiral's flag, but with the anchor flag as a substitute when the presence of the king rendered the use of the standard by the Lord Admiral undesirable.

When William of Orange came over in 1688 to take possession of the throne of Great Britain for himself and his wife he flew a red standard containing in an escutcheon his arms impaled with the Stuart royal arms, with the legend "For the Protestant Religion and the Liberties of England" above the escutcheon and his motto "je maintiendray" below[234]; but when the joint sovereigns had been formally proclaimed king and queen they adopted the Stuart standard with an inescutcheon of Nassau already described.

The restriction in the use of the standard which had been rapidly growing[235] since the beginning of the seventeenth century, reached its culmination in 1702, when the anchor flag definitely superseded it as the Lord Admiral's flag, although, curiously enough, the standard remained in use as a signal flag (for calling a council of flag officers) for nearly another century.

The reason of the abandonment of the royal standard in 1702 does not appear. In February the Earl of Pembroke, recently appointed Lord High Admiral by William III, had given instructions for his flagship, the 'Britannia,' then fitting out at Chatham in preparation for the French War, to be supplied with a standard, but on the 20th March, just after the accession of Queen Anne, he wrote to the Navy Board:

> Notwithstanding any former Orders from me for your preparing any of the Royal Standards of England, I do hereby desire and direct you to forbear doing thereof, but you are to cause to be prepar'd for me as soon as conveniently may be, so many of these flags[236] which particularly have been worn by the Lord high Admll of England &c., by vertue of his Office, as may be necessary

---

[234] These arms and device were also used on Proclamations issued in January, 1689.

[235] This is especially seen in the case of the Earl of Lindsey, who had nevertheless been granted the extraordinary privilege of pardoning penalties inflicted by Martial Law in his fleet, a power that did not appertain even to the Lord High Admiral.

[236] I.e. the anchor flag; this is confirmed by a sketch of the flags ordered on 20th March, 1702, in *Rawlinson MS.* C 914.

for my Shipp and Boat[237],

and with this the long-continued existence of the royal standard as a naval flag of command came to an end.

A number of interesting examples of the use of the standard at sea by the king and by the Lord High Admiral (the Duke of York) in 1672 are given in the Journal of Sir John Narborough, then lieutenant in the Lord High Admiral's flagship, among them the following:

> Tuesday being 23rd.... This day the King came on board.... At his coming this day we put abroad a silk Ensigne and a silk Jack and all silk Pendants at every yard arm and Top mast head, and at the Main topmasthead the silk Standard of England, and at the Fore topmasthead a silk Flagg Red with a yellow anchor and cable in the Fly: and at the mizen topmasthead a Union Flagg. These we wore all flying while the King was aboard: But when the King went out of the Ship and left the Duke aboard the Red flagg was taken in at the Foremasthead, which had the Anchor and Cable in it, and hoisted up at the Maintopmasthead. The Standard being struck there, and the Union Flagg at the Mizen topmasthead was struck....

> Wednesday being 5th. (June 1672).... This day the King and several of the noblemen came on board the Prince[238]. His Royal Highness caused the Standard to be struck when the King's Standard was in sight, and when the King was on board the Standard was hoisted at the Maintopmasthead, and the Red Standard with the anchor in it at the Foretopmasthead and the Union Flag at the Mizentopmasthead.

> Tuesday being 18.... The King had a Standard flying all night at ye head of the Yacht's mast, the Queen had a Standard flying at the head of the Prince's Main topmasthead Flaggstaff, and his R.H. the anchor Flagg at the head of his Yacht's mast and Prince Rupert had the Union Flagg at the head of his Yacht's mast....

> Monday being 9th. (Sept. 1672).... This afternoon at 4 of the Clock the King came on board, and Prince Rupert and several of the nobility were with His Majesty. When His Majesty came within two miles of the Prince his R.H. commanded the Standard to be struck until such time as his Majesty came on board. At the striking of his R.H.'s Standard all the Flaggs in the Fleet were struck immediately and kept down until the Standard on board the Prince was hoisted, then they hoisted theirs.

(II) THE ADMIRALTY FLAG

The Admiralty Flag appears to have originated as a purely ornamental flag

[237] *Adm. Sec. Out Lrs.* 182.
[238] I.e. H.M.S. *Prince.*

displaying the official badge of the Lord High Admiral for the decoration of his ship on ceremonial occasions. Its use for such a purpose would be analogous with the display, in the fourteenth, fifteenth and sixteenth centuries, of the royal badges, such as the dragon, swan, antelope, portcullis, ostrich feather or rose.

The office of "Great" or "High" Admiral of England may be dated from the appointment of John de Beauchamp as Admiral of all the fleets, in 1360, but although the Anchor badge is found upon the seals of the Lord Admirals of Scotland as early as 1515, no such early instance has yet been brought to light in England[239]. It may, however, be presumed that it was in use south of the Tweed from an earlier date, for the anchor was certainly in use in the sixteenth century as a mark placed upon ships or goods arrested by the Admiralty Court. The earliest known instance of the anchor in conjunction with the English Lord High Admiral's arms occurs at the end of Queen Mary's reign in a volume of Acts of the High Court of Admiralty dated 11th February, 1558. Here the arms of Lord Clinton and Saye are surrounded by four anchors without cable[240].

For the earliest instance of the anchor in a flag we must turn to the well-known engraving supposed to represent the 'Ark Royal,' Howard's flagship in 1588, which shows an anchor in the head of a streamer flown from the foretop[241].

The foul anchor[242] is first found in the seal of Howard after he had become Earl of Nottingham, and may be seen in a specimen attached to a document dated April, 1601, now in the British Museum. The badge appears on the reverse of this seal on the trappings of the horse which the earl bestrides. In 1623 Buckingham, who had succeeded Nottingham as Lord High Admiral, was provided with "an Ensigne with ye Ld Admiralls Badge & Motto." This badge was evidently the anchor and cable, for the badge of the foul anchor appears prominently four times on the York Water Gate (Thames Embankment) built for Buckingham in 1626, and in 1627 Buckingham was using as his official seal the anchor and cable surrounded by the garter and surmounted by a coronet. In the badges on the gate the end of the cable hangs down over one of the arms, but in the seal the end is neatly flemished down in three coils upon the shank.

In 1633, when Buckingham was dead and the Admiralty in commission, the flags surveyed at Deptford included among them a silk "red ensigne with ye Lo. Admiralls badge." At this date the badge could not have been a personal one, and there seems no doubt that it was the official anchor and cable, possibly of the same design as in Buckingham's seal, for the Commissioners had adopted this form for use in their own seal, replacing the coronet and garter by the legend "Sig.

---

[239] This is perhaps due to the fact that the English Lord Admirals adopted a ship in full sail upon the obverse of their seals. We have no specimen of the reverse or counter-seal earlier than that of Nottingham. As the anchor is found on the reverse of this seal it is possible that it was upon the reverse in the earlier seals.

[240] The author is indebted to Mr R. G. Marsden for this reference.

[241] Reproduced in Hakluyt Society's edition of *Hakluyt's Voyages*, iv, 208. The engraving may be dated circa 1600.

[242] A conventional design of an anchor and cable, in which the cable is entwined about (or, as seamen say, foul of) the stock and shank.

Com. Reg. Ma. Pro. Adm. Ang[243]." It will be observed that the field of this flag is red, as at the present day. The anchor with coiled cable appears again during the Commonwealth on the seals of the Generals at Sea, but the design had begun to deteriorate even in Buckingham's time. In his seals in 1628 some of the turns of the coil pass below the shank, and in the later seals the coil lays round the shank instead of upon it.

When the Commission was dissolved in 1638 and the office granted to the Earl of Northumberland (as substitute for the young Duke of York), Northumberland adopted for his seal a design in which the cable was draped in graceful turns as a border round the anchor, ending at the ring on the side opposite to that at which it was made fast. This design was used by the Committee of the Admiralty and Navy under the Commonwealth and was adopted by James Duke of York in 1660[244], but in the eighteenth century it in turn deteriorated, until it reached the form used in the present flag[245], in which the cable is not made fast to the anchor at all, but simply passes loosely through the ring and hangs down stiffly on either side.

The anchor flag was not used during the Commonwealth, but it was restored in 1661, when the contractor was paid £2. 10s. "ffor shading the Standard and Ensigne and Jack with a ancor," £5. 10s. "ffor sowing silke and cloth for the sockett and markeing the Ensigne with the ancor and cable," and £4. 10s. "ffor sowing silke and cloth for socketing & markeing the flag with a ancor and cable[246]."

The subordinate "badge" flag was now promoted to the dignity of a "standard" and flown at the masthead as a substitute for the royal standard when the Lord Admiral was unable to fly the latter, because of the presence of the king in the fleet.

In 1673 the Test Act deprived the Duke of York of his office, which for the next eleven years was placed in commission. Charles II, just before his death, revoked the commission, and the office fell in to the crown. When the Duke of York succeeded to the throne in 1685 as James II, he retained the office in his own hands, and in token of this placed "a crown over the anchor as being himself his own Admiral[247]."

In addition to the anchor flag (which when used by the sovereign is flown at the fore, as the main is already occupied by the royal standard) a flag of similar design, but with the St George's cross in the upper canton, was also flown as an ensign at the stern[248].

---

[243] The seal of the Royal Commissioners for the High Admiralty of England.

[244] A variation of it, in which the cable passes loosely through the ring and ends in extravagant flourishes on either side, was in use by Pepys in 1673.

[245] Plate VIII, fig. 1. On the seals the anchor was vertical, but in the flags it was usually placed horizontally. The foul anchor in the Admiralty seal since 1725 has, however, been of a design similar to that on the York Water Gate.

[246] *S. P. D. Chas II.* LXVI. 74.

[247] *Pepys MSS.* Miscellanea, IX.

[248] *Pepys MSS.* Miscellanea, IX.

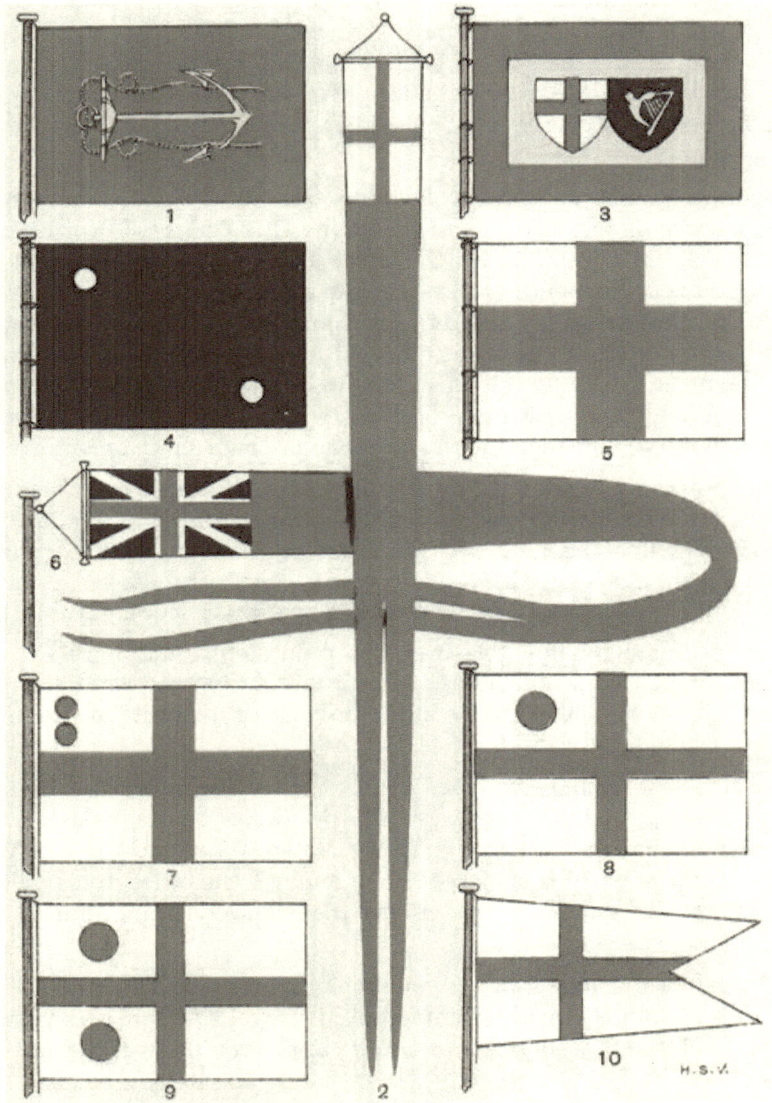

Plate VIII

Admirals' Flags

1. Admiralty Flag
2. Distinction Pendant
3. Commonwealth Admiral
4. Rear Admiral of Blue, 1702
5. Rear Admiral of White, 1702
6. Budgee Pendant
7. Rear Admiral of White, 1824
8. Vice Admiral, 1889
9. Rear Admiral, 1889
10. Broad Pendant (modern)

At this period, according to Lieut. Graydon's flag-book, the Scots Lord Admiral flew a white flag containing a blue anchor and cable. The Admiral of Scotland, who according to Pepys[249] was "no officer of State" and had "no precedence at all given him from his office," was abolished after the Union of 1707, when the three small ships representing the navy of that country were absorbed in the English, henceforth the British, fleet.

After the Revolution of 1688 the Office of Lord High Admiral was placed in commission, but it was revived by William III in June, 1702, when the Earl of Pembroke was appointed. Pembroke had intended to proceed to sea in command of the fleet then being fitted out in anticipation of the outbreak of the war with France and Spain, known as the War of the Spanish Succession, and he would have flown the royal standard in his flagship. William, however, died on 8th March, and Queen Anne, immediately after her accession, deprived the Lord High Admiral of the right to fly the standard, among other perquisites and *droits*. Pembroke then gave instructions for the anchor flag to be supplied instead. But as he was not a seaman his proposal to take command of the fleet had naturally aroused much opposition, and in the end it was dropped. In May he was replaced as Lord High Admiral by Prince George of Denmark, the Queen's consort, and although Pembroke again held the office for a short time after the Prince's death in 1708, no opportunity arose for the anchor flag to be flown at sea in military command during his or the Prince's tenure.

In 1709 the office of Lord High Admiral was again placed in commission and it remained in commission for over a hundred years. During this period the anchor flag was on one occasion flown at sea in executive command. At the end of March, 1719, Admiral the Earl of Berkeley, then First Lord of the Admiralty, was appointed to the command of a fleet then fitting out to repel a naval raid threatened from Cadiz in support of the claims of the Pretender. Having been given the extraordinary rank of "Admiral and Commander in Chief of his Majesty's Navy and Fleets," he was authorised by the king (George I) to fly the anchor flag at the main whilst so serving, and the flag was in fact flown for a few weeks at the end of March and beginning of April. The next occasion on which this flag was flown in executive command at sea occurred in July, 1828, when the Duke of Clarence (afterwards William IV), who had been appointed Lord High Admiral in 1827, with the express understanding that he should exercise no military command, suddenly put to sea from Plymouth, flying the anchor flag, in command of a squadron of manoeuvre that it had been intended to place under Vice-Admiral Sir Henry Blackwood. This extraordinary escapade and the friction which had been caused by the duke's method of conducting affairs, led to his removal, and to the office being once more placed in commission. It is very improbable that it will ever again be conferred upon an individual. In May, and again in August, 1869, Mr Childers, the First Lord, accompanied by Vice-Admiral Sir Sydney Dacres, the First Sea Lord, embarked in H.M.S. 'Agincourt' and took command, first of the reserve fleet, and then of an experimental squadron, under the Admiralty flag. This proceeding gave rise to much comment, but since the Letters Patent appointing a Board of

---

[249] *Ibid.* Naval Minutes.

Admiralty give power to "any two or more" of the Commissioners to exercise all the functions of the Lord High Admiral, the action of Mr Childers does not seem to have been *ultra vires*, though it is not one that is likely to be repeated.

Since 1850 the anchor flag has been flown over the Admiralty Office in London. At sea it is flown in the royal yacht when the sovereign is present, in recognition of the fact that, under the Constitution, he is the source from which the Lord High Admiral's powers are derived; the anchor flag being flown at the fore, the royal standard at the main, and the Union flag at the mizen. In the Admiralty yacht the anchor flag is flown at the main when members of the Board are embarked in her. It is the custom (a custom that was in existence in the early years of the eighteenth century) to fly the anchor flag on men-of-war during the ceremony of launching. A similar flag, with the lower half of the field blue, has been recently adopted as the flag of the Australian Naval Board.

(III) ADMIRALS' FLAGS

> And so the Admiral of a Fleet or Squadron hath his flag in the Main-top; the Vice-Admiral in the Fore-top and the Rere Admiral in the Missen-top, with the Crosses or Colours of their Nation and Countrymen, And thus far it is usual and common even with Fleets of Merchant men, agreeing amongst themselves for the Admiral[250] ships in this kind.

In these words Boteler, writing in 1634, sums up the method of distinguishing the flags of the principal officers of a fleet which had been made possible by the appearance of the three-masted ship of war in the fifteenth century, was adopted by the English in the sixteenth, and remained in vogue until the disappearance of the sailing ship of war in the nineteenth century.

But, it may well be asked, what was done to distinguish the admirals before ships had three masts? It is not easy to answer this question, for the records throw no light on it and the information vouchsafed by contemporary chroniclers is very scanty. Perhaps the answer nearest the truth would be: "nothing, for there were then no grades to distinguish." Before the sixteenth century there was rarely more than one admiral in a fleet, and on those rare occasions on which two or more admirals appear they were usually given the command "jointly and severally," that is, as co-equals[251]. In such cases it may be presumed that both, if indeed they were not embarked in the same ship, bore the St George's flag or royal standard at the masthead and were distinguished by banners of their personal arms.

[250] Throughout the sixteenth and seventeenth centuries the term "Admiral" was used of the ship as well as of the officer in command. The rank, moreover, until the latter part of the seventeenth century, was purely local and temporary, and simply denoted the senior officer for the time being of the ships in company.

[251] See lists in Nicolas, *History of the Royal Navy*, i, 435, and ii, 524. It is a curious circumstance that in nearly all these cases the fleet was directed against Scotland. One exception to the rule occurs in 1315 when John of Argyle was appointed "Captain of our fleet of ships which we are shortly about to send to the Scottish parts." Under him were placed "William de Crey and Thomas de Hewys, Admirals of the fleet of the King's ships," who were "commanded that they be obedient and responsive to the same John."

In the fleet that attempted invasion under Eustace the Monk in 1217, only one ship (that of the Commander-in-Chief) appears to have flown a flag at the masthead, for we are told by a contemporary chronicler[252] that one of Hubert de Burgh's men agreed, when they engaged Eustace's ship, "to climb up the mast and cut down the banner, that the other vessels may be dispersed from want of a leader."

In 1346 there seems to have been still only one flag of command in a fleet. Edward III had in that year fitted out a fleet in order to make an incursion into Gascony, but after a false start which had been frustrated by contrary winds, the king, on the advice of Godefroy de Harcourt, suddenly changed his mind and set out for Normandy, taking the flag of command from his Admiral and leading the fleet himself.

> Et il meismes prist l'ensengne[253] de l'amiral le conte de War-
> vich, et volt estre amiraus pour ce voiage, et se mist tout devant,
> comme patrons et gouvrenères de toute le Navie[254].

We have no further evidence as to the method of bearing admirals' flags in the English fleet until we come to the "Book of Orders for the War by Sea and Land[255]," drawn up by Thos. Audley *c.* 1530 at the request of Henry VIII. Here provision is made for only one admiral, who is to bear two flags; one at the main and the other at the fore, while all the other ships are to bear one at the mizen. The orders drawn up by Lisle fifteen years later provide for a fleet divided into three squadrons, and in this case also each admiral had two flags, but here the two flags were necessary to distinguish the flagships, as the private ships had each one flag, at the fore, main, or mizen respectively, to denote the squadrons to which they belonged.

> 5. Item the lord Admiral shall beare one banner of the Kings
> maits Armes in his mayne topp and one flag of saint George crosse
> in his fore topp, and every shipp appoynted to the battaill, shall
> beare one flag of saint Georges crosse in his mayne toppe.

> 6. Item thadmirall of the vanwarde ys appoynted to beare too
> flaggs of saint George crosse, thone in his mayne topp and thoth-
> er in his fore topp. And every shipp appoynted to the vanwarde
> shall weare one flag of sainte Georges crosse in his fore toppe.

> 7. Item thadmirall of the wyng shall beare a flag of saint Georg
> crosse in either[256] of his mesyn toppes, and every Shipp Galliasse
> pynnesse and Shalupe appoynted to the wyng shall have in ther
> mesyn toppe one flag of saint George crosse[257].

[252] *Vide* Nicolas, *History of the Royal Navy*, i, 178.

[253] Ensign, in the original sense of insignia; the modern "ensign" does not appear to have been used in the English navy before the latter part of Elizabeth's reign.

[254] Froissart, i, 255.

[255] *Harl. MS.* 309, fol. 4.

[256] I.e. in *both* the main-mizen and the bonaventure (or after) mizen tops; the large ships of this period were four-masted.

[257] *S. P. Henry VIII*, ccv, 160.

The relative dignity of the mastheads, main, fore and mizen, is seen underlying this arrangement, for the Lord Admiral places his standard at the main masthead and his St George, as next in rank, at the masthead next in importance; the second admiral occupies the two foremost mastheads with his flags and the third admiral the two aftermost, each being, of course, in a four-masted ship.

It will be observed that there is as yet no mention of "Vice" or "Rear" Admiral, but the term Vice-Admiral, which is much the older of the two, was in use in the English fleet in 1547 and in the French fleet at least as early as 1338. The term Rear-Admiral is more modern. This is pointed out by Monson[258], but indeed sufficient proof is to be seen in the fact that the term is not used in either the French or Dutch navies[259].

The Instructions drawn up in March, 1558, by Wm Wynter, Admiral of a fleet of ships about to go to Portsmouth, contain "an order for beringe of the flagge":

> Item that every Shippe of Warre do set up a flage of St. George uppon her Bonaventure myson, excepte Mr. Broke, Captaine of the reed Gallie, who is apointed to ware the flagge of vize Admyrall for this present Jorney: And the Victuellers, Hoyes and others for to ware there flagge bytwyne the myzon and the aftermost shrowde[260].

Here the Vice-Admiral has but one flag, and although we are not explicitly told where the Admiral and Vice-Admiral are to fly their flags, it is evident that it is intended they should be at the main and fore respectively.

We have no further definite information as to the mode in which the junior admirals bore their flags until we reach the year 1596. For the important expedition to Cadiz in the summer of that year a large combined English and Dutch fleet was assembled, and was divided into five squadrons; four English and one Dutch. The English ships were under the command of the Earl of Essex and the Lord Admiral (Howard) as "Joint Generalls of the Armies by sea and land." Under them were Lord Thomas Howard as Vice-Admiral of the fleet and Sir Walter Raleigh as Rear-Admiral. Each of these officers had command of one of the English squadrons with a Vice- and a Rear-Admiral of that squadron under him.

A contemporary account of the expedition among the Duke of Northumberland's MSS.[261] contains a series of coloured diagrams showing the flags flown by the various Admirals. From these we see that Howard, as Lord High Admiral, flew the royal standard at the main and the St George at the fore. The Vice- and Rear-Admirals of his squadron flew, at the fore and mizen respectively, a flag with

---

[258] "Though the use of a Rear Admiral is but a late invention in comparison with the other two and is allowed but the ordinary pay of a Captain" (*Naval Tracts of Sir Wm Monson* (N. R. S.), IV, 1).

[259] The French employ the term "contre-amiral" and the Dutch the curious locution "Schout-bij nacht," i.e. "Bailiff by night." The offices of Lord High Admiral, Admiral, and Vice-Admiral were adopted by England from the French.

[260] *Pepys MS.* and *Rawlinson MS.* c, 846.

[261] Edited by Sir Julian Corbett and published by the Navy Records Society in 1902 (*Miscellany*, vol. I) with facsimiles of the diagrams.

striped field (red, white and blue in seven horizontal stripes) and the St George in the canton. Essex, although superior to Howard in social rank and named before him in the joint proclamation which they issued, flew only the St George at the main. The Vice- and Rear-Admirals of his squadron flew at the fore the St George barred with blue horizontally.

The Vice-Admiral of the fleet flew the St George at the fore, and at the main, as Admiral of his squadron, a flag with the St George in a canton and a field striped horizontally green and white. The Vice- and Rear-Admirals of this squadron flew a similar flag at their proper mastheads. The Rear-Admiral of the fleet flew the St George at the mizen, and he and the Vice- and Rear-Admirals of his squadron flew plain white flags at the main, fore, and mizen respectively. The squadronal flags of the first three squadrons as depicted in this manuscript are unique as admirals' flags; they appear to have been stern ensigns promoted for this special occasion.

Originally it had been intended to use plain flags of different colours for the four squadrons, as is shown by the following entry in the Navy Accounts to which Mr Oppenheim drew attention in his *Administration of the Royal Navy*.

> Richerde Waters of London Upholster for iiij^{er} large fflagges or Ensignes made of fine Bewpers conteyning in each of them iiij v (85) yards of the same stuffe being each of them of severall Cullers viz One white, one Orengtawnie, one Blew and the iiijth Crimson Color which were appointed to be so made for the distinguishing of the iiij^{er} squadrons of the flete ffor the service then intended, finding at his owne chardges all manner of stuffe & workman-shippe. xvi^{li} viiij^{s} viij$^{d[262]}$.

Apart from the fact that "the unusual particularity of the item suggests that it was thought to require some justification, which would be natural if the flags referred to had never been used[263]," it may be pointed out that ten squadronal flags were needed, while this item only refers to four. There is, moreover, another entry in the same account which gives the sizes and prices of the "Ensignes & fflagges" provided for the expedition, at a total cost of £371. 8s. 4d. Descriptions of these flags are unfortunately not given, but it is a significant fact that of the largest size, sixteen breadths[264], ten were supplied.

The reason for the abandonment of the original intention to use plain-coloured flags for the squadrons of the 1596 expedition is not known, but when, in 1625, another expedition was sent out against Cadiz the fleet was divided into three squadrons, each under three admirals, with red, blue, and white flags respectively.

This expedition set sail in October, 1625, but four months earlier a much smaller fleet, also divided into three squadrons, had been sent to conduct the Queen from Boulogne to England. The difference in the Admirals' flags worn on these two occasions is significant, for it shows that there was no established practice

---

[262] Pipe Off. Dec. Acc. 2232.

[263] Corbett, *op. cit.* Descriptions of flags are very rarely given in the accounts; usually only the size and price appear.

[264] These flags would be about 6 yards long by 5 yards deep.

applicable to large fleets.

The Instructions[265] issued by Buckingham in June for the Boulogne fleet provide that the Admiral shall wear the Union flag at the main, and each ship of his squadron a pendant at the main masthead. The Vice- and Rear-Admirals are to have the Union at the fore and mizen respectively, and the private ships[266] of their squadrons pendants at those mastheads.

But when the larger fleet was set forth in October each of its three squadrons had three flag officers. The instructions issued by the Commander-in-Chief, Sir Edward Cecil (afterwards Lord Wimbledon) on 3rd October, contained the following provision:

> 17. The whole fleet is to be divided into three squadrons: the admiral's squadron is to wear red flags and red pendants on the main topmasthead; the vice-admiral's squadron to wear blue flags and blue pendants on the fore topmasthead; the rear admiral's squadron to wear white flags and white pendants on the mizen topmast heads.

The wording of this instruction is somewhat ambiguous. Owing to the absence of a comma after "flags," it may be taken to read that every ship was to have both a flag and a pendant in one of the three tops, but this would leave no ready means of distinguishing the flag-ships. Monson and Boteler, who wrote shortly after this date, say that the squadrons of a fleet were distinguished by coloured pendants hung from the main, fore, and mizen tops respectively[267], so that we may conclude that the arrangement of flags on this occasion was as follows:

The Admiral commanding in chief, although he was not Lord High Admiral, flew the royal standard at the main.

The Vice- and Rear-Admirals of his squadron flew "a redd flagg with a little white, and St George's Crosse therein at the topp of the flaggstaff[268]" (i.e. a red flag with St George in the upper canton next the staff, as in the red ensign), while the private ships of this squadron flew red pendants at the main.

The Vice-Admiral of the fleet and the Vice-Admiral and Rear-Admiral of his squadron bore plain blue flags at the appropriate mastheads, and the private ships of this squadron wore blue pendants at the fore topmast head.

[265] *S. P. D. Chas I*, v, 31.

[266] A ship not bearing an admiral's flag was called a "private ship"; but before 1650 the term "private man-of-war" almost invariably denotes a merchant ship having letters of marque, afterwards called a "privateer."

[267] Cf. *Boteler Dialogue*, 5: "The use of them is in Fleets to distinguish the Squadrons, by hanging of them out in the Tops; as all those Ships of the Admirals Squadron hang them out in the Main-top; those of the Vice Admirals in the Fore-top; and those of the Rere Admirals in the Missen-top; and here also they are of different Colours." See also Monson, Book III.

[268] *A Relation Touching the Fleet and Army of the King's most excellent majesty King Charles, set forth in the first year of his highness's reign, and touching the order, proceedings and actions of the same fleet and army,* by Sir John Glanville, secretary to the Council of War (*Camden Soc.* N. S. vol. XXXII, p. 83).

The Rear-Admiral of the fleet and the Vice- and Rear-Admirals of his squadron had white flags[269], while the private ships of this squadron had white pendants at the mizen topmast head.

No mention is made of the Union flag, which should normally have been flown by the Vice-Admiral and Rear-Admiral of the fleet at the fore and mizen respectively, but as "every flag officer both of the fleet and of the squadrons was a soldier[270]" anomalies were to be expected. Sir Francis Stewart, the original Rear-Admiral of the fleet, and the only seaman among the flag officers, was left on shore at the last moment because his ship, the 'Lion,' was found to be leaky. Wimbledon sent for his flag and conferred it on Denbigh, the Vice-Admiral of his squadron. Denbigh's former place was given to Delaware, the Rear-Admiral of the second, or blue squadron. This naturally gave offence to the Vice-Admirals of the second and third squadrons, and a furious squabble arose, which only interests us in two points so far as the flags were concerned. One is that in the course of the squabble the red flag, which became the object of contention, is referred to repeatedly as the "flag of St George," the other is that in a weak attempt at a solution of the difficulty created by his action Wimbledon authorised Valentia, the Vice-Admiral of the blue squadron to

> carrie the redd flagg with the St George's Cross in the maine topp
> as a kind of extraordinary or cheife deputy or Vice Admirall to
> the Admirall or to his Squadron, soe to distinguish him from my
> Lo. Delaware with some preferment alsoe to my Lord of Valencia.

A few days later Wimbledon requested him "to weare his flagg no longer in the maine topp," and finally both Valentia and Delaware "for reasons best known to themselves took downe their flagges." The whole episode forms a truly comic opera performance that must have greatly amused, if it did not disgust, the seamen of the fleet.

The main interest in this miserable expedition lies in the fact that it was the first occasion of the division of the fleet into red, blue, and white squadrons.

Two years later an expedition was fitted out under the command of Buckingham, the Lord High Admiral, intended for the capture of the Ile de Ré. On this occasion, in addition to the main fleet, which was again divided into red, blue, and white squadrons under three principal officers:—the Lord Admiral, with the standard at the main; the Vice-Admiral, with the Union at the fore and a blue flag at the main; and a Rear-Admiral, with the Union at the mizen and a white flag at the main, each of these having a Vice- and Rear-Admiral under him—there were two subsidiary squadrons, one under Lord Denbigh, who flew the St George at the main, and the other under Sir John Pennington, who flew the St Andrew's cross at the main, the only occasion on which the Scots' flag has been flown by an admiral of an English fleet.

The method of bearing Admirals' flags now became regularised. If the fleet

---

[269] *Op. cit.* "The Rere Admirals place with the white flagg to be borne in the mayne topp was assigned ... to my Lord Denbigh."

[270] Corbett, *Fighting Instructions*, 1530-1816 (N. R. S.), p. 49.

was small and had only three flag officers, the senior flew the Union flag at the main—unless he were the Lord Admiral, or had special permission to fly the standard—and the other two flew the Union at the fore and mizen respectively. If the fleet were larger the number of flag officers, who, it must be remembered, had as yet no permanent tenure of the rank, was increased to nine and the fleet was divided into squadrons distinguished by the red, blue and white flags of their Admirals and by the corresponding pendants of the ships; but this distinction of colour did not as yet extend to the ensigns on the poop.

This arrangement persisted until the end of the reign of Charles I, but in the first great fleet fitted out by the Commonwealth, at the beginning of the First Dutch War, the precedence of the colours was changed. As already related, the standard and Union flag flown by the principal admirals had been replaced by flags containing the cross and harp, but from the following proposals referred by the Commissioners for the Admiralty and Navy to their subordinate Board, the Navy Commissioners, it will be seen that it had been at first intended to adhere to the order of colours—red, blue, white.

> The 3 Generals to weare each of them a Standard, the one to have a pendent under the Standard & an Ensigne of Redd, the second a pendant under the Standard & an Ensigne of Blew, the third a Pendant under ye Standard & an ensigne of White.

> One Vice Admirall of the ffleet to weare the usuall fflagg in his foretopp wth a pendant under his fflagg and an ensigne of Redd.

> One Rere-admirall to the ffleet to be a Vice-admirall of a grand Squadron, to weare the usuall fflagg in his mizon topp & a blew fflagg in his foretopp wth a pendant under it & an ensigne of Blew.

> One Vice admirall to the Grand Squadron to weare a white flagg in his foretopp & a Pendent & Ensigne of white.

> Three other Rere-admirals: one of them to weare a Redd flagg, another a blew flagg & ye other a White in their mizon topps, wth Pendents & Ensignes of their respective Colors.

> The rest of the fleet to be devided into 9 parts & to be put under the 9 flags before mentioned & to weare the colors of the flagg they are put under, vizt. A pendent & Ensigne of the same colors the flagg is off under wch they are put.

> All the shipps to weare Jacks as formerly.

> If any of the Generals shall goe out of their shipps then that shipp to take downe ye Standard & to putt upp a flagg of the colors of thet pendant yt shipp weares[271].

---

[271] *S. P. D. Inter.* xxxii, 39.

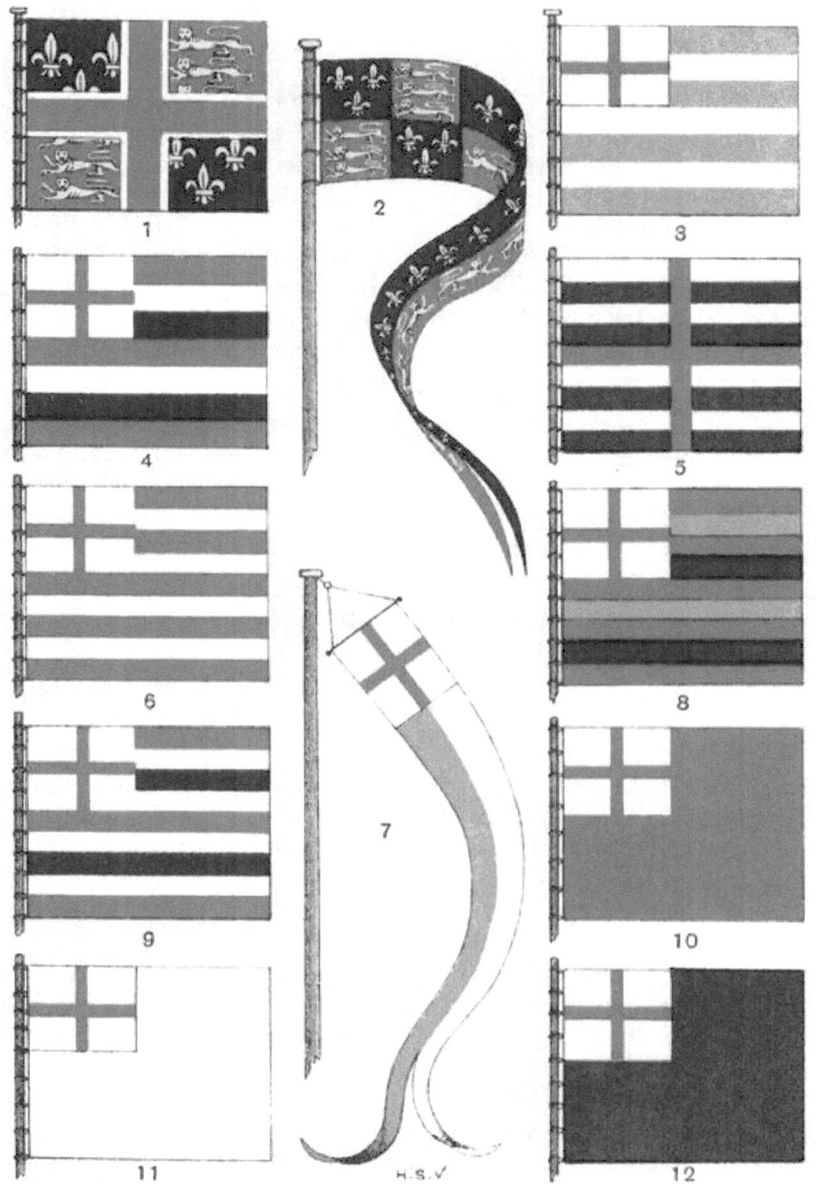

Plate IX

Early Ensigns, etc.

1. Levant Co., 1581
2. Streamer of Royal Arms
3, 4, and 5. Elizabethan Ensigns
6. Jacobean Ensign
7. Green and White Pendant
8. Jacobean Ensign, 1615

9. Jacobean Ensign, 1618   10. Red Ensign, early 17th cent.

11. White Ensign, early 17th cent.   12. Blue Ensign, early 17th cent.

The arrangements here proposed merit attention, for they contain several departures from the custom hitherto prevailing. The three principal admirals, being of co-equal authority, are each to fly the same standard at the main masthead, but to distinguish them they are to have pendants and ensigns of three different colours. The Vice- and Rear-Admiral of the fleet are retained, but they no longer have separate squadrons, the senior becomes Vice-Admiral to the first, or red squadron, and the junior, Vice-Admiral of the second, or blue squadron. To these are added a squadronal or "occasional" Vice-Admiral for the third or white squadron, and three Rear-Admirals, one for each squadron. The private ships are to have an ensign, as well as the customary pendant, of the squadronal colour.

The Navy Commissioners, after remarking upon rates of pay suitable to the various grades of flag officers, confess their incompetence to advise about the flags. "As to the distinguishment of weareing the fflaggs, Pendants and Ensignes, wee are not capable to give our advice therein, but must leave it to those Comand[rs] at Sea (whoe best knowe the causes of such kind of distinctions) to advise."

This was on the 14th January, 1653, but in the order to hasten the supply of flags to the fleet dated 4th February these flags are named in the order red, white, and blue. The reason for the change is not known, but it may be remarked that the white escutcheon of England had precedence of the blue escutcheon of Ireland in the Generals' standard, and this may have led the Generals at Sea to change the order of precedence of the squadronal colours.

On the 18th February the fleet came into collision with the Dutch at the Battle of Portland. On that occasion Blake and Deane, two of the original Generals at Sea, were embarked together in the flagship of the Red Squadron, which flew the standard, but Monck, who had recently been appointed as the third General in the vacancy caused by the death of Popham, took command of the White Squadron, while Penn, the Vice-Admiral of the fleet, commanded the Blue. The Admiral's flags, other than the standard, were "clear" colours, in other words plain flags, but the pendants and ensigns all had "a red cross in chief." The Vice- and the Rear-Admiral of the Fleet, who acted as Admiral of the Blue and Vice-Admiral of the Red respectively, probably flew, in addition to their plain blue and red flags, the Commonwealth "Union" flag of the cross and harp, but about this time the latter flag seems to have lost its red and yellow border and to have been of the same form as the "Jack." Thus in an order dated 2nd March for a further supply of flags to be hastened to the fleet, then re-fitting for a renewal of the conflict, these flags are described as "of ye Jack colours[272]."

3 Standerds of ye usuall colo[rs] wth ye field Red

4 fflags of ye Jack colors

---

[272] *Rawlinson MS.* A 227. Cf. also the Instructions of Goodson to Penn 21st June, 1655. "You shall wear the jack-flag upon the maintopmasthead" (*Memorials of Penn*, II, 116).

6 fflags cleare white

6 fflags cleare blue

40 pendants red

40 pendants blue

40 pendants white

40 Ensignes red

40 Ensignes blue

40 Ensignes white

100 Jacks

as ye last was wth the red crosse in chiefe[273]

At the Restoration the standard and jack flags reverted to the forms in use before 1649. The existing method of displaying the admirals' flags and the precedence of the squadronal colours remained unaltered, but a more strict regulation of their use gradually makes itself felt, and precise instructions as to the wearing of their flags begin to appear in the commissions of appointment issued to the flag officers. This was no doubt the logical outcome of the improved methods of naval administration, and especially of such improvements in the status of officers as the establishment of "Half-pay," of the introduction into the fleet of suitable youths with the express purpose of training them as officers, and the institution of qualifying tests before promotion to the rank of lieutenant. All these reforms tended to make the navy a regular profession for its higher officers instead of a mere haphazard calling, but it must be remembered that as yet the only established "Flag" ranks were those of Lord Admiral and Vice- and Rear-Admiral of England (or "of the Fleet"). All other Admirals were only "occasional," and officers holding such "occasional" rank yielded up the dignity on hauling down their flag and may frequently be found serving later as simple "Captain."

An important step forward was made in recognising that there might be two or more ships in company without either of them necessarily becoming an "Admiral" ship. This led to the institution in 1674 of the "Distinction-Pendant," which will be discussed in detail later. (See Broad Pendant, p. 106.)

When the Revolution of 1688 put an end to Pepys' activities at the Admiralty he was engaged in codifying the regulations relating to flags, and had laid before the king (as Lord High Admiral) a "new establishment" under which "no flags are to be issued but by particular warrant, which I suppose is to express their no., colors, and dimensions according to the occasions which they are issued for[274]."

The position at the end of Pepys' career is well summarised in the table overleaf drawn up by him—one of the many instances of his fondness for methodical statements.

---

[273] Strictly speaking, the "chief" embraced the whole of the hoist. In the ensigns the cross occupied only the upper part of it, being placed in a white canton in the red and blue ensigns. See Plate IX, figs. 10, 11, and 12.

[274] *Pepys MS.* Miscellanea, IX. Pepys proposed also to restrict the number of admirals' flags flown, according to the number of ships in a fleet.

The last entry is of especial interest. When the stricter regulation enforced had prevented many officers from wearing flags who would, in similar circumstances, undoubtedly have had that privilege in the first half of the century, much importance was attached to the right to exhibit a naked flagstaff. One striking instance of this occurs in 1687, when Sir Roger Strickland was appointed Vice-Admiral of the fleet under the Duke of Grafton, ordered to transport the Queen of Portugal (the king's sister) to Lisbon. Strickland, not unnaturally, wanted to wear a flag as Vice-Admiral. Not many years earlier he would have done this as a matter of course; now he had to obtain the king's permission, which was granted. But he had omitted Pepys from his reckoning. The king's sign manual warrant was accompanied by a long letter from Pepys dissuading him from exercising the right:

> a thing so extraordinary, so irregular, and so unjustified by any practice past, and unlikely to be ever imitated in time to come, as this which you have thus contended for, of having two of the Top Flags of England exposed to sea, in view of the two greatest Rivalls of England for Sea Dominion and Glory (I mean the Dutch and French) with no better provision for supporting the Honour thereof, then Six Ships, and two of them such as carry not above 190 men and 54 guns between them, and this too obtained through meer force of Importunity,

and hinting that the king will take it well if he does not hoist the flag, though he may bear the flagstaff. Like a wise man, he took Mr Secretary's hint, and resigned the honour. The king thereupon authorised Strickland to bear the naked staff only, and informed that officer that he was pleased to find that Pepys' advice had been taken, for it had been offered with his privity.

Although Pepys' influence ceased at the Revolution, and his proposed "establishment" of flags was never ratified, the work of regulation and restriction went on through the reigns of William and Mary and Anne, culminating in the abolition of the Lord Admiral's standard and the confining of the Union flag at the masthead to the "Admiral of the Fleet." Nevertheless, several curious anomalies remained until the opening years of the eighteenth century. Officers appointed to the chief command of squadrons sent to the Mediterranean or West Indies were, whatever their rank, usually authorised to wear the Union flag at the main so soon as they had left the Channel. Thus in 1690 Captain Lawrence Wright was authorised to wear the Union flag at the main when sent to the West Indies in command of a small squadron.

A DESIGNATION OF THE SEVERAL FLAGS AND COLOURS USED IN THE ROYAL NAVY OF ENGLAND FOR DISTINGUISHING DEGREES OF COMMAND THEREIN (Table Part 1)						
The several Degrees of Command in use in the Navy of England	The various Flags and Colours used in the Navy of England denoting command					
	Standard	Anchor of the Ld Admiral	Union or Jack Flag	Red Flag	White Flag	Blue Flag
Ld High Adm¹ of England	At the Main-top the King being aboard or not at all in the Fleet	At the Main-top the King being in the Fleet aboard another ship	—	—	—	—
Vice Adm¹ of England	—	—	At the Foretop wʰ a distinction pendant under it	—	—	—
Rear Adm¹ of England	—	—	At the Mizentop wʰ a Distinction Pendant under it	—	—	—
Admiral of a Fleet of 3 Squadrons with nine flags	—	—	At the Main-top	—	—	—
Admiral of the White Squadron	—	—	—	—	At the Main-top	—
Admiral of the Blue Squadron	—	—	—	—	—	At the Main-top

The several Degrees of Command	Colour						
Vice Admiral of the	Red	—	—	—	At the Foretop	—	—
Vice Admiral of the	White or	—	—	—	—	At the Foretop	—
Vice Admiral of the	Blue	—	—	—	—	—	At the Foretop
Rear Admiral of the	Red	—	—	—	At the Mizen-top	—	—
Rear Admiral of the	White or	—	—	—	—	At the Mizen-top	—
Rear Admiral of the	Blue	—	—	—	—	—	At the Mizen-top
Admiral of the Fleet w^h 3 flags only		—	—	At the Main-top	—	—	—
Vice Adm^l of the same		—	—	At the Foretop	—	—	—
Rear Adm^l of the same		—	—	At the Mizen-top	—	—	—
Adm^l or Commander in Chief of a squadron with one flag		—	—	At the Main-top	—	—	—
Private Captain		—	—	—	—	—	—

A DESIGNATION OF THE SEVERAL FLAGS AND COLOURS USED IN THE ROYAL NAVY OF ENGLAND FOR DISTINGUISHING DEGREES OF COMMAND THEREIN (Table Part 1 *continued*)					
The several Degrees of Command in use in the Navy of England	The various Flags and Colours used in the Navy of England denoting command				
	Jack	Ensigne Ordinary	Pendant Ordinary	Pendant of Distinction	Flag Staff Naked

	At the Bowsprit	At the Poop with an anchor in it			At the Fore and Mizen tops
Ld High Adm¹ of England	At the Bowsprit	At the Poop with an anchor in it	—	—	At the Fore and Mizen tops
Vice Adm¹ of England	Do	At the poop	—	At the Foretop under the Union Flag	At the Main and Mizen tops
Rear Adm¹ of England	Do	Do	—	At the Mizentop under the Union Flag	At the Main and Fore tops
Admiral of a Fleet of 3 Squadrons with nine flags	Do	Do	—	—	At the Fore and Mizen tops
Admiral of the White Squadron	Do	Do White	—	—	At the Fore and Mizen tops
Admiral of the Blue Squadron	Do	Do Blue	—	—	At the Fore and Mizen tops
Vice Admiral of the { Red	Do	Do Red	—	—	At the Main and Mizen tops
Vice Admiral of the { White or	Do	Do White	—	—	At the Main and Mizen tops
Vice Admiral of the { Blue	Do	Do Blue	—	—	At the Main and Mizen tops
Rear Admiral of the { Red	Do	Do Red	—	—	At the Main and Fore tops
Rear Admiral of the { White or	Do	Do White	—	—	At the Main and Fore tops
Rear Admiral of the { Blue	Do	Do Blue	—	—	At the Main and Fore tops
Admiral of the Fleet wʰ 3 flags only	Do	Do Ordinary	—	—	At the Fore and Mizen tops

Vice Adm^l of the same	Do	Do	—	—	At the Main and Mizen tops
Rear Adm^l of the same	Do	Do	—	—	At the Main and Fore tops
Adm^l or Commander in Chief of a squadron with one flag	Do	Do	—	—	At the Mizen and Fore tops
Private Captain	Do	Do White or Blue, when of either of those squadrons	At the Maintop when alone or in Comp^y with a Senior Captn, and in the Colour to be answerable to the Squadron	At the Maintop when eldest captain in company with Private ships	At the Maintop or Mizentop according to the highest flag he may at any time before have had the Honour of wearing

Whereas his Matie thinks fitting for his Service that in ye present Employment on which you are going of Commander in cheife of the Squadron of their Mats Shipps appointed for service in ye West Indies you should weare a fflagg at the Maintop. These are in pursuance of his Mats pleasure signified to this Board on that behalfe to authorize and require you that in your Voyage outwards bound to ye West Indies, soe soon as you shall be out of ye English Channell, you weare ye Union fflagg at the maintop-mast head of their Mats Shipp on board wh you shall be in person in your aforesaid Employment as Comandr in cheife, and to continue soe to doe untill in your returne from the West Indies you shall againe arrive in the Channell. And for soe doing this shall be your Warrant. Given under our hands & ye Seale of ye Office of Adty this Sixth day of ffeby 1689 (1690)

> To Capt[n] Lawrence Wright
> Commander in cheife of their Ma[ts] Ships
> now bound to ye West Indies[275].

The position occupied by Captain Wright was equivalent to that for which, at a later date, the title "Commodore" was borrowed from the Dutch. The Distinction Pendant, which it might be thought would be more applicable to such cases, was as yet confined in its use to the Downs. Ten months later Captain Aylmer was sent to the Mediterranean in a similar position, but instead of being allowed the Union flag he was only granted a special distinction pendant with the Union instead of the St George's cross at the head. Cases in which captains were ordered to wear the Union flag at the main are rare, but junior flag officers in command of squadrons were, during the reigns of William III and Anne, frequently directed to wear the Union flag as though they were full admirals. Thus Sir George Rooke, when appointed Commander-in-Chief in February, 1693, of a fleet destined for the Mediterranean was instructed:

> 12. So soone as you shalbe out of ye English Channell in your voyage outwards bound, you are to wear the Union Flag at ye Mainetopmast head and to continue so to do untill in your returne you shalbe againe in the Channell[276].

At that date Rooke was Vice-Admiral of the Red, and flew, while in the Channel, the red flag at the fore.

---

[275] *Admiralty* 2/5.
[276] *Admiralty* 2/11.

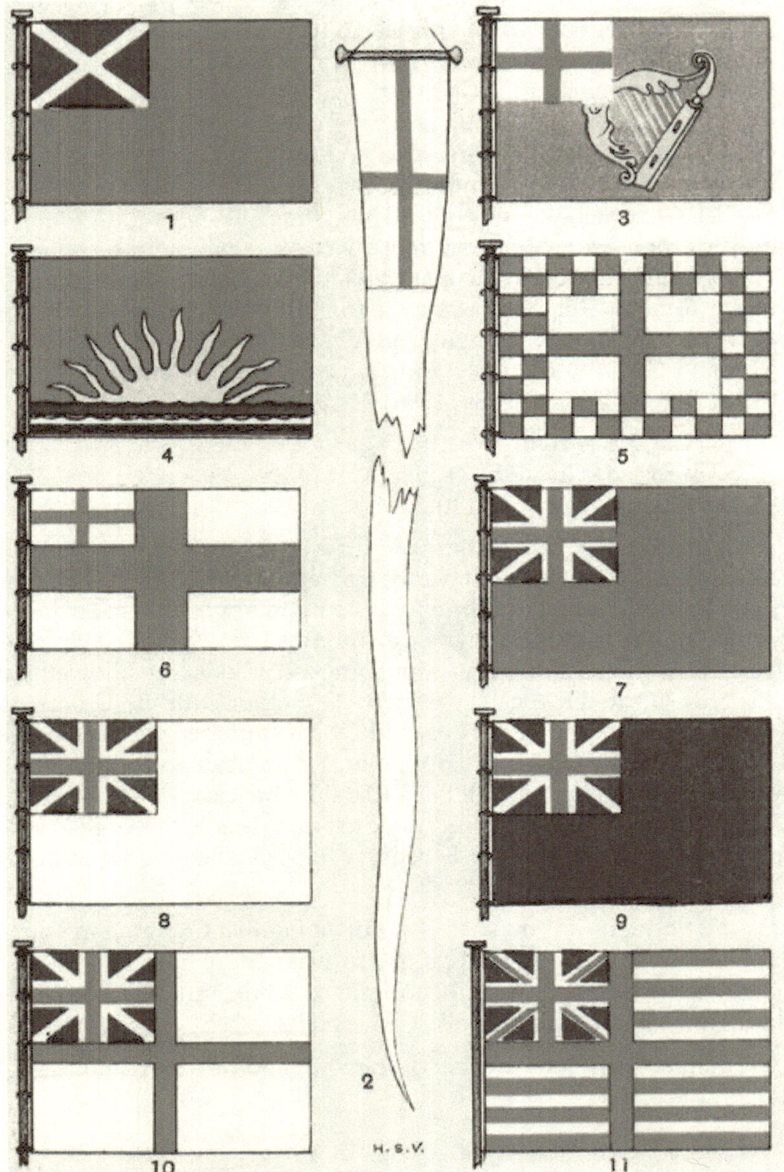

Plate X

Ensigns, etc.

1. Scots Ensign, 1686   2. White Pendant

3. Irish Ensign, 1686   4. Scottish East India Co.

5. Guinea Jack   6. White Ensign, 1702

7. Red Ensign, 1707
8. White Ensign, 1707
9. Blue Ensign, 1707
10. White (St George) Ensign, 1707
11. East India Co., 1822

Early in 1702 an important alteration was made in the white squadronal colours, which led to the introduction of the St George's cross in the admiral's flag and in the fly of the ensign. It will be remembered that hitherto the white colours consisted of: (1) a plain white flag for the admirals; (2) a plain white ensign with a small St George's cross in the upper canton next the staff; (3) a plain white pendant with a St George's cross at the head. In February, 1702, the Earl of Pembroke, then Lord High Admiral, sent the Navy Board instructions for fitting out the fleet intended to operate against the French; these instructions included:

An account of what Flagg-Ships are ordered to be fitted out at Chatham and Portsmouth, and what Flags they are to wear.

Chatham:

Britannia	Ld High Admiral	The Standard
	Sr George Rook	
Soveraigne	Adml of ye White	Union Flagg
	Marq^s of Carmarthen	
Prince George	Rear Adml to Ld Adml.	Redd flagg
	Sr Dav^d Mitchell	
Boyne	Vice Adm^l of ye White	Union fflagg
	Sr Clo. Shovell	
Queen	Adm^l of ye Blue	Blue Flagg

Portsmouth:

Roy^l William	Mr Aylmer	
	Vice Adm^l to ye Ld Adm	Redd fflagg
Victory	Sr Jno. Munden	
	R^r Adm^l of ye White	Union Flagg
St George	Sr Staff^d Fairborne	
	Rear Adml of ye Blue	Blue Flagg

The Vice Adml of the Blue vacant by Mr. Benbow being in the West Indies.

The Lord High Adml and the Flagg Ships of his squadron to have Redd Ensignes and Pendants as usual to ye Private Ships.

The Admiral of the White to have Ensignes with the usual Cross in the Canton, with this distinction; that a third part of the said Ensignes for himself and the Flaggs and private Ships of his Squadron are to be White in the middle of the Flye:—and this to be in the whole length of the Ensigne.

> The Admrll of the Blue and the Flagg Ships of his Squadron to wear blue Flaggs and Blue Ensignes and Pendants to the private ships with the usual Cross in the Canton of each as hath been usually worne by ships of the Blue Squadron.

> But as for the Pendants to the Private Ships of each Squadron, and the Flaggs to wear in the Boats by the fflagg Officers, particular directions will be suddenly given therein[277].

The white admirals' flag was to be replaced by the Union, and the white ensign by a red one with a broad white horizontal stripe through it. The reason for some such change is obvious when we recollect that at this date the French flag was white. Six weeks later were given the further directions that had been promised "suddenly." After cancelling the order for the standard, as already related[278], Pembroke instructs the Navy Board:

> And whereas it may be necessary to distinguish the Vice and Rear Admll of each squadron by some particular mark in the fflaggs which they carry in the heads of their Boats, I do hereby desire and direct you to cause the distinctions exprest in ye papers herewith sent you to be made in the Flaggs which the respective Vice and Rear Admlls shall be furnished with for the Boats as aforesaid: as also that what Pendents there shall now or for the future be wanting for the Fleet, be made somewhat broader than they now are, and shorter according to the draught in one of the said papers, that so the inconveniencys that attend the present Lengths of them by entangling in the Rigging or otherwise may be prevented[279].

This was accompanied by a diagram showing the following boat flags.

Vice Admiral of the Red	Plain red flag[280]
Rear Admiral of the Red	Red flag with a white ball in hoist
Vice Admiral of the White	Union flag with a white ball in hoist
Rear Admiral of the White	Union flag with two white balls placed diagonally
Vice Admiral of the Blue	Blue flag with a white ball in hoist
Rear Admiral of the Blue	Blue flag with two white balls placed diagonally[281]

The need for some distinction in the flags of the admirals of the same squad-

[277] *Admiralty* 2/182.

[278] See p. 80.

[279] *Admiralty* 2/182.

[280] The rank of Admiral of the Red was not created until Nov. 1805. The Admiral of the Red Squadron was either the Lord High Admiral, flying the anchor flag, or the Admiral of the Fleet, flying the Union.

[281] See Plate VIII, fig. 4.

ronal colour, when displayed in a boat, or indeed any small craft in which only one position was available, must, one would suppose, have been felt often before, but this was the first attempt to solve the difficulty. Its main interest lies in the fact that it supplied the solution of the similar difficulty which arose, nearly three hundred years later, when the three-masted sailing-ship had given place to the two-masted iron ship, which often had only a single masthead available for the Admiral's flag.

The changes promulgated by the orders of the 5th February and the 20th March, 1702, already quoted, did not end there, for the officers of the fleet were not satisfied with an arrangement that made over the Union flag to the admirals of the second squadron of the fleet and introduced a red and white ensign. Accordingly, on the 6th of May, Pembroke issued the following further order:

> Whereas I did some time since direct in what manner the Flaggs and Ensignes should be made for such ships as should be appointed to be of the Squadron of the Adml of the White, and whereas upon consulting with the Flagg Officers of the Fleet, it is thought more advisable that the said Flaggs and Ensignes should be rather made white with a large St George's Cross, according to the sample herewith sent you: and I do therefore hereby desire and direct you, to cause all such of the said Flaggs and Ensignes as have already been made by your orders to be altered, and that such as are still to be made be conformable to what is before directed, as also the Flaggs necessary for the Boats of the Ships of the aforesaid Squadron[282].

The drawing included with the order shows a very broad red cross, in width equal to one-third of the depth of the whole flag[283].

This alteration necessitated a change in the boat flags of the Vice- and Rear-Admirals of the White. The balls became blue and were gathered into the upper canton instead of being placed diagonally across the flag; the white balls in the red and blue flags also underwent the same alteration in position.

In November, 1805, as a special compliment to the navy, the rank of Admiral of the Red was created. As this introduced three red flags in place of two, the boats' flags of the Vice- and Rear-Admiral of the Red were altered so as to have the same number of balls as the other Vice- and Rear-Admirals.

No further alteration took place in the Admirals' flags until 1864, when the division of Flag Officers into the three categories "of the Red," "of the White," and "of the Blue" was abolished and the squadronal colours discontinued. The reason for this change will be discussed in dealing with "Flags of Distinction," and it will therefore be sufficient to note here that the white colours were retained for the navy, red balls being substituted for blue in the "boat" flags.

The invention of the modern battleship, with only two masts (one of which was often unfitted for the display of the Admiral's flag owing to the presence of a masthead semaphore) had caused the general adoption by Vice- and Rear-Admi-

[282] *Admiralty* 2/182.
[283] See Plate X, fig. 6.

rals of the "boat" form of their flags instead of the plain flag at the fore or mizen respectively, and this led to the question being raised in 1898 of a suitable flag for Vice- and Rear-Admirals, who often found the main masthead alone available for their flag, while on the contrary an Admiral was, in other ships, often obliged to hoist his on the foremast. In view of the fact that many of the great maritime nations had adopted the British method of differencing by balls (or stars) it was not thought desirable to abandon this method, but to make the flags more easily distinguishable the balls were increased in size to one-half of the depth of the canton, which necessitated placing the second ball of the Rear-Admiral in the lower canton next the staff, instead of in the upper one.

With the arrangement then adopted, which clearly distinguishes the flags of the three grades in all conceivable circumstances, we may assume that finality has been reached.

(IV) PENDANTS OF COMMAND

(a) *The Commodore's Broad Pendant*

Although the use of a specially large pendant to denote the presence of the officer in command of a squadron was not unknown in early days[284], the custom was not adopted in the English fleet until the latter part of the seventeenth century. Introduced first in 1674 simply to denote the ship of the officer in command for the time being of that important roadstead the Downs, the natural rendezvous of all ships going to and from the Thames and Medway, the custom was extended in 1690 to embrace the case in which a small squadron was sent abroad under a captain for whom there was no room on a Flag List which had become restricted to the nine admirals of the red, white, and blue colours.

On 14th November, 1674, in the course of a debate by the King and the Admiralty Board concerning the flying of pendants by foreign men-of-war in the Downs, the question was raised as to the desirability of marking the ship of the officer in command there, when that officer was not of flag rank. The summary of this discussion, recorded by Pepys in the Admiralty "Journal," contains so many points of interest that it seems desirable to reproduce it in full.

14 Novr 74

Present

The King

Prince Rupert   Mr Sec^y Coventry

Lord Treasurer   Mr Sec^y Williamson

Mr Vice Chamberlaine

Navy Offrs attending

Upon readeing another Lre from Capt Dickinson in ye Hunter, Commandr in Cheife in ye Downes, disireing direction how

---

[284] A broad green pendant was used by Doria at Lepanto (see p. 115), and Drake was noted by the Spaniards for the inordinate size of the pendant he displayed.

to demeane himselfe in reference to any forreigne Men of Warr which shall come into and remaine in ye Downes with ye Pendant in ye Mainetop, while his Mats ship at ye same time Comanding there shall ride without other Marke or distinction then that of a Pendant in ye Maintop, vizt whether hee shall suffer ye said forreigne Man of Warr to continue rideing with his Pendant up, or cause it to be taken downe; and it being, upon discourse thereon, observed first that Pendants originally were not at all designed as a mark or distinction, but only ornament. Next, That at this day ye weareing of a Pendant at ye Maintopp is yt which is everywhere become ye Marke of distinguishing a Man of Warr from a Mercht man. Thirdly, That our Ensigns and Jacke, together with their lyeing in ye Admls Birth, will sufficiently informe as well straingers as his Mats Subjects which is ye Comandr in Cheife without ye helpe of ye Pendants, soe as noe mistake can arise from ye want of it either on occasion of applications to be made or respect to be paid to her. Lastly, That noe difficulty has at any time heretofore been made of permitting Straingers Men of Warr to weare their Pendants in presence of ye Comandr in Cheife in ye Downes, noe more than elsewhere. The respect challenged by his Maty lying not in ye lowreing of ye Pendant but ye fflagg or Topsaile which was now avered by Mr Vice Chamberlaine and Sr Jeremy Smith, as it had lately been to Mr Pepys by ye body of ye Trinity House of whom hee had on this occasion lately inquired after the knowledge and observation of ye Eldest Seamen there. Whereupon it was resolved by his Maty and their Lordps, that ye loureing of ye Pendant and kepeing of it downe is not in this case to be exacted, and yt Capt Dickinson should be accordingly directed therein, But in case upon further inquiry into this matter (wch Mr Pepys was ordered to make wth ye Offrs of the Navy) it should be found needfull (with respect either to decency or use) that some distinction be observed betweene his Mats Ship Commanding in Cheife (and not beareing a Flagg) and others of his Mats Ships or his Subjects rideing in ye Downes at ye same time, some convenient marke or distinction be by them Propounded to his Maty & my Lords on that behalfe in order to their further determination thereon.

On the 18th Pepys sent the Navy Board a memorandum

to put them in mind of considering how far it may be necessary for the ship which shall command in chief there, and which from her quality and the saving of charge shall not be allowed to wear a flag, be appointed to bear some mark of difference, and if so what may be proper to be established without exposing the King to the extraordinary charge of a flag[285].

---

[285] *Catalogue of Pepysian MSS.* (N. R. S.), ii, 400.

After a week's consideration the Navy Board replied that

> in case the evills that may arise from the want of this distinction
> are such as shalbee thought necessary to bee prevented, wee doe
> humbly acquaint yo[r] Lo[pps] that in our opinion severall inconve-
> niences fitt to be prevented may accrew in case severall of his
> Ma[ties] Shipps doe at one and the same tyme ride in the Downes
> and it bee not knowne which of the said shipps doeth command
> there in cheife[286].

They therefore humbly conceived it expedient to appoint, as a mark of distinction,
a Red Pendant, somewhat larger than ordinary, on a small flagstaff at the main
topmast head. With a view to saving expense they were careful to suggest that the

> Flaggstaff & Pendant when the shipp by whome it was worne
> happens to leave the Downes shall bee delivered to such other
> shipp there as shall bee appointed to succeed in the roome of the
> former, or if there bee noe such shipp there, then that the same
> bee sent on shore to Deale and lodged there with his Ma[ties] Muster
> Master[287]

until it was again wanted. Their fear that they might have to supply every likely
ship with a staff and distinction pendant is perhaps the reason of the hesitating
reluctance which their letter displays.

The Admiralty approved their proposals, and on the 12th December issued
the necessary order, being careful to add that it was done "without any extra wages to be allowed for the same[288]."

The arrangement seems to have been viewed with some apathy by those concerned, probably because there were no extra wages attached, for in June, 1676,
Pepys wrote to his brother-in-law, the Muster Master at Deal, reminding him that
it was his duty to see the order complied with, and at the same time informing
Captain Sir R. Robinson, then Commander-in-Chief in the Downs:

> I am to note to you that his Majesty's last orders authorised
> you to wear the pendant of distinction which was some time since
> established ... the wearing which pendant I fear hath been for
> some time neglected, but the King's said orders will remedy it
> by your calling for it from his Agent at Deal and putting it up
> according to the establishment ... which will abundantly I hope
> distinguish you[289].

Pepys in his *Miscellanea* has given us a drawing and description of this pendant, from which it appears that it had the St George's cross in a white field in
chief and was five breadths (4 ft 7 ins.) broad at the head, and 21 yards in length,
whereas the ordinary pendants were only three breadths (2 ft 9 ins.) at the head
and varied in length from 22 to 32 yards according to the size of the ship. Both

[286] *Admiralty* ⅓₃₅₄₆.
[287] *Admiralty* ⅓₃₄₅₆.
[288] *Admiralty* ⅔₁.
[289] *Catalogue of Pepysian MSS.* (N. R. S.), iii, 210.

were "swallow-tailed" (i.e. slit at the end of the fly).

In 1683 the Navy Board had again to be reminded that this distinction pendant was to be used, but by 1692 it had become so popular that "some Commanders of their Ma[ts] ships do take the liberty to wear distinction pendants without order for the same[290]," and they were strictly forbidden to do so.

In 1695 the use of this pendant was extended to the senior captain of ships cruising in the "Soundings" at the entrance to the Channel.

In the meantime another form of distinction pendant was introduced, in which the St George at the head was replaced by the Union. This form was for use abroad, in analogy with the practice by which Admirals sent abroad were ordered to wear the Union flag when out of the Channel, instead of their squadronal flag. As early as 1687 Pepys had noted the use abroad of a red ensign with the Union instead of the St George in its canton. At this date the St George's flag was still being flown by Genoese ships, and it was doubtless the desire to avoid any misunderstandings on this account that led to the disuse, before 1707, of the St George's flag by English men-of-war outside home waters. For some unexplained reason this form of ensign had become known as the Budgee flag, and this name was later transferred to the Union Broad Pendant, which became known as the Budgee Pendant[291] and was no doubt the parent of the modern word "Burgee."

The first instance of the use of the Budgee Pendant occurs in December, 1690, when Captain Aylmer, appointed Commander-in-Chief of the squadron intended for the Mediterranean, was ordered to be supplied with a distinction pendant "made with ye Union Crosses in place where other Distinction Pendants have only St Georges Crosse[292]."

Three years later the Earl of Danby, Captain of the 'Royal William' in the fleet under the three joint-admirals, was ordered to wear this same pendant and given precedence next to the Flag Officers[293], and in 1697 Captain J. Norris was appointed Commander-in-Chief of a squadron bound to Newfoundland and ordered, when out of the Channel, to "wear such a swallow tail pendant as Mr Aylmer had when he commanded a squadron in the streights, and which was afterwards worne by the Earle of Danby[294]."

All these officers, whether commanding-in-chief like Aylmer or in subordinate command like Danby, were serving in a position afterwards known as that of "Commodore." This title, derived from the Dutch "Commandeur" (originally the senior officer of a merchant fleet) which had been adopted in the Dutch navy from their merchant service at the end of the sixteenth century, was introduced into the English navy about 1695, no doubt as a consequence of the close connection between the two navies under "Dutch William." It was, however, not yet officially

[290] *Admiralty* 2/9.

[291] In 1710 Captain Warwick was refused permission to use the "Bugee Pendant"; *Admiralty* 2/453. Millan's Signal Book (1746) contains an illustration of the "Budgee Broad Pendant."

[292] *Admiralty* 2/171.

[293] *Admiralty* 2/11. Orders of 31st March and 1st May, 1693.

[294] *Admiralty* 2/23, 15th March, 1697.

recognised; in their official orders the officers were simply "Captain" or "Captain and Commander in chief." They received a special allowance, usually 10s. a day, while so acting. Later on the importance of some of these positions was enhanced by the introduction, in certain cases, of a second captain into the Commodore's ship. This practice, which was in vogue at least as early as 1720, does not seem at first to have entailed any difference in flag or pay, but it made an important difference in prize money, for those Commodores who had Captains under them were treated in this respect as though they were flag officers.

In 1731 the Admiralty attempted to establish the rank of Commodore by providing for three posts of this rank in the *Regulations and Instructions for his Majesty's service at sea*, then for the first time gathered together in one book, but the Privy Council struck out all the articles relating to this proposal before recommending the book for the king's approval. The title was, however, formally recognised in 1734 by an Order in Council which, in laying down the relative precedence of Sea and Land Officers, provided "That Commodores with Broad Pendants have the same respects as Brigadiers-General," but the rank remains to this day a "temporary" one, carrying special pay and privileges but giving the captain holding it no authority over captains senior to him on the list.

Regulations governing the rank first appeared in the *King's Regulations* of 1806. The Broad Pendant was to be of the squadronal colour and was to have the further distinction of a white ball if the Commodore had no second captain in his ship.

> There shall be a temporary rank of Commodore which shall
> be distinguished by a Broad Pendant, Red, White or Blue....

> If the Commodore commands the ship himself the Pendant
> shall have a large white Ball near the staff and he shall not rank as
> a Rear Admiral.

Prior to 1806, Commodores appear to have kept their pendants flying in all circumstances. The new regulations, however, directed that if the Commodore met a senior captain, that captain was also to hoist a broad pendant, but if there were more than one senior to him then the Commodore was to strike his broad pendant instead.

This anomalous arrangement was altered in the Regulations of 1824, which provided that no Commodore should fly his broad pendant, or even hold the rank, while in the presence of a senior captain; but the difference in the two positions, dependant on the presence or absence of a second captain in the commodore's ship, was accentuated by dividing the commodores into two distinct classes on this basis; the first class flying the red or white pendant and the second the blue only.

> A plain Red Broad Pendant, or a White Broad Pendant with a
> Red Cross in it, is to be worn by Commodores of the First Class;
> but when more than one such Commodore shall be present, the
> Senior only shall wear the Red Pendant, and the other, or others,
> the White Pendant.

A Blue Pendant is to be worn by Commodores of the Second Class.

With the abolition of the squadronal colours in 1864, the red and blue broad pendants disappeared. Commodores of the first class were to wear the white broad pendant at the main and those of the second class the same pendant at the fore. In boats the latter were to have a red ball in the upper canton of their pendants. From the same cause as that which affected the admirals' flags, this form with the ball soon became the only one in use for the second class.

Originally fourteen times as long as it was wide at the head, the broad pendant became gradually shorter. By the time the red and blue forms were abandoned it had reached its present proportions, in which it is only twice as long as its greatest breadth.

In 1913 the provision that Commodores should strike their broad pendant while in the presence of a senior captain was deleted from the *King's Regulations*. Commodores take rank and command of each other according to their seniority as captains and without regard to the class to which they belong, so that a Second Class Commodore flying a Broad Pendant with a ball might be the superior officer of a First Class Commodore flying the pendant without the ball, normally the superior flag, and the relative precedence of these flags would thereby become inverted while these two Commodores were in company or in the same port.

(b) *The Senior Officers' Pendant*

Ten years after the institution of the Distinction Pendant to denote a Commander-in-Chief who did not hold flag rank, Lord Dartmouth, then in command of an expedition against Algiers, hit upon the idea of granting a similar pendant to the senior captain of three or more ships that might casually happen to be in company. His orders, dated 1st January, 1684[295], contain the following provisions:

1. That every younger captain, upon his meeting with an elder Captain at sea or in port (though the rate of the ship which he is in be superior to the other) pay all fitting respect and obedience by taking in his Pendant....

3. That (abroad) wheresoever more than 2 ships happen to be or meet together the eldest Captain shall put up and wear a Pendant of distinction and the other captains shall wear the Ordinary Pendant.

4. That the said Pendant of distinction in this Fleet shall be red with a large Cross at the head and double the breadth of the ordinary Pendant, two thirds the length of it, and cut with a long and narrow swallow tayle.

It was within the competence of Dartmouth to give such an order to the squadron serving under him, but the practice seems to have been kept up after he had left the Mediterranean, for Captain Sir Roger Strickland, writing to Pepys from the Bay of Bulls in September, 1686, complained

[295] *Pepys MS.* 2867.

> Had I wore a Flag in this Expedition, I might then have had a sight of Capt. Priestman's orders for his keeping the King's Ships under his command so long here, at so extra an expence, & I am no less surprised at his wearing a swallow-tail'd flag at his main topmast head much broader than his ensign, having a St Andrew's Cross in it as well as St George's, being indeed such a thing as I never saw, seeming to turn the King's flag & Pendt into ridicule when at ye same time ye D. of Mortmar rides by him wh only a small Pendt...[296].

From a "particular draft" of this pendant given to Pepys it appears that it was very broad and short, with a red swallow-tailed fly, and a blue saltire, surmounted by a red cross, on a white ground at the head. Captain Priestman was brought to book and had to apologise to the king for his action.

The practice of wearing a senior officers' pendant, although never officially recognised, appears to have extended and to have been put down by the following order issued in July, 1692:

> Whereas we are informed that some of the Comanders of their Mats ships do take the liberty to wear Distinction Pendants without any order for the same, contrary to the Rules of the Navy: We do hereby strictly charge & require all Captns & Comanders of their Mats Ships & Vessels & others hired into their service That they do not presume upon any pretence whatsoever to wear any other Pendants in the Ships they comand, then the Ordinary Pendants wh have by the constant practice of the Navy been worne in their Mats Ships of Warre without particular order in writing from this Board for soe doeing[297].

After this we hear no more of this pendant until the great change of 1864, when the following provision was made in the regulations promulgated on that occasion:

> When two or more of Her Majesty's Ships are present in Ports or Roadsteads, a small Broad Pendant (White, with the St George's Cross) is to be hoisted at the mizen-top-gallant-mast-head of the Ship of the Senior Officer.

A slight modification was introduced in the *King's Regulations* of 1906, which ordered that in ships with less than three masts this pendant should be hoisted at the "starboard topsail-yard-arm." This was again modified in 1913 when the senior captain at a port, if the senior naval officer there present, was instructed to hoist this pendant at the masthead while any Commodore junior to him on the list of captains was also present in that port.

---

[296] *Pepys MSS.* Miscellanea, ix.
[297] *Admiralty* 2/9.

CHAPTER V

COLOURS OF DISTINCTION

Boteler, in his *Dialogues*, reminds us that "Flaggs (to speake properly) are only those which are borne out in the Topps of Shyps, and they serve as Badges, and that as well for the distinguishing of Nations as Commanders ... the others are named the Colours or Ensigns and Pendants." To these was added in 1633, while he was writing these Dialogues, the jack, or small Union flag flown at the bowsprit, which, with the ensign and pendant, completed the "suit of colours" for a ship of war. The differentiation by this means of the various classes of public and private ships reached its culminating point by the middle of the nineteenth century. At that period British ships were divided into five categories, each with its own special flags of distinction, according to their employment, as:

1 Public ships of war.

2 Private men-of-war.

3 Public ships for uses other than war.

4 Merchant ships.

5 Pleasure craft.

Since that date the "colours" of the first of these five classes (and incidentally those of the third and fourth classes) have been simplified by the abandonment of the squadronal colours in 1864, while the second class has disappeared in consequence of the abolition of privateering by the Declaration of Paris in 1856.

(I) PUBLIC SHIPS OF WAR

The Distinction Colours proper to a British ship of war are the Pendant, Ensign and Jack. Of these three flags the pendant (or streamer, as it was originally named) is by far the most ancient, dating back to the days when there was no rigid distinction between public and private men-of-war, when every ship owned by an Englishman was, in the eyes of the law, the king's ship, and might be requisitioned for his use at a moment's notice and, with the aid of a few planks and balks of timber, be converted into an efficient ship-of-war, with fore and after castle and fighting-top complete. Besides such "castles" a ship, devoted for the time being to warlike purposes, whether in a national or semi-private quarrel, had as a distinctive mark, from the end of the thirteenth century onwards (and probably from an even earlier date) a huge streamer displayed from the masthead, or hung from the fighting-top, and often reaching down to the water.

These colours, first the pendant, then from 1634 to 1864 the pendant and jack, and finally all three of them together, have served to distinguish ships "of war" from ships not fitted out for war, but the pendant and ensign, with occasional assistance from a masthead flag, have also served for a secondary distinction within the main category "of war," namely, that tactical distinction of lesser groups among a collected body of ships of war which may be termed squadronal distinction.

Squadronal distinction colours were the outcome of the development of naval tactics. So long as a battle between two opposing fleets of any size is to be fought pell mell, like a gigantic football scrimmage, there is obviously no need for other flags than such as mark out the two opposing parties, with perhaps the addition of special flags of command to denote the ships of the two leaders. But directly the attempt is made to bring intelligence to bear as well as courage and brute force, to derive advantage from superior skill in manoeuvring, and to use the ship itself as an actual weapon instead of a mere transport to carry opposing warriors into touch with each other, it becomes necessary to co-ordinate the movements of the various ships under the direction of some master mind. If these ships are few in number their movements can be readily directed from one centre; but if they are many, experience shows that the whole fleet must be divided into distinct parts (called squadrons) of which the principal one will remain under the direct control of the commander of the whole fleet, while each of the others is placed under the immediate control of a subordinate commander, who is directly in touch with the Commander-in-Chief and acquainted with his intentions and wishes.

It then becomes necessary to furnish the ships comprising the various squadrons with some means whereby they may be readily distinguished should they become separated, or should the fleet fall into temporary disorder.

Among the ancient Egyptians, Greeks, and Romans this appears occasionally to have been provided for by painting some part of the ship in a distinctive colour[298], but this method has the disadvantage that the ships of the various squadrons are not readily interchangeable, and it appears to have gone out of use before the Christian era.

With the passing of the great days of the Greek states the art of sea warfare suffered an eclipse from which it did not recover for many centuries, and we meet with no further indication of the existence of fleets organised in squadrons until the thirteenth century of our era. The proper stimulus for the development of the art of fleet tactics can only be supplied by the collision of two maritime powers of fairly equal intelligence and resources. This condition was first supplied by the rivalry of Genoa, Pisa, and Venice for the sea-borne trade of the Mediterranean.

The great fleet fitted out by Genoa in 1242 affords one of the earliest recorded instances (perhaps the earliest) of a tactical division into squadrons by means of flags. The circumstances have already been related, and it will be remembered that the squadron leaders were then distinguished by flags appropriate to the district from which they had been selected. This method is evidently insufficient, for although it enables the individual ships of a squadron to recognise their leader, it does not enable that leader to distinguish his own ships in the confusion of battle.

[298] See Maspero, *Popular Stories of Ancient Egypt*, p. 231, and Torr, *Ancient Ships*, Cambridge, 1895, p. 60.

The next step is to distinguish the individual ships by suitable flags according to their squadrons. We do not know when this step was taken, but it appears from the Instructions issued by Amadeo of Savoy in 1366 to the combined fleet under his orders[299] that each galley then carried the standard of the Commune whence it came, so that it is possible that the galleys were at that time organised in squadrons according to their respective Communes. At the great Battle of Lepanto in 1571, which marked the culmination of galley tactics, the combined fleet under the command of Don John of Austria was divided into squadrons with distinguishing pendants.

> The first division or right wing numbered fifty-four galleys, and was commanded by Giovanni Andrea Doria, whose galley was distinguished by a broad green pennant at the peak of the mainyard, smaller pennants of the same colour being displayed in the same position by the other vessels of the division. The centre, under Don John of Austria, consisted of sixty-four galleys, with blue pennants flying at the masthead. The left wing of fifty-three galleys was commanded by Agostino Barbarigo, and was marked by yellow banderoles on the foreyard, that of the leader flying at the peak of the mainyard. A rearguard or reserve followed the line of battle, and was composed of thirty galleys under the Marquis of Santa Cruz. They displayed white pennants from a flagstaff over the stern lamp[300].

But in the stormy seas of northern Europe the galley never became naturalised, and it was long before the teaching of the school of tactics that had grown up in connection with it came to be applied to the larger vessels required for the navigation of these waters. The fleet under Hubert de Burgh, which in 1217 put an end to Lewis the Dauphin's hopes of adding the Crown of England to that of France, made use of only elementary tactics, though indeed these proved amply sufficient, and very little advance had been made three centuries and a half later, when the Spanish Armada was crushed and driven away from the shores of England[301].

No attempt appears to have been made to divide an English fleet into squadrons with distinctive signs until the reign of Henry VIII. After the rather unsatisfactory battle with the French fleet off Portsmouth in July, 1545, Henry, who was of no mean ability in naval affairs[302], had evidently seen the need for better organisation, for when the fleet put into the Channel to deter the French from raiding the Sussex coast it was divided into three divisions distinguished by having the English flag at different mastheads, as is shown by the orders issued for the occasion:

> ... every ship appoynted to the battaill shall beare one flag of saint

---

[299] See p. 145.

[300] Stirling Maxwell, *Don John of Austria*, 1883, i, 387.

[301] Corbett, *Fighting Instructions* 1530-1816 (N. R. S.), 1905, p. 27: "Even Howard's great fleet of 1588 had twice been in action with the Armada before it was so much as organised into Squadrons."

[302] It was Henry who first organised navy administration by the institution of the Navy Board in 1546.

> George's crosse in his mayne toppe ... and every ship appoynted
> to the vanward shall beare one flag of sainte George's crosse in
> his fore toppe ... and every Shipp Galliasse pynnesse and Shalupe
> appoynted to the wyng shall have in ther mesyn toppe one flag of
> saint George's crosse[303].

This seems to have been the only occasion on which an English fleet was divided into squadrons distinguished by means of the same flag flown at different mastheads. In two years from that date Henry was dead, and the organisation of the navy sustained a set-back from which it took many years to recover. It was not until the results of the first day's fighting against the Spanish Armada in 1588 had shown the necessity for better organisation that any further attempt was made to divide the fleet into squadrons. There is no indication in the State Papers of the steps then taken to mark the squadrons, but from the fact that the arrangement was impromptu and that there was no time available for providing special colours it is probable that only the squadron leaders were distinguished by their flags.

In his expedition against Lisbon in the following year Drake made an attempt to remedy the prevailing want of method.

> The Armada campaign, as we have seen, had taught the sailors the danger of entirely discarding the old military methods; they had learnt the strength that the Spaniards gained by their squadronal system, and under the soldiers' influence we find an elaborate scheme for "squadronising" the fleet that is something entirely new, and obviously founded on the existing military system[304].

Here, again, we know nothing of the method adopted to distinguish the squadrons, but it seems to have been largely a paper one.

> Such was the first attempt to remedy the vices of the radical revolution which the sailor-admirals had brought about. That it smacked too much of the camp to please the seamen is not to be doubted. Excellent as it looked on paper, for some reason it took no hold; and for a thorough and lasting fleet system the English navy had to wait till half a century later, when the exploits of the new school of soldiers had so entirely weaned the country from its "idolatry of Neptune" that Cromwell and his soldier-admirals were able to force their ideas upon the seamen[305].

It is evident that the plan took no hold upon the navy, for the Instructions for a fleet at sea drawn up by Sir John Hawkins some time between this date and his departure on his and Drake's last voyage in 1595 contain no provision for any such division by squadrons[306].

The first instance, after 1545, of the systematic division of the fleet into squad-

[303] *S. P. D. Henry VIII*, ccv, fol. 163.
[304] Corbett, *Drake and the Tudor Navy*, ii, 203.
[305] *Ibid.* ii, 203.
[306] Rules in Sir John Hawkins his tyme, *S. P. D. Jas I*, clvii, 67.

rons occurs in the Cadiz Expedition of 1596. There were four English squadrons and one Dutch. The squadronal colours of the admirals have already been fully described, but, unfortunately, we have no record of the colours worn by the private ships. There were in this fleet sixteen ships belonging to the Crown: these were supplied with 145 flags and ensigns at a cost of £371. 8s. 4d., but although the size and price of each flag is given, the colours are never once mentioned in the accounts[307]. From the variations in the prices of flags of the same size, it is clear that they were of many different patterns. Possibly each ship wore an ensign of the same colours as the squadronal flags of the admirals; if so it was the first occasion on which this method was used.

One thing alone is clear; the distinction was not made by the pendants, which appear all to have been white[308] and hung only from the mizen yards. Yet it was the pendant which was ultimately adopted as the squadronal distinction colour. The first definite proposal to this end occurs in the "Notes on Sea Service"[309] submitted by Captain John Young to the Earl of Essex, probably just before the Cadiz Expedition of 1596. Young, who commanded merchant ships in the naval operations of 1588, 1589, and 1596, writes:

> That the Lord High Admiral, or any of the Admirals having charge of their several squadrants or quarters, and companies unto them appointed, and if they would know which of all their companies or squadrants so appointed do come into the fight or no. Then it is very convenient and very necessary to know who doth or doth not come in, and that every Admiral and all his own company must wear upon their mizen yardarms pendants, and look how many Admirals you have—so many several colours of pendants you must have also, unto the full complement of your ships, barks, and pinnaces. By which means and being accomplished you shall easily see and perceive who doth come into the fight or not, which without these sundry colours of your pendants it cannot be otherwise perceived, for that divers ships being something afar off may resemble one another and not be known the one from the other for these sundry coloured pendants[310].

This proposal was not adopted in 1596, but in the Algiers Expedition of 1620 the fleet was divided into three squadrons, the ships of which were distinguished by pendants at the main, fore, and mizen tops respectively.

> ... the Admirall Squadron was kept six leagues from the shore with pendants in the maine toppes for their signes: the Vice Admiral's squadron three leagues without him, on his bowe, with

---

[307] Chardges in equipping & setting forth xvj^en of her Ma^ts shippes and pinnaces to the seas. Pipe Off. Dec. Acct. 2232.

[308] See Arts 16 and 31 of the Instructions (*Naval Miscellany* (N. R. S.), vol. i). The greenish edge in the accompanying diagrams is apparently the artist's shading.

[309] *S. P. D. Eliz.* cclix, 48, printed in Oppenheim's *Naval Tracts of Sir Wm. Monson* (N. R. S.), iv, 202 et seq.

[310] Oppenheim, *Monson Tracts* (N. R. S.), iv, 209.

pendants on his foretops, the Rear Admirall three leagues within
him, on his quarter, with pendants on their mysentops.

The colours of these pendants are not stated, but from the pictures of the home-
coming of the Prince of Wales in 1623, now at Hampton Court and Hinchinbrook,
it appears that the pendant was still white, as in 1596, with the St George's cross
at the head. The same arrangement of pendants was employed for the fleet which
transported the Queen from Boulogne in June, 1625[311].

For the great expedition to Cadiz which set forth in October, 1625, the pendants, while still displayed at the three different mastheads according to the
squadron, were further distinguished by being made of different colours. The Admiral's Squadron had red pendants at the main; the Vice-Admiral's, blue pendants
at the fore; and the Rear-Admiral's, white pendants at the mizen.

The field of the ensign had, since its introduction about 1574, been of striped
design[312]. In 1621 a large red ensign was manufactured at a cost of £4. 16s., and a
few more were made in the following years. The suggestion for a general change
to this colour emanated from Sir F. Stewart, the Rear-Admiral of the fleet, who
had been nominated Admiral of the White Squadron for the Cadiz Expedition.
Writing to Sir John Coke from the 'Lion' on 2nd July, 1625, he says: "A red ancient would become every one of the King's ships." Owing to the defective state
of his ship, Stewart did not accompany the expedition when it finally sailed, but
his suggestion was evidently adopted, for the surveys of ships' rigging made in
January of the following year contain several entries of red ensigns, "serviceable"
or "decayed," but as these are accompanied by other entries for the same ships
of "ancients" which are not particularised, it is clear that the older ensigns were
not all immediately withdrawn from service. Probably, from motives of economy,
they were retained in use until worn out.

The flags flown by the Admirals of the various squadrons of the fleet that
sailed to the Ile de Ré in 1627 have already been described; no record has, however, been preserved of the method (if any) by which the private ships of those
squadrons (which were composed largely of merchantmen) were distinguished.
The probability is that they did not wear any special ensigns or pendants.

A survey of the stores at Deptford carried out in April, 1633, gives the following flags:

Standard for the maintop	1
Red Ensigne for yᵉ mainmizen	1
White Ensigne with yᵉ kings armes	1
Red and White Ensigne with yᵉ St George's crosse	1
fflower de luce & roase	1

[311] *S. P. D. Chas I*, v, 31.

[312] See Plate IX, figs. 3-6, 8 and 9. In the earlier ensigns, towards the end of Elizabeth's
reign, the stripes were sometimes diagonal, and different designs appear to have been used
to distinguish individual ships, much as the ensigns were used to distinguish regiments
ashore.

Standard for the barges head	1
White ensigne with ye guilded lyon	1
White ensigne guilded lyon & crowne	1
White ensigne guilded unicorne	1
White ensigne with rose and crowne	1
White ensigne flower de luce & crowne	1
White ensigne with ye Scotch armes	1
Red ensigne with ye Lo. Admiralls badge	1
Brittaine Flagge	1
Pendants	26

*   *   *   *

fflags of 18 breadthes	1	
fflags of 16 breadthes	1	
fflags of 12 breadthes	5	
Ensignes 18 breadthes	1	
Ensignes 14 breadthes	6	
Striped ensignes	4	new but unsbl.
Red ensignes returned from sea	2	unsbl.
Chest to put fflaggs in	1	

As the four striped ensigns are reported "new but unserviceable" it may be inferred that the old striped form had now been definitely abandoned. Moreover, a similar survey carried out the month before at Portsmouth contains entries of four new "White Ensignes" and two new "Blew Ensignes," so that the white and blue ensigns had by 1633 made their appearance in the fleet. Unfortunately, the almost complete disappearance of the naval records of this period prevents us from ascertaining the precise occasion of the birth of these two ensigns; but they do not appear to have been yet in general use for distinguishing the private ships of squadrons, for Boteler, in his Six Dialogues written at this date, states that pendants were employed for that purpose.

> *Admiral.* Colours and Ensignes I take to be all one, but wher are they to be placed and wherefore serve they?

> *Captain.* They are placed in the Sternes or Poops of Ships; and very few Ships there are, whether Men of Warre or Merchantmen, that are without them. And their especial Service is, that when any strange Shypps meet one with another at Sea, or fynde one another in any Harbour or Rode, by the shewinge abroade thes Ensigns or Colours, it is knowne one to another of what country they are and to what place they belong.

> *Adm.* Serve thes Colours or Ensigns for noe other employ-

ments but only this?

Capt. Yes to many other, by waye of direction[313], as shall be sett downe largely in our next dayes discourse.

Adml. What are the Pendants you mentioned even now, and wherefore serve they?

Capt. A Pendant is a long Piece of silk or other stuff, cut out pointed wise towards the end in form of a streamer, wher they are slit into two partes, and the use of them, to distinguish the Squadrons of great fleetes by hanging them out in the topps of suche shyps as carry noe flaggs. As, for example, all suche Shypps as are of the Admiralls Squadron are to hang them out in their maine topps, thoes of the Vice Admiralls Squadron in their Foretops and thoes of the Reare Admiralls in their Missen-tops. And here alsoe they are to be of severall Colours. But besides this use, in great ships and especially suche as belong to the King, they are often used by way of trimme and braverye, and are then hung out att every Yarde-arme and att the heades of the Masts. And thes only are their uses and employments.

It was not until the crucial period of the First Dutch War that the practice of supplying all the ships of a squadron with ensigns of the squadronal colour became established. The proposal to divide the fleet into three squadrons, one under each of the three "Generals at Sea," with red, blue and white ensigns and pendants respectively, was first made in January, 1653. This was apparently one of the results of the attempt then being made to improve the fleet tactics in view of the unsatisfactory results of the earlier actions of the war[314]. It was, however, not until early in March that definite steps were taken for this purpose. The Navy Commissioners then gave orders for the urgent manufacture of a number of pendants and ensigns, forty of each colour, all having the "red crosse in chief," the order of precedence of the colours being at the same time changed from red, blue, white, to red, white, blue. This new order of precedence remained unchanged until squadronal colours were abandoned in 1864.

The circumstances in which the St George's cross was introduced into the fly of the white ensign in May, 1702, have already been detailed. The old form with plain fly was, however, not immediately superseded; both forms were in use as late as 1717, but by 1744 the older form had entirely disappeared. It is difficult to understand why the two forms should have been allowed to continue after the short time requisite for wearing out any ensigns of the earlier pattern that might be in existence when the change was ordered in 1702, but the surveys of stocks and orders for stores establish the fact that it was so, and that the form with the cross through the fly, known as the "St George's ensign," was at first issued only to ships which were appointed to serve outside home waters.

---

[313] I.e. as signals.
[314] Corbett, *Fighting Instructions* (N. R. S.), p. 83.

Plate XI

Modern Ensigns, etc.

1. White Ensign, 1801

2. Blue Ensign, 1801

3. Red Ensign, 1801

4. Admiralty, Blue Ensign

5. Naval Ordnance, Blue Ensign   6. Blue Pendant

7. War Office Badge   8. Military Auth. Afloat

9. Post Office   10. Royal Mail

11. North Sea Fishery

On the legislative union of England and Scotland in 1707 the tiny Scots navy came to an end as a separate force, and the "Union" colours, invented on the union of the two crowns a hundred years before, were inserted in all ensigns, naval and mercantile. An Order in Council of 21st July, 1707, established as naval flags the royal standard, the Union flag and "the ensign directed by her Majesty since the said Union of the two Kingdoms," which from the coloured draughts attached to the order is seen to be the red ensign. The white and blue ensigns are not mentioned in this Order; evidently the red ensign was alone regarded as the legal ensign of Great Britain and the others as merely variations of it for tactical purposes. In conveying this Order to the Navy Board, the Lord High Admiral instructed that body

> to cause the several ships and vessels of the Royal Navy to be with all possible dispatch furnished with Colours accordingly, and for the speedier and cheaper doing the same ... to order St George's Cross to be taken out of all the ensigns and a Union Jack Flagg put into them in the roome thereof, or to alter the said Colours in such other manner as you shall judge best for the Service.

It was found that the jacks in store were not of the same shape as the old canton, so finally all the ensigns were returned to the contractor "to be made Union."

Except for the slight change caused by the insertion of the Irish Saltire in accordance with the Royal Proclamation of 1st January, 1801, on the legislative union of the Irish Parliament with that of Great Britain, no further change in the design of the three ensigns has taken place, though the shape has been gradually altered from a proportion of roughly 5 by 4 to that of 2 to 1. By Order in Council of 9th July, 1864, the squadronal use of the ensigns in the navy was abandoned, and the principal ensign, the red, was made the exclusive property of the Mercantile Marine, which had shared it in common with the navy since the time of Charles I. The second ensign, the white, was retained for H.M. ships, and the third—the blue—assigned to the Naval Reserve, then recently formed, and to ships belonging to the Civil Departments of the navy and other departments of State.

The reason for this change is set forth in the Memorial of the Admiralty Board to the Council in the following words:

> The Flag Officers of the Fleet, whether Admirals, Vice-Admirals or Rear-Admirals, are classed in Squadrons of the Red, White and Blue, and are (with the exception of the Admiral of the Fleet) authorised to fly their Flags of the colour of the Squadron to which they belong, this regulation necessitating the adoption of ensigns and pendants of a corresponding colour in every ship and vessel employed under their orders, each vessel is therefore

supplied with three sets of colours, and the frequent alterations that have to be made when the Fleet is distributed as at present, under the orders of many Flag Officers, is attended with much inconvenience from the uncertainty and expense which the system entails.

The increased number and size of merchant steamships render it a matter of importance to distinguish on all occasions men-of-war and private ships by a distinctive flag; the latter vessels bearing at present the same Red Ensign as Your Majesty's Ships when employed under an Admiral of the Red Squadron. It also appears to us to be desirable to grant (under such conditions as we may from time to time impose) the use of a distinguishing flag to such ships of the Merchant Service as may be employed in the public service, whose Commanding Officer (with a given portion of the crew) may belong to the Royal Naval Reserve. We therefore most humbly submit that Your Majesty may be pleased by Your Order in Council to prescribe the discontinuance of the division of Flag Officers into Red, White and Blue Squadrons, and to order and direct that the White Ensign with its broad and narrow pendant be henceforward established and recognised as the colours of the Royal Naval Service, reserving the use of the Red and Blue colours for such special occasions as may appear to us or to officers in command of Fleets and Squadrons to require their adoption.

It will be seen that the reasons for the change given in this memorial are, first, the inconvenience and expense of keeping up the three sets of colours, and then (apparently as an afterthought) the need of a distinctive flag for the mercantile steamship. But in fact the man-of-war was already clearly distinguishable from the merchantman by its pendant and jack, a distinction that had been found sufficient for a period of two hundred years; a period during which the merchantman was, for the most part, much more like the man-of-war in outward appearance than it was in 1864. The real reason undoubtedly was that the squadronal organisation of the days when squadronal colours were first invented had become obsolete, and changes in tactics had rendered the squadronal colours unnecessary.

Before the change was made the opinions of a number of the leading admirals were taken. The majority agreed that the squadronal colours were no longer necessary and that their abandonment would be for the good of the Service. There were one or two, however, who thought otherwise, and it was pointed out that it had been found convenient during the Russian war of 1854-5 to divide the fleets in the Baltic and Black Sea by means of these colours. When Vice-Admiral Sir Charles Napier took command of the Baltic fleet he found that he and his two Rear-Admirals were all "of the Blue," and he therefore told one of them to hoist the red colours and the other the white, retaining the blue for himself, so that for this occasion the blue was the principal colour. Similarly, both Rear-Admirals in the Black Sea being "of the Red," one temporarily hoisted the white colours.

The fact that the division of fleets into red, white and blue squadrons was no longer a tactical necessity had been to some extent recognised before the end of the eighteenth century, for Howe concluded his fighting instructions, issued in 1782, with the following article:

> In action, all the ships in the fleet are to wear red ensigns.

Probably this was inspired largely from fear of the inconvenience that might arise from the white ensign being mistaken for the French national flag, but the fact that Howe issued such an instruction would seem to indicate that he did not regard the squadronal colours as indispensable. Nevertheless, in the battle of the "Glorious First of June" in 1794 his fleet was divided by squadronal colours, and the 'Marlborough' suffered through having her white ensign mistaken for the French national flag, then white with a tricolour canton[315].

Shortly after this the French fleet began to fly the new tricolour flag (as at present used) which had been adopted in February, 1794, but was not supplied to the fleet until October. Thereafter there was no danger of confusing it with the white ensign, and as that was now the ensign most unlike the French flag, it was usually ordered to be flown in action by the Admiral in command. Thus on the 10th October, 1805, Nelson issued the following memorandum:

> When in presence of an Enemy, all the Ships under my command are to bear White Colours, and a Union Jack is to be suspended from the fore-topgallant stay[316].

And when the enemy opened fire at Trafalgar, Collingwood (who was a Vice-Admiral of the Blue) hoisted his blue flag, but all the fleet, including his own flagship, hoisted white ensigns. Nelson's device of displaying an extra Union flag to ensure that no mistake should arise as to nationality is of interest, for the same course was at first adopted in the recent war, the British and German ensigns being very much alike at a distance. Early in the war the red ensign was substituted for this Union flag, and the practice of hoisting additional red ensigns on H.M. ships was followed to the end.

By the Colonial Naval Defence Act of 1865 it became lawful for any colony, subject to certain conditions, to provide and maintain its own vessels of war, and these were authorised to wear the blue ensign with the seal or badge of the colony in the fly and a blue pendant. In 1913, as an outcome of the Imperial Conference of 1911, the ships of the Naval Forces of the Dominion of Canada and the Commonwealth of Australia were further authorised to

> wear at the stern the White Ensign as the symbol of the authority of the Crown, a White Pendant at the masthead, and at the

---

[315] "Observed the Gibraltar and Culloden firing at us, probably by mistaking our St George's Ensign for the national flag, on which we cut off the fly." (Master's Log, *vide* Sturges Jackson, *Logs of the Great Sea Fights* (N. R. S.), p. 130.)

[316] Nicolas, *Despatches and Letters of Lord Nelson*, vii, p. 104. In a footnote (the volume was published in 1846) Nicolas says: "It may be hoped that the time is not distant when the anomalous distinctions of Blue, White and Red Admirals will be abolished, so that St George's banner will be the only flag borne by *all* British Admirals."

jack-staff the distinctive flag of the Dominion, viz: the Blue Ensign with the badge or emblem of the Dominion in the fly.

The ships of the Royal Indian Marine occupy a somewhat ambiguous position. Some of them—the floating defences—may be regarded as a Colonial Navy, others might more properly be included in class (3), Public Vessels. The old Indian marine took its rise in 1613, when the East India Company found it necessary to fit out for use only in Indian waters small vessels, which although employed to a certain extent in local carrying trade were sufficiently well armed to be of use in keeping in check the numerous native pirates who sought to prey upon the East Indiaman in those waters, and also to afford protection to the Company's vessels and factories against the ill-will of their European rivals, particularly the Portuguese. After the transfer of Bombay to the Company in 1668 that town developed into the principal seat of the Company's power, and the Indian Marine became known as the Bombay Marine. This gradually rose to such importance locally that from 1759 to 1829 a Captain of this service was annually appointed, as a deputy of the Company, to the post of Admiral of the Mogul Emperor, flying the flag of the Mogul at the main-mast-head and the Company's colours at the stern of his flagship.

From the earliest years the Company's ships were in the habit of flying pendants, and the proclamations of 1694 and subsequent years that forbade the use of these flags by other than H.M. ships were not obeyed—perhaps their existence was not known—in Indian waters. From the beginning of the eighteenth century it became customary to describe the senior officer of the Bombay Marine as "Commodore," and for him to fly a broad pendant. This practice had never received the sanction of the home authorities, though Admiral Watson, who was in command of H.M. ships in the East Indies station from 1754 to 1757, appears to have approved of the use of a common pendant[317] by the Company's armed ships.

In 1764, while carrying out arrangements connected with the evacuation of Manilla, Captain Brereton arrived at Batavia in H.M.S. 'Falmouth' and found there Commodore Watson, of the Bombay Marine, in the Company's ship 'Revenge' flying a red broad pendant. On the approach of the 'Falmouth' this was hauled down and a common pendant substituted. Brereton ordered this to be struck, and Watson thereupon hoisted the Company's colours and a broad distinguishing pendant. Brereton then sent an officer on board to demand that this also should be struck, and after a stormy scene it was done, but the pendant was again hoisted a short time afterwards. A second officer was sent to the 'Revenge,' but Watson positively refused to strike it. The next morning the 'Revenge' was seen clearing for action, with a number of armed men in her maintop to repel any attempt to touch the pendant. A third officer was then sent to the 'Revenge,' and when the junior officers of that ship realised what the result of proceeding to extremities was likely to be they gave up the pendant to him.

This example illustrates well the anomalous position in which the Indian navy stood; on the one hand it was recognised as a Colonial naval force, on the other it was treated as though it were merely a part of the British merchant service.

[317] I.e. a narrow pendant with striped red, white and blue fly.

The position does not appear to have been regularised until 1827, when the Admiralty issued a warrant that granted the ships of the Bombay Marine

> the privilege of wearing in addition to the Red Ensign, which all ships belonging to His Majesty's subjects should legally wear, the Union Jack and a long pennant having St George's Cross on a white field in the upper part next the mast with a red fly.

The curious expression "should legally wear" seems to have reference to the fact that the legality of the old striped ensign of the Company had recently been called in question, and its use, except as a jack, had in consequence been abandoned. It will be observed that the Warrant makes no mention of a broad pendant, but the Bombay Marine (or Indian navy as it was called after 1830) evidently still made use of it, for in 1848 the officer acting as commander-in-chief of H.M. ships on the East Indies Station objected to the flying of the red broad pendant, and as a result it was decided that the Commander-in-Chief of the Indian navy should fly a broad pendant, red with a yellow cross, and the Company's cognisance of the yellow lion rampant, holding a crown, in the upper quarter next the staff, the Commodore of the Indian navy serving in the Persian Gulf being allowed a similar flag with a blue field[318].

In 1858, when the Government of India was transferred to the Crown, the military and naval forces were transferred with it, but the Indian navy did not find favour in the eyes of its new masters, and it was abolished. This took place in 1863, when the following ceremony was observed:

> At noon on the 30th inst. the broad pennant of Commodore Frushard will be saluted by eleven guns from the battery at the Apollo Pier. The flag of the Indian Navy, long known as "the Company's Jack," will then be hoisted at the Castle flagstaff and saluted by twenty-one guns. At the close of the salute the Indian Jack will be hauled down, the broad pennant of Commodore Frushard and the pennants of all the Indian Naval vessels in harbour will be struck, and the Indian Navy will cease to exist as an effective service[319].

A new "Bombay Marine," consisting of a few small vessels engaged in the local transport and pilotage service of that port, similar to one that had already come into existence at Calcutta, was thereupon instituted. The Indian Marine Service Act of 1884 made provision for placing the vessels belonging to the Government of India under the Naval Discipline Act in time of war, and for constituting such ships vessels of war in the Royal navy. At the same time a warrant was issued authorising the vessels of the Indian Marine (to which the Prefix "Royal" was added in 1892) to fly a blue ensign with a badge of the Star of India in the fly, and a Union jack with a blue border. These vessels were in November, 1921, authorised to fly a red pendant when in commission.

[318] Low, *History of the Indian Navy*, ii, 201. A similar red pendant has recently been approved as the flag of the Director of the Royal Indian Marine.

[319] Order of the Governor in Council quoted by Low, *History of the Indian Navy*, ii, 570.

(II) PRIVATE MEN-OF-WAR

The "private man-of-war" or "privateer[320]" was a vessel the owner (or owners) of which had received from the Crown, or from the Lord High Admiral, "Letters of Marque and Reprisal." The occasion for the issue of such a licence, which was originally granted in the form of Letters Patent—whence the name—might be either special or general. It might be issued "specially" to some merchant who was able to prove that he had suffered certain losses from the action of the subjects of some foreign power, and who was thereupon authorised to make seizure of any ships or goods belonging to subjects of that State until he had by that means taken sufficient plunder to make good the losses formerly sustained by him, but no more. Such licences were also issued "generally" upon the outbreak of hostilities with a foreign state, to any subjects who wished to make war upon enemy vessels on the chance of making some profit by it, and who were able to give satisfactory security that they would comply with the regulations laid down for their conduct, particularly in the matter of the disposal of prizes taken. During the wars of the late seventeenth and eighteenth centuries merchants frequently sought Letters of Marque for their vessels, not because they wished them to take the offensive as regular privateers, but because they were thereby freed of all danger of being classed as "pirates" should they attempt to turn the tables upon any enemy that attacked them. For this reason many, perhaps most, of the ships of the East India and Guinea Companies fitted out in the seventeenth century carried Letters of Marque and displayed the Union jack.

Indeed, despite the issue of the Proclamations of 1634 and 1674, it seems that all privateers in the seventeenth century were in the habit of wearing the Union jack—sometimes with the permission of the authorities, but more often without it—with the object of making themselves look (so far as flags were concerned) as much like the king's ships as possible. The instructions for privateers issued toward the end of that century indicate that there was some infirmity of purpose on the part of the authorities in enforcing the existing law as regards the wearing of the Union jack. Thus the Instructions for privateers operating against Algiers[321], issued in December, 1681, provided

> That the merchants, captains, and others who shall have such letters of marque or commissions as aforesaid shall not weare in their said ships our Union flagg or jack (which is intended to distinguish our owne ships of warr from all others) at no time nor upon no pretence whatsoever, unless they be warranted for so doing by an order of leave under our hands and seal of our lord high Admirall or Commissioners of the Admiralty,

whereas the Instructions for Privateers fitted out against France issued in May, 1693, merely ordered that the Union jack or pendant (which actually were illegal without special warrant) should not be worn in presence of H.M. ships or in circumstances in which they might give occasion to a salute by a friendly foreign power.

[320] This word first appears about 1650, and soon replaced the earlier term.
[321] Marsden, *Law and Custom of the Sea* (N. R. S.), II, 412.

> That such merchants, commanders of ships, and others, who shall obtain such letters of marque or commissions as aforesaid shall not wear our colours, commonly called the Union Jack or pendant on board such ship or vessell by them fitted out in pursuance of such our commission, in company of any our men of warr, or so near any other men of warr belonging to any nation in amity with us, so as to occasion any salute from them, or in or near any port or road whatsoever.

A special distinguishing flag for privateers was first provided in the Royal Proclamation issued in July, 1694, which ordained that vessels receiving "Commissions of Letters of Mart or Reprisals" should wear, in addition to the St George's flag at the masthead and the red ensign with canton of St George at the stern, "a Red Jack with the Union Jack described in a Canton of the upper corner thereof next the staff"—the flag that Pepys in 1687 called the Budgee jack—which was in fact of the same design as the red ensign adopted in 1707, though apparently the canton occupied a larger proportion of the area of the flag in the jack than in the ensign[322].

Despite this precise direction, the privateer Instructions issued against France and Spain in December, 1704, contain the same instructions as those of 1693 quoted above, which presuppose that these vessels would fly the Union jack and pendant, which the Proclamation of 1694 had forbidden—but indeed, this muddle-headed attitude is not uncommon in official instructions. It is clear that privateers did carry pendants, for Woodes Rogers relates that he was ordered to strike his pendant by the 'Arundel' in August, 1708, "which we immediately did, all private commissioned ships being obliged by their Instructions to pay that respect to all her Majesty's ships and fortifications." The Distinction Jack of 1694 (subject to the necessary modification of the Union in 1801) remained the distinguishing flag of a privateer until privateering was abolished in 1856.

(III) PUBLIC SHIPS FOR USES OTHER THAN WAR

The first suggestion that public ships which were not men-of-war should wear some distinctive flag is found in the *Sub Notes about Flags and Colours* drawn up by Pepys about the year 1687. He writes:

> And here above all it is to be reflected on what distinction is to be made (as to the wearing of the Union Flag) between the King's own Ships, great or small, and hired ones, either as men-of-war (many of which both at Home and in the Plantations have been made up of hired Merchant Men) or for lower uses, as little as Victuallers, Water Ships, Store Ships, Pressing boats, Transporters etc. Wherein is to be considered whether if it be wholly necessary even in some of these occasions, as well as those of the Custom House, Green Cloth &c. some kind of distinction-flag might not be found sufficient to answer all the ends suggested for wearing the Jack Flag, without prostituting that to such low uses and ready

[322] About two-thirds, instead of less than one-fourth.

insults[323], which so much deference is expected to by us from the ships of foreign Princes and States of the greatest force and rate.

The Revolution of 1688 put an end to Pepys' reforming activities, and no steps were taken to distinguish such ships until 1694, when a Royal Proclamation issued 12th July provided that

> Such Ships and Vessels as shall be employed for Their Majesties' Service by the Principal Officers and Commissioners of Their Majesties' Navy, the Principal Officers of T.M. Ordnance, the Commissioners for Victualling T.M. Navy, the Commissioners for T.M. Customs, and the Commissioners for Transportation for T.M. Services, relating particularly to those Offices shall wear a Red Jack with the Union Jack in a Canton at the upper corner thereof next the staff, as aforesaid, and in the other part of the said Jack shall be described the Seal used in the respective Offices aforesaid by which the said ships and vessels shall be employed.

An Order in Council of 19th November in the same year provided further that "boats imployed in the service of the Generall Post Office be permitted to carry colours to distinguish them from other boats, and that in the said Colours there be represented a man on horseback blowing a Post horne," and from later papers in the same year it appears that the intention was that this device should be placed in the fly of the red jack, like the seals of the other government departments.

The proclamations of 1702 and 1707 confirmed the use of the red jack with the seal of office, but the King's Regulations of 1731 introduced a slight variation by providing that the seal might be placed in the body of the jack *or* ensign; the Regulations of 1806 completed the transfer by directing that the seal should be described "in the fly of the ensign," and the Regulations of 1844, not content with this, provided that the seal or badges should be placed "in the centre of both Ensign and Jack."

In July, 1864, the colour of the Ensign was altered to blue, and the red jack became an Union jack with a white border, both with the seals or badges as before, but the introduction of the "white bordered Jack" into this clause of the Order in Council appears to have been a slip, for the Addenda to the Regulations published in 1868 specified that the jack was to be of the same design as before but blue, like the ensign, and thus it remains; the difference between the jack and the ensign being that the former is smaller and square[324], instead of oblong in the proportion of two to one.

The badges of the offices referred to in the proclamation of 1694 were as follows:

> *Navy Office.* An anchor without cable in pale, with two smaller anchors on each side of the shank.

> *Ordnance Office.* This badge was similar to that now used by

[323] E.g. in 1636 the people of Calais stoned the Dover mail packet which carried the Union flag at the stern, "rending the said Unite coullers."

[324] See Plate V, fig. 7.

the War Office (Plate XI, 7), but the colour of the shield appears to have been originally red with a yellow chief.

Victualling Office. Two anchors with cables in saltire.

Customs. A castle gate. A regal crown was substituted for this in 1817. From that date until the Coastguard Service was transferred to the Admiralty in 1856 all vessels engaged in prevention of smuggling under the Customs, Excise and Admiralty flew red ensigns and pendants with this crown upon them.

Transport Office. A plain anchor.

In 1701 the Admiralty complained to the King that the Governors of the plantations—the English Colonies of North America and the West Indies—were in the habit of authorising certain merchant ships, to which they gave commissions, to wear the colours of the king's ships. This the Governors claimed to do in virtue of their Vice-Admiralty commissions and because they conceived

> it necessary for the security of ships sent out by them for H.M. Service, as well as for the honour of H.M. Commissions that these ships be authorised to bear such colours as may distinguish them from ordinary merchants' ships and other common trading vessels.

Presumably these ships, which certainly engaged in "common trade," were also employed on protection and police duties that would normally have been performed by ships of the Royal navy, had such ships been present there in sufficient numbers. On the 31st July of the same year an Order in Council was issued directing such ships to wear a jack with a white escutcheon[325] in the centre, and forbidding them to wear the ordinary Union jack. I have not met with this special form of jack at any later date, and it seems probable that the use of these colonial hired ships was discontinued after Benbow arrived in these waters in the late autumn of that year, though an Article providing for the use of the jack appeared some years after in the Instructions issued to the Governors of these colonies. It might seem that these vessels should be classed as hired men-of-war or as privateers, but the memorial of the Admiralty to the Council places them in the category of "those employed by the Officers of the Navy, Ordnance, Victualling and others."

After the disappearance of this jack there were no special distinguishing flags for colonial vessels until 1866, when it was laid down that ships in the public service of a colony might fly the blue ensign with the distinguishing badge of the colony.

Besides the Public Offices there are a number of corporate bodies whose functions are of a public nature and who have the right to fly a special flag upon their vessels at sea. The most ancient of these is the Corporation of Trinity House, a body first incorporated by Henry VIII in 1514. Its flag (Plate XII, fig. 4) may be seen flying upon the Trinity yacht when leading the Admiralty and Royal yachts during a review of the fleet, or when escorting the sovereign at sea; on such occasions the

---

[325] See p. 68.

Trinity yacht flies also a white ensign. The duties of this Corporation are, however, mainly concerned with the erection and maintenance of lighthouses, beacons and other sea marks around the English coast. Similar duties in Scottish waters are performed by the Commissioners of Northern Lighthouses, who fly upon their vessels a blue ensign with a white lighthouse in the fly, the Commissioners' own flag being a form of white ensign without the St Patrick's cross in the Union, and with a blue lighthouse but no St George's cross in the fly. Vessels belonging to Lloyds fly a blue ensign with the badge shown in Plate XII, fig. 10. The Port of London Authority, Thames Conservancy, Humber Conservancy, and Mersey Docks and Harbour Board have each their special badge, but these are of no historical interest. The modern Cinque Ports flag (Plate XII, fig. 5) is now never flown at sea, but is flown upon Walmer Castle, the residence of the Lord Warden.

(IV) MERCHANT SHIPS

As already remarked, the first legislative enactment providing for a distinction between the flags of merchantmen and ships belonging to the Crown was in the year 1634. We shall briefly review the position of affairs in the earlier years of that century. When James I united the crowns of England and Scotland in 1603 the English merchant ships were in the habit of flying the St George's flag at one or more mastheads, while those of Scotland flew the St Andrew's flag in a similar manner. It seems that in the great majority of these ships no other flags were flown, but some of the larger ships, especially those engaged in voyages to foreign parts, seem to have allowed themselves the additional luxury of a striped ensign (which appears to have been displayed only when attacking or resisting attack from pirates or other foreign ships, or when signalling to consorts), and also a number of pendants or streamers, which were probably only used on like occasion, or on occasions of special ceremony or rejoicing. Thus, for the ships fitted out by the East India Company in January, 1601, there was provided "for eche of the shippes 12 Streemers, 2 fflagges and one Auncient." In an inventory of the Company's ship 'Hector' of the preceding September there is mentioned besides "2 ancyents and 28 pendaunts," "a smale flag for the boat spirrit." This is the earliest instance in which I have met with a jack flag for the bowsprit in an inventory, and its use at this date must have been extremely rare and exceptional.

On the union of the two crowns, disputes as to precedence of flags appear to have broken out between the English and Scots merchant seamen, hitherto "foreigners" to each other. James attempted to remove the cause of these by providing in 1606 a combined flag, which was to be borne by both parties in their maintop, the English retaining the St George's cross at the foretop and the Scots the St Andrew's cross. So far as the Scots were concerned this attempt at compromise appears to have been rejected, for reasons already related in Chapter III, but the English adopted it. Thus, in the period between 1606 and 1634 the English merchantmen were bearing aloft two flags: the "Britain" flag, as it was then called, and the St George's flag, and although they were warned in the Proclamation of 1606 not "to bear their flags in any other sort" it is clear that some were also using on the poop a striped ensign with a St George's cross in a canton. The colours of the stripes appear to have been a matter of individual taste. Thus the ensign illustrated in the contemporary map[326] of Baffin's voyage for the discovery of the North-west Passage in 1615 displays red, green and blue stripes[327].

In 1634 the inconveniences arising from the fact that the king's ships and merchant ships wore the same flags had become so pronounced that a Proclamation was issued withdrawing the right to use the Union flag for the merchant ships and confining those of England to the St George's flag and those of Scotland to the St Andrew. No mention is made of any poop ensign, from which it may be inferred that this flag was not yet in common use among merchantmen. By the time of the Commonwealth the striped ensign appears to have gone out of use, and the merchantmen seem to have gradually adopted the red ensign introduced into the fleet in 1625. The order of 1649 requiring the ships in the service of the State to bear the St George's flag only does not seem to have been applied to merchant ships, and from a reference in 1656 to the flying of the "English Collers" improperly by a merchant ship lying at the Brill, when these colours were worn "with the Cross downewards" (i.e. the flag being inverted in contempt) it is clear that the English ensign at that date had the cross in a canton, and was not the plain St George's flag. The use of the red ensign was for the first time legally recognised as the distinctive flag of a British merchant ship in a Proclamation of 1674[328], in which the colours are expressly laid down as being

> those usually heretofore worn on merchants' ships, viz: the Flag and Jack white with a red cross (commonly called Saint George's Cross) passing right through the same; and the Ensign red with a like cross in a canton white at the upper corner thereof next the staff.

This order definitely abolished the use of any striped ensign, if any such still survived outside of the East India Company's ships. The red and white striped ensign[329] of that Company, which was probably adopted on its formation in 1600, remained, however, unchanged in spite of the Proclamation, and in 1676 the Commander-in-Chief in the Downs drew Pepys' attention to the fact. In his reply of the 20th November Pepys wrote:

> For that of the different colours assumed by the East India Company and ordinarily worn in their ships, I am very glad you take notice of it, though it be not of any so near resemblance to the King's as to create any mistake, which some have heretofore offered at, yet it being contrary to the letter of the proclamation it will be fit that his Majesty's pleasure be known in it[330].

Pepys mentioned the matter to Sir John Bankes, one of the principal members of the Company, urging him to get the use of this flag regularised, and in the Decem-

[326] B. M. *Add. MS.* 12206.
[327] Plate IX, fig. 8.
[328] See p. 66.
[329] See Plate IX, fig. 6. The number of stripes varied from nine to thirteen, the odd numbers being red.
[330] Tanner, *Catalogue of the Pepysian MSS.* (N. R. S.), iii, 325.

ber of this same year he wrote to Bankes as follows:

> I have fresh occasion of repeating what I lately mentioned to you about colours worn by the ships belonging to the East India Company different from what the merchant ships of other his Majesty's subjects generally do, and by his Majesty's proclamation of 18th Sept. 1674 ... are bound to use, without any provisional exception made therein on behalf of the said Company; for want thereof, not only his Majesty's commander-in-chief in the Downs but others of his captains and officers are under an obligation of interrupting your ships in the wearing the said colours, and have several of them applied themselves to me at sundry times (and now lately) for direction therein, with answer still given them by me in favour of the Company as knowing their and their predecessors' usage in that matter, and the moment it may be of to them that the same should be continued; but, forasmuch as it cannot be thought fit for me to remain under a constant accountableness for any behaviour of his Majesty's officers different from his pleasure signified by a proclamation, I desire you will please to take an opportunity of mentioning this thing to my honoured friends of your Company, to the end that (in case their service be indeed concerned in the continuance of this their usage) they may take some way of making their desires therein known to his Majesty, that so what he shall think fit to indulge to them upon it may be done by an order pursuant to the said proclamation, and his officers thereby indemnified in their obedience of it[331].

Apparently the matter was adjusted to the satisfaction of Pepys, for the striped flag[332] continued to be used by the Company until the year 1824, when, on the question of its legal position being again raised, its use as an ensign was discontinued, though it remained in existence until 1863 on the Company's ships as a jack or signal flag[333].

The flags laid down for the merchant ships by the Proclamation of 1674 were confirmed by further Proclamations in July, 1694, and December, 1702, with the additional restriction that such ships were expressly forbidden to wear "any kind of pendant whatsoever." As these proclamations were addressed to all "loving subjects" they were presumably binding on the Scots as well as on the English, but the use of the St Andrew canton certainly persisted in the ships of the Scots navy, and therefore presumably in the merchant ships of Scotland.

On the legislative union between England and Scotland in 1707 a further Proclamation was issued, which contained a fundamental difference. In the Proclama-

---

[331] Tanner, *Catalogue of the Pepysian MSS.* (N. R. S.), iii, 334.

[332] There are, however, instances during the eighteenth century of these ships flying a red or blue ensign.

[333] The Union replaced the St George's cross in the canton; and the St George's cross appears to have been introduced into the fly, by adding a vertical bar and thickening the middle stripe, about 1820. (See Plate X, fig. 11.)

tion of 1674, 1694, and 1702 the merchant ships had been forbidden to use any other colours than "those usually worn," but they were not expressly ordered to wear
any colours at all. In the Proclamation of 1707, under which the Union replaced the
St George in the canton of the red ensign, a clause was inserted

> strictly charging and commanding the Masters of all Merchant
> Ships and vessels belonging to any of our subjects, whether em-
> ployed in Our service or otherwise, and all other persons whom
> it may concern, to wear the said ensign on board their ships or
> vessels.

They were further forbidden to wear "any Flags, Jacks, Pendants or Colours made
in imitation of ours, or any kind of Pendant whatsoever, or any other ensign than
the ensign described." This did not prohibit the use of the St George's jack on the
bowsprit, which was expressly recognised by the *King's Regulations* for the navy[334]
as being, together with the red ensign, the appropriate colours for a British merchant ship.

In consequence of the legislative union with Ireland, a proclamation was issued on 1st January, 1801, substituting the new form of the Union in the canton
of the ensign, but leaving the existing regulations unaltered. The provision for the
use of the St George's jack by merchant ships last appeared in the 1808 edition of
the *Regulations and Instructions relating to His Majesty's Service at Sea* in the following terms:

> Merchant Ships are to carry a Red Ensign with the Union Jack
> in a canton, at the upper corner next the staff, and a White Jack
> with a Red Cross, commonly called St. George's Cross, passing
> quite through it.

How far such regulations, which in the preamble are expressly stated to be drawn
up for the "Naval Service at Sea," can have been legally binding on the Mercantile Marine is a matter for lawyers to decide, but it seems probable that the merchant service did not generally observe the regulation as to the jack, for in the next
edition (that of 1824) all reference to it is omitted. From that date the red ensign
alone has been the legal national colours of a British merchant vessel. It must be
displayed

(*a*) On a signal being made from one of H.M. ships or from a vessel under the
command of an officer of the Royal Navy on full pay.

(*b*) On entering or leaving any foreign port.

(*c*) If the vessel is of 50 tons gross tonnage or more, on entering or leaving any
British port.

Merchant ships commanded by officers on the retired list of the Royal Navy or
by officers of the Royal Naval Reserve may, on certain conditions laid down in the
King's Regulations, be allowed to wear a blue ensign instead of a red one.

No British merchantman may, under penalty of £500 and confiscation of the
colours, wear any other "distinctive national colours," nor any other flags or pen-

[334] First issued in a collected form in 1731.

dants in any way resembling those of H.M. ships, but there is nothing in the Merchant Shipping Act to prevent any such ship from wearing any fancy flags that it likes—even if some covert disloyalty is intended thereby—provided that such flags are not "distinctively" national and do not imitate the flags of the navy, and that it displays the red ensign upon the proper occasions.

The law on the subject of the flags to be flown by British merchantmen was, as will have been seen, sufficiently explicit, and the flags allowed by no means inferior in dignity or traditional sentiment to those withheld; nevertheless, the merchant skipper, until a comparatively recent period which may be dated roughly as the beginning of the reign of Queen Victoria, seems to have taken an especial delight in attempting to evade the law. Attempts to fly the Union jack have already been sufficiently illustrated. Another idiosyncracy was the flying of the blue instead of the red ensign. St Lo dealt with this at Jamaica in 1728 by an ingenious device, that of using the Crown's right of impressment to deprive such ships of one of the most important members of the crew: "rather than be troubling their Lordships with complaints of taking them away, I have found out another expedient, which is to get a Carpenter or Caulker from them, so that I hope in a little time to bring them to better reason."

In 1819 the master of a ship in home waters who had persisted in flying a blue ensign and pendant although repeatedly fired at, was prosecuted by the Admiralty, but upon his appeal the prosecution was dropped with the hope that "it will be understood that any future violation of the law will be punished strictly." Two other ships were, in the following year, prosecuted for flying pendants, and in 1821 the attention of the Commanders-in-Chief was called to the existing regulations "relative to Colours to be worn by private ships which it has been apprehended have not been generally attended to."

Not long after this date the custom of flying at a masthead a "house" flag denoting the ownership of the vessel became general, and perhaps for this reason or because they were living in a more prosaic age the captains of merchantmen ceased to give further trouble by attempts to display illegal colours. There are now many hundreds of house flags[335] in existence, but nearly all of them have come into use since 1840. An older practice with some of the larger merchantmen, which seems to date from the early years of the eighteenth century, was to fly the arms of the town in which the master lived at the mizen, and the arms of the town where the freighter resided at the fore. Some passenger ships plying on regular lines (such as the cross-Channel steamers) fly at the fore the national flag of the country to and from which they sail.

The somewhat anomalous position of the ships of the East India Company, many of which were given Letters of Marque in order to regularise their position as combatants if they came into conflict with ships of native states (or possibly with those of other European powers) in Indian waters, has already been remarked. No trace can be found of any formal grant of the Company's flag, and it seems most probable that it was really the survivor of an early striped ensign such as many ships, men-of-war or merchant, wore in the latter part of the reign of Elizabeth

[335] See *Lloyds Book of House Flags and Funnels.*

and the early part of the reign of James. There was, however, an early precedent of the grant of a special flag to specified merchantmen to denote a privileged position. In 1581 Elizabeth, anxious to encourage the trade then being opened up with Turkey, granted a Charter of Incorporation for a term of seven years to Sir Edward Osborn and three other merchants, who might add other Englishmen, not exceeding twelve in all, to their number. These were allowed "to set and place in the tops of their ships and other vessels the Arms of England with the red crosse over the same, as heretofore they have used the red crosse, any matter or thing to the contrary notwithstanding." On its expiry in 1588 this charter was not renewed, but in 1593 Osborn and others were incorporated in a company to be known as the Governor and Company of Merchants of the Levant, and they were "to set and place in the toppes of their ships or other vessels the Armes of England with the redde crosse in white over the same as heretofore they have used." It would appear from these words that the red cross in the original flag was bordered with white, although it is not so described in the earlier charter. The Charter of 1593 was found defective, and a new one was issued in 1601 which contained the same clause, the name of the company being changed to the "Governor and Company of Merchants of London trading into the Levant Seas." On the death of Elizabeth this charter lapsed, and it was not until the 14th December, 1605, that another charter was issued. This charter, which remained in force until 1825, omits all reference to the flag. Possibly James already had in mind the Union flag that was established early in the next year, and indeed the design of the Union flag is distinctly reminiscent of the old Levant Company's flag—the banner of Scotland taking the place of the Arms of England. The omission from this charter of any provision for a special flag cannot have been other than intentional, nevertheless the ships of the company seem to have continued to use the old flag in Levant waters, for in 1625 Sir Thomas Roe, then Ambassador to Turkey, issued a general proclamation "To all Captaynes, Maisters, pursers and officers of any English shipps and all other his Matie Subjects serving or sailing in them within ye Levant Seas," ordering "that from hence forth they, nor none of them presume to use or beare any other flagg or coulers than ye usuall flagge and Red Crosse of England, or St Andrewe of Scotland, neither in the Levant Seas nor in any Port of the Grand Signior's Dominion, upon what pretence soever." From this time the "usual flag and Red Cross of England" became very prominent in those waters and gradually replaced the French flag as protector of the lives and goods of foreign merchants trading within the Sultan's dominions. The various capitulations by which this was effected were consolidated in 1675 by a Treaty of Commerce made between Mahomet IV and Charles II[336], which, among other things, provided "that the Merchants of Spain, Portugal, Ancona, Seville, Florence, Catalonia, and all sorts of Dutch and other foreign Merchants ... might always come under the Flag and Protection of the Ambassadors or Consuls of England."

---

[336] *A General Collection of Treatys of Peace and Commerce* (1732), iii, 282.

Plate XII

Modern Ensigns, etc.

1. New Zealand Ensign, 1831   2. New Zealand Blue Ensign
3. Australian Blue Ensign   4. Trinity House

5. Cinque Ports	6. Red Pendant
7. Canada Badge	8. South Africa Badge
9. Indian Marine Badge	10. Lloyds Badge

There were other trading companies that, like the East India Company, had or assumed the right to fly a special flag, in this case probably only as a jack. One was the Guinea, or Africa, Company, the ships of which from the time of Charles II onwards flew a St George's flag with a chequered border of two rows of red and white squares. This practice probably originated with the third company, chartered in 1662, and of course expired on the dissolution of the fourth company in 1752. Another was the so-called Scottish East India Company which started its short life in 1695 and is best known from its disastrous attempt to colonise the Isthmus of Darien. Its emblem of the rising sun (Plate X, fig. 4) indicated the dawn of hopes that were doomed to an early eclipse.

Special forms of the red ensign may be flown by merchant ships of three of the British Dominions, viz. Canada, Australia and New Zealand. This privilege was first granted to Canada in the year 1892, the badge of Canada without the Crown (see Plate XII, fig. 7) being placed in the centre of the fly.

In 1899 merchant ships registered in New Zealand were authorised to wear a red ensign having in the fly four white stars, representing the constellation of the Southern Cross. In this connection it may be remarked that in 1834 the British resident in New Zealand proposed that the New Zealanders should have a national flag. Three patterns were sent over by the Governor of New South Wales, and by a narrow majority the chiefs voted for the one represented in Plate XII, fig. 1. New Zealand was then an independent country; in 1839 it was added to the British dominions and after the grant of its Constitution in 1852 this flag appears to have been dropped, to be subsequently revived by the Shaw Savill and Albion Shipping Company, which now uses it as a "house flag."

A red ensign for Australian merchant vessels was first approved in 1903. It had a six-pointed white star (indicating the six states) in the centre of the lower canton and five smaller stars, representing the Southern Cross, in the fly. In 1908 the large star under the Union had the number of its points increased to seven (see the similar blue ensign in Plate XII, fig. 3).

No other dominion or colony is at present allowed the privilege of "defacing" the red ensign, but any colonial merchant vessel is at liberty to carry, in addition to the red ensign, a flag containing the badge of the colony, provided that such a flag is not "distinctive national colours" (i.e. does not contain or imitate the Union).

A merchant ship commanded by a retired officer of the Royal Navy or by an officer of the Royal Naval Reserve may fly the blue ensign under Admiralty Warrant if the crew includes ten officers or men belonging to the Reserve. The formation of a reserve among officers of the merchant service was first authorised by Act of Parliament in 1861, and in the following year it was decided that a merchant ship commanded by such an officer might fly a blue ensign with a crown and the letters R.N.R. in the fly; the abolition of the squadronal colours of the navy in 1864, however, enabled the blue ensign undefaced by a device to be assigned to the Reserves, and the device was thereafter omitted.

(V) PLEASURE CRAFT

For the introduction into Great Britain of craft built solely for pleasure and large enough to navigate the open sea or the estuaries of large rivers we need look no further back than the restoration of Charles II. From the earlier years of the seventeenth century the wealthy inhabitants of the Netherlands had included among their recreations the sailing of specially designed boats upon their numerous waterways. With the presentation to Charles in 1660 of two of the Dutch yachts we may, for all practical purposes, date the inauguration of this form of recreation in England. The fashion set by the King and his brother gradually spread among the wealthier classes.

Except those belonging to the King, all such pleasure craft would legally form part of the mercantile marine, and in the absence of special permission to the contrary could only wear the flags appropriated to that service. Yet from an early date the owners attempted to appropriate to themselves some special distinction. The failure of the Governor of Dover in 1676 to obtain the King's permission to fly the Union jack on his private yacht has already been noticed. This failure did not deter others from assuming such a right. In 1686 the question of the liberty taken by private yachts to wear the King's jack without license came before the Navy Board, and Pepys, who was present, has left us the note upon the motives leading to such evasions of the law, which has been already considered in Chapter III (page 68).

The yachts belonging to James II (who reserved the Office of Lord High Admiral to himself throughout his reign) flew, in addition to the royal standard at the masthead and Union jack, a special red ensign, with St George's cross in the canton, and in the fly an anchor and cable surmounted by the royal crown.

The first attempt to democratise yachting and to form a club to facilitate its enjoyment came, oddly enough, from the Irish, a nation that has never, in spite of its natural advantages, shown any marked liking for the sea. Yet by the formation of the Cork Water Club in 1720 Ireland took a lead that was not followed in England for nearly a hundred years. The Club adopted as their distinctive flag the Union jack with the harp on a green escutcheon in the centre, as in the jack of the Protectorate; this escutcheon was also placed on the Union in the canton of their ensign. Dissolved in 1765, this Club was resuscitated in 1806, and was the progenitor of the existing Royal Cork Yacht Club.

The first corporate body of yachtsmen to be formed in England was the Royal Yacht Club (now the Royal Yacht Squadron) founded at Cowes in 1815, when the close of the long war with France rendered the Channel safe for such a form of amusement. As a distinctive flag, this Club chose a white ensign with the Union in the canton but without the St George's cross in the fly. For six years the Admiralty took no notice of the breach of the law involved in flying such a flag, but in 1821 the number of yachts had so increased that the Commander-in-Chief at Portsmouth drew attention to the fact that a large number of small craft were flying an unauthorised flag. He received instructions to enforce the law, and the Club had to content itself with the legal red ensign. In 1829, however, the Admiralty granted the yachts of the club permission to wear "a St George's or white ensign," and the club thereupon adopted the modern white ensign which its members still fly.

This was followed in 1831 by the grant of a blue ensign to the Royal Northern Yacht Club; a white ensign with "the Arms of Ireland" in the lower canton next the staff to the Royal Irish Yacht Club; and a formal grant of the red ensign with "the Union (with the harp and crown on a green field in the centre) in the corner" to the Royal Cork Yacht Club.

In 1832 a newly formed Irish club, the "Western Yacht Club," which had assumed a green ensign, approached the Admiralty with a view to the confirmation of this flag on the ground that "a white ensign has been granted to the 'Royal Yacht Club,' a red ensign to the 'Royal Cork,' a blue ensign to the 'Royal Northern,' and as the only unoccupied national flag we have assumed the green ensign[337]." They were informed "You may have as the flag for this Club either a red, white or blue ensign, with such device within as you may point out, but that their Lordships cannot sanction the introduction of a new colour to be worn by British ships." They then chose a white St George's ensign with "a crown in the centre surrounded with a wreath of shamrock."

There followed other grants of the white ensign, plain or with the St George's cross in the fly and with or without special badges.

In 1842 the Royal Yacht Squadron, moved by frequent complaints of the improper conduct in foreign waters of British yachts, erroneously supposed, from the fact of their having a white ensign, to belong to that club, asked that they might have "the sole permission to carry the white ensign," at the same time suggesting that the other clubs should have a blue one. The Admiralty acceded to this request and issued the following circular letter:

22 July 1842.

Sir

My Lords Commissioners of the Admiralty having, by their order of the 6th June 1829, granted permission to the Royal Yacht Squadron, as having been the first recognised club, and enjoying sundry privileges, to wear the White St George's ensign and other distinctions, that their vessels might be generally known, and particularly in Foreign ports, and much inconvenience having arisen in consequence of other Yacht Clubs having been allowed by this Board to wear somewhat similar colours, my Lords have cancelled the warrant enabling the ___________ to wear the white ensign, and have directed me to send you herewith a warrant, authorizing the vessels belonging to the club to wear the blue ensign of Her Majesty's fleet, with the distinguishing marks of the club, as heretofore worn on the white ensign; and as it is an ensign not allowed to be worn by merchant vessels, my Lords trust that it

[337] *Parl. Paper* 1859, III, Sess. 2.

will be equally acceptable to the members of the club.

This letter was sent to the Royal Western, the Royal Thames, the Royal Southampton, the Royal Eastern and the Gibraltar Yacht Clubs and to the Wharncliffe Sailing Club, but from a misapprehension the Royal Western Yacht Club of Ireland, once incorporated with its English namesake, was overlooked. In 1853 this point was raised in Parliament, but no action was then taken. In 1858, however, the exemption of the Irish Club was again made a grievance by other clubs desiring the same privilege, and the warrant of the Irish Club was then cancelled. The outcry raised led to the papers connected with the grants of the white ensign being laid before the House of Commons in 1859[338].

From that date the privilege of flying the white ensign has remained the prerogative of the Royal Yacht Squadron, a privilege enhanced in 1864 by its becoming the distinctive ensign of the Royal Navy.

At the present day forty-four clubs have the privilege of flying the blue ensign, either plain or "defaced" with some distinctive badge, and eight are allowed to "deface" the red ensign with their special badge. Other clubs may fly only the ordinary red ensign of the Mercantile Marine.

---

[338] *Parl. Paper 1859*, III, Sess. 2. Further particulars of the various devices adopted by the clubs will be found therein.

CHAPTER VI

FLAG SIGNALS

(I) EARLY SIGNALS

THE few scattered references to signals found in early Greek literature are so vague in their terms that they leave us in doubt whether the ancient Greeks or their predecessors on the waters of the Eastern Mediterranean made any use of flags for signalling purposes. It seems probable that the earliest signals were given by raising the naval standard which, as we have seen, found a place at the stern of the Phoenician ships of war at least as early as 400 B.C., and that the Greeks adopted this method from the Phoenicians, substituting a cruciform standard for the Phoenician Crescent and Globe.

When Thucydides tells us that the "semeion" was raised in the Greek fleet we may, in default of some better explanation, assume that the officer in command seized the cruciform standard and elevated it at arms' length. Such a signal might be rendered more conspicuous by throwing a military cloak of bright colour over the arms of the cross before raising it and, as already remarked, it seems highly probable that the sign known as Phoinikis (φοινικὶς) originated in this manner.

The earliest recorded instance of a signal at sea is probably that mentioned by Herodotus[339] as having been made by Xerxes in the year 480 B.C., when on quitting Therma in his expedition to Greece he embarked in a Sidonian ship and "gave the signal (σημήιον) to the rest of the fleet to get under way." A more characteristic—or more frequently mentioned—use of the "semeion" was as a signal to commence action. The fleet fitted out by the Corinthians against the Corcyreans in the year 433 B.C. met with a joint fleet of Corcyrean and Athenian ships. Both the opposing fleets drew up in rank and the "semeia" were then raised on both sides (τὰ σημεῖα ἑκατέροις ἤρθη) as a signal for beginning action[340].

Thucydides mentions two other instances[341] in which a fleet awaited the signal before commencing to fight, but the only strictly tactical signal which he has recorded was one made to the Peloponnesian fleet in 429 B.C. The Peloponnesians had enticed the Athenian fleet into a disadvantageous position by a feigned attack upon Naupactus. At a given signal (ἀπὸ σημείου) the Peloponnesians suddenly turned their ships round and attacked the Athenians[342].

Towards the end of the Peloponnesian War (if we may suppose that Polyae-

---

[339] Herodotus, VII, 128.
[340] Thucydides, I, 49.
[341] *Ibid.* II, 84; VII, 34.
[342] Thucydides, III, 90.

nus, writing in the second century A.D., was not guilty of anachronism) the purple cloak signal (φοινικὶς) comes into evidence. Conon, the Athenian commander, was in the year 406 B.C. off Mitylene, flying before Callicratidas the Spartan, who had twice as many ships. Observing that the Lacedaemonian ships had, in the ardour of pursuit, broken their ranks, Conon raised the "Phoinikis," which was the signal he had pre-arranged with the commanders of his ships, and, turning together, the Athenian ships bore down on their pursuers, then in disorder[343].

The Rhodians, in the second century B.C., made signals in the early manner by raising the "signum" or military ensign. Livy relates that Eudamus, when hard pressed in his action against the Syrian fleet under Hannibal (191 B.C.) made use of such a signal to call his unengaged ships to the rescue[344].

The earliest code of naval signals is that drawn up in the ninth century A.D. by the Emperor Leo VI in his treatise on Tactics[345]. Leo in the Introduction to his nineteenth chapter explains that he has been unable to find anything on this subject among ancient Greek writers except a few scattered references and that his knowledge is mainly derived from the experience of his Generals.

In this nineteenth chapter, which deals with Naval Warfare (Περὶ ναυμαχίας) he says:

> 39. Let there be some standard (σημεῖον) in your ship, either a banner (βάνδον) or a streamer (φλάμουλον) or something else in some conspicuous position, to the end that you may be able, thereby, to make known what requires to be done, and that the rest may set themselves to carry out the course of action decided on, whether it be to fight or to withdraw from fighting; to open out to surround the enemy, or to concentrate to the relief of an endangered portion of the fleet; to slow the rowing or increase speed; to make an ambush, or, emerging from ambush to attack the enemy; or, in general, whatever the signal that has its origin in your ship, that the others, by keeping an eye on her, may be able to execute it.
>
> 40. For in such an emergency you will not be able to make use either of the voice or of the trumpet to communicate what is necessary, because of the uproar and the tumult, and the sound of the sea, and the crash of ship against ship, the noise of the oars, and above all the clamour of the combatants.
>
> 41. Further, let the signal be given by setting the standard up-

---

[343] Polyaenus, *Strategemata*, I, 48 (2).

[344] Livy, XXXVII, 24: "Eudamum in alto multitudine navium maxime Hannibal, ceteris omnibus longe praestantem, urgebat; et circumvenisset ni signo sublato ex praetoria nave, quo dispersam classem in unum colligi mos erat, omnes quae in dextro cornu vicerant naves ad opem ferendam suis concurrissent."

[345] This work Λέοντος ἐν Χριστῷ τῷ Θεῷ αὐτοκράτος τῶν ἐν Πολέμοις τακτικῶν σύντομος παράδοσις is usually assigned to Leo VI (the philosopher), but it is possible that it may have been written by Leo III (the Isaurian) and dates therefore from the eighth century. It has not been translated into English.

right or by inclining it to the right or to the left, or by moving it twice to the right or left, or by shaking it, or lifting it up, or lowering it or altogether withdrawing it or altering its position, or by varying the appearance of the head by means of devices or colours as was the practice amongst the ancients; for in time of war they gave the signal for battle by raising what was called the Phoinikis (φοινικίδα). There was also what was called the "cap" (μαμελαύκιον) raised upon a pole, red in colour, and they had some other signals which were made known in like manner. Perhaps however it would be safer to make your signals by your own hand.

42. And thus, O General, let the exercise of these signals be practised, so that all the officers in command of ships under you may have certain knowledge of all such signs; of the reason why each is made, and when, and how, and may not fail. So that, well familiarised with the signals, they may readily understand them in time of emergency and carry out the orders indicated.

In reading the above paragraphs one cannot fail to be impressed by the profound grasp of the essential requirements of the subject exhibited by the writer. Nothing like it appears again until modern times, and the concluding words might well have been written by Kempenfelt and the other reformers of the Signal System in the British navy at the end of the eighteenth century.

After Leo we meet with nothing further on this subject until the middle of the fourteenth century, and from what we then find it is clear that the art had not only made no progress in the interval, but on the contrary had decidedly deteriorated. Two sets of instructions preserved in the *Black Book of the Admiralty*, to which Sir Travers Twiss assigns a date between 1337 and 1351[346], contain each one flag signal; one for calling a council, the other for notifying the presence of the enemy:

A xviii. Item est assavoir que a quel temps convenable il plest a ladmiral dassembler les capitaynes et les maistres de la flotte conseiller avecques eulx il prendra hault en mylieu du mast de sa nef une banniere de conseil parainsi que en toutes parties de la flotte, soit en ports ou dehors sur la mer, ce pourra estre congnu et apperceu &c et doncques tantost les capitaynes et maistres de nefs sont tenuz dassembler sans delay avec leurs bateaux bien eskippez de mariners pour nager et aler en la nef de ladmiral pour illecques oyr et faire ce

xviii. Also it is to be noted that at whatever convenient time it pleases the admiral to call together the captains and masters of the fleet to take counsel with them he will carry high in the middle of the mast of his ship a banner of council so that in all parts of the fleet, whether in ports or out at sea, this may be recognised and perceived etc., and then immediately the captains and masters of ships are bound to assemble without delay with their boats well manned with seamen to row and go on board the ship of the admiral there to

---

[346] Probably 1338, *vide Monumenta Juridica; The Black Book of the Admiralty*, ed. by Sir Travers Twiss (Rolls Series), Introduction, p. xxx.

que le conseil de ladmiral aura ordonne.

hear and do what the council of the admiral shall have ordained.

B vi. Item en cas que aucune nef ou outre vessel de la flotte apperceyue aucun vessel ennemy sur la mer doncques il mettra une banere en hault par laquelle la nef de ladmiral et autres nefz de la flotte pourront avoir congnoissance qu'il a veu ung vessel ennemy ou plusieurs et ainsi apres ordonner le mieulx quilz sauront pour lencontrer, &c.

Item in case any ship or other vessel of the fleet perceive any enemy vessel upon the sea then he shall put a banner aloft by which the ship of the admiral and other ships of the fleet may have knowledge that he has seen one or more enemy vessels and thus afterwards give the best orders they know of to encounter it.

The very primitive tactics in use at this period in northern waters called for none but the most primitive signals. When at sea, the fleet gathered each evening round the admiral to take his orders for the next day, and if by any chance he wished to consult the captains or had orders to communicate before that hour he took the banner, which was normally planted on the aftercastle, and placed it halfway up the mast. When the enemy was seen, the sighting ship displayed a banner in the top, and thereupon all the ships met together to discuss what to do. Nothing could be simpler; nothing, one would suppose, more inefficient in time of emergency; certainly nothing could be farther from the well-practised organisation inculcated by the Emperor Leo.

In the waters of the Mediterranean the tradition of a more scientific method of warfare than simple *mêlée* fighting had its natural influence on the method of signalling. The orders issued by Amadeo VI of Savoy in 1366 for the combined fleet of galleys provided by Genoa, Venice and Marseilles and sailing under his command[347] show a considerable advance upon those recorded in the *Black Book.* This may be judged from the following excerpts which include all the articles relating to flag signals.

Ce sunt les chouses ordonnees pour larmee Monseigneur de Savoye sur le gouvernement daler sur la Mer.

These are the ordinances for the armed force of My Lord of Savoy concerning the regulation of going upon the sea.

10. Item quand le dit seigneur voudra avoir conseil qui facet mettre son estendart aut et que toutes les gallees doivent venir vers le dit seigneur et oui ce quil voudra ordonner des autres gallees ce que le dit seigneur voudra ordonner.

10. Item when the said Lord wishes to take counsel let him order his standard to be placed on high and then let all the galleys come towards the said Lord and hear what he shall wish to command of the other galleys what the said Lord shall wish to command.

---

[347] *Due Ordinanze Militari Marittime del Conte Verde,* Anno 1366, by Capitano di Corvetta Prasca in *Rivista Marittima,* June 1891. I have supplied as literal a translation as the state of the text admits.

11. ... et que la ou ilz sont dessen-
du a terre que chascun tirat celle part
soubz la banniere quil est.

22. Item se ensi est que monseigneur vueille parler es gallees que
monseigneur doye lever une banniere
a ses armes a muy de la galee et tantost
chascune des gallees se doit aprochier
du dit seigneur sur la penne dicte.

23. Item se ainsi est que monseigneur vueille parler a lung ou a deux
ou au plus des gallees que quant monseigneur fera lever une bandiere a dues
ou plus que le patron du quel seront les
armes de la bannere ou dues bannieres
que monseigneur fera lever se doivent
tantost aprochier de la galee de monseigneur pour oir ce que leur voudra
dire sur la penne dessus dicte.

26. Item si ainsi fut que aucune des
dictes galee veist aucune nef ou galee
ou autre navile estrange que tantost
deust lever une bandiere e baissier la
bannere vers celle part ou il verra le
naviles estrange sur la penne dicte et ti-
enne tant la bandiere que la galee monseigneur li ait rendu enseigne et quil ait
lever sa bannere.

27. Item en cas avenoit que au-
cunes des dites galees eist aucun cas de
necessite quil eust besoing dayde que
elle doye fere enseigne dune banniere
onmy de la galee et tantost les autres
galees doivent aprochier celle par vers
telle gallee pour ly aydier sur la dicte
penne.

28. Item que nulle des gallees ne
doivent esguarder lune contre lautre
devant que elles verront pointer une
banniere sur la galee monseigneur

11. ... and there where they have
landed let each one go to that place
where is the banner under which he
serves.

22. Item, if it happens that my Lord
wishes to speak to the galleys then my
Lord shall raise a banner of his arms
amidships of the galley, and immediately each one of the galleys shall approach the said Lord under the penalty
named.

23. Item if it happens that my Lord
wishes to speak to one or to two or to
more of the galleys, then, when my
Lord shall cause to be raised one banner or two or more; the captains whose
arms are those of the banner or two
banners that my Lord shall cause to
be raised shall immediately approach
the galley of my Lord to hear what he
wishes to say to them, under the penalty aforesaid.

26. Item if it has happened that any
one of the said galleys has seen any
strange ship or galley or other vessel
then immediately it shall raise a banner and lower the banner towards that
part where it sees the strange vessels,
under the penalty named, and hold the
banner in that position until the galley
of my Lord has returned the signal and
has raised its banner.

27. Item in case it shall happen that
any of the said galleys has any occasion
of necessity that it has need of aid, then
it shall make a signal with a banner
amidships of the galley and immediately the other galleys shall approach
that place, towards such galley to aid
it, under the penalty named.

28. Item none of the galleys shall
face one another before they shall see
a banner on my Lord's galley pointed
from the poop towards the prow, and

de pope en proue et tantost chascune des galees sur la penne dicte regardera lune contre lautre.

29. Item se ainsi estoit que une des galees fut esperdue des autres et ensi fut quelle se retornast avec les autres pour faire seigne de cognoissance de jour celle qui sera dessoubz vent ou celle doivent ou qui sera lancre doivent lever lestandart de son commun onmj lieu de sa galee et l'autre galee li doit rendre l'enseigne et lever lestandart de son commun en la proue chascune doit porter son estandart en lon lieu de la poupe adonques se feront cognostre qui sont amis et ce sur la penne dessus dict.

immediately each of the galleys, under the penalty named, shall face one another[348].

29. Item if it has happened that one of the galleys has lost the others and then returns to them to make a recognition signal by day, that one which shall be to leeward, either that one or the one which is at anchor, shall raise the standard of its Commune amidships of the galley and the other galley shall return the signal and raise the standard of its Commune in the prow. Each one shall (then) carry its standard to its place on the poop[349]. Then they will know which are friends, and this under the penalty aforesaid.

It will be seen that both these sets of instructions give prominence to a signal for calling a Council and both, curiously enough, betray the same confusion of thought. From the opening sentence it would be supposed that the captains of the ships are assembled to advise the Admiral in Council; from the closing sentence it would appear that they are only called to hear the result of the council's deliberations. The "etc." in the English Instructions and the repetition at the end of Article 10 in the Savoy Instructions seem, however, to indicate that the texts have not reached us in their original state. In the English fleet the "Banner of Council" signal remained in use until the close of the eighteenth century[350]. As a rule this signal was made with the royal standard, though in 1369 a special gonfanon was provided and in the reign of Henry V the "Trinity Royal" had a banner of council containing the royal arms and the cross of St George[351]. When the fleet was large, as in the Cadiz Expedition of 1596, the royal standard was hoisted for the "selected" or inner council while the flag of St George called the captain and the master of every ship to the flagship for a general council.

But while in the English fleet the Banner of Council signal underwent no development until the end of the sixteenth century, the Mediterranean instructions of 1366 contain three signals of this nature: one to call the council, another to call all the ships when some order had to be communicated, and a third to call one or more particular vessels. These, with the addition of one signal for calling aid, one

[348] The object of this manoeuvre is not clear, but since the ram and the guns pointing forward were the only weapons of the galley it can be readily understood that friendly galleys would only face one another in exceptional circumstances.

[349] Commander Prasca suggests that *lon* should be read as *bon* and that the meaning is: to a place on the poop where the banner can be well seen. I suggest that it should be read as *son*.

[350] It was omitted from Howe's signal-book of 1790.

[351] *Exchequer Accounts,* 49/29 (7-10 Hen. V): "j banner de consilio de Armis Regis et Sancti Georgii."

manoeuvring signal, and a recognition signal, to which were added signals by sails and, at night, by lanterns, contain the germ of a complete system of signalling.

It is not until the middle of the seventeenth century that we meet with so advanced a system in the English navy. If an explanation of this be sought it will be found in the fact that the rowing galley was not suited to the waters of the English Channel and North Sea. If the Mediterranean nations had, in the Middle Ages, a comparatively advanced system of tactics and therefore—for the one inevitably follows the other—a comparatively complete method of signalling, it was because they had inherited the foundations of it with the galley from the Romans and Greeks. The sailing-ship did not assert its superiority over the older weapon until the early part of the sixteenth century, and it was another century before the seamen who manned it could be persuaded that the methods of tactics invented for the despised galley could be of use when applied to vessels whose motive power was of another order. It was the soldier-admirals, who were well acquainted with the value of formal tactics on shore, who taught the English navy the lesson it was so loath to learn.

The Instructions of 1366 just quoted may be taken as representative of the fourteenth century. For the fifteenth century we have at least two good examples; the orders for the Venetian navy drawn up by Mocenigo[352] in the year 1420 and the orders for the navy of Castile drawn up by Fadrique Henriquez[353] in 1430. It will be sufficient to extract from the Venetian orders, which are the more interesting for our immediate purpose, the various articles relating to flag signals.

Questi sono i ordeni et commandamenti dati per il magnifico M. Piero Mozenigo del mar Zeneral Capitan—1420—

5. Quinto che andando à uela nulla Galia ardisca passar el fogo à Misser lo capetanio saluo quella Galia che sarà de guarda, ma tuttauia debia attendere à non spartirse da lui sotto pena de lire diese à zaschedun che contrefarà, massime quando se uorà raggattar. Misser lo capetano farà metter la bandiera al mezzo. In quella uolta à chi piaserà ragattar habbi libertà di poterlo fare non si luntanando da lui mia dò al più, sotto la detta pena.

These are the ordinances and commands given by the eminent Mr Piero Mocenigo, Captain General at Sea—1420—

5. Fifthly, when proceeding under sail, no galley shall attempt to pass the lantern of the Captain except the galley which shall be on guard, but should always take care not to part company from him under penalty of 10 lira for each one contravening, especially when they are racing. The Captain will place the flag amidships. In that case anyone wishing to race shall have liberty to do so; not however outdistancing him more than two miles at the most, under the aforesaid penalty.

---

[352] Transcribed from a Vatican MS. in Jal's *Archéologie Navale*, II, 107 et seq.

[353] Fernandez de Navarrete, *Coleccion de los Viages y Descubrimientos que hicieron por mar los Espanoles*, I, 410 et seq.

13. Quando messer lo capitanio uorà domandar da parte el farà meter una bandiera in la popa, in quella fiada tutte le Galie se debia accostar à lui perche el possa saper el sò parer.

14. Quando misser lo capitanio uorà che alguna de so Galie uegna da lui, el farà leuare in pope la bandiera di qual sopracomito el uorà che uegna da lui. In quella fiada quel tal sopracomito di chi sarà la bandiera uegni de presente à lui sotto quella pena che à lui piaserà.

13. When the Captain desires to call the ships to him he will put a flag on the poop, in which case all the galleys ought to approach him in order to learn his intentions.

14. When the Captain desires any particular galley to come to him, he will raise on the poop the flag of that commander whom he wishes to come to him. In that case the commander whose flag it is shall at once repair to him under such penalty as seems fit.

Signals for the galley on guard.

Primà sel uederà fusta over fusto armado, debia leuar l' Insegna di misier San Marco et puoi tor quela uia tante fiade quanti sarà i nauilij che l' hauerà descouerto, et se queli sarano da uno in suso debia uegnir du miser lo capitanio, et farli sauer de queli fusti lui hauerà descouerto. Se la sara coca zoe naue lieue la soa bandiera dal ladi sinestro, se la sarà barca leua un penon dal ladi destro; fazando segni cum quela bandiera in la qual uia queli nauiglij i sarà descouerti et se miser lo capitanio uorà che la Galia de guarda uada ad algun de quali nauiglij i quali sarà descouerti el farà leuar una bandiera quara à pope al ladi destro à la uia del nauilio, obseruando i ordini infrascritti. Et se l' occorese che la Galia de guarda andando ad algun nauilio per l' ordene dato de sopra, et se miser lo capitanio uolese che quela tornase, non andase più auanti, se miser lo capetanio andarà à remi el farà fer uela de presente, et fara calar, et uezudo questo segno la Galia de guarda debia tornar subito à lui.

First, if he shall see a light galley or armed galley, he ought to raise the Ensign of Saint Mark and then lower it as many times as there may be ships which he has discovered, and if there are more he should go to the Captain and acquaint him how many galleys he shall have discovered. If that be a boat or ship he shall raise his flag on the left side, if a bark, a pennant on the right side, making signals with this flag in the direction in which these ships are discovered, and if the Captain wishes the Guard-galley to go to any of these ships which shall be discovered, he will raise a square flag on the right side of the poop towards that ship, in conformity with the regulations given below. And if it shall come to pass that the guard-galley on going to any ship under the above order and the Captain should wish her to turn back and not to advance further, if the Captain shall proceed under oars, he shall order sail to be taken in at once and shall strike sail, then having seen this signal the guard-galley ought to turn at once to him.

Item comanda misier lo capetanio che sel fose descouerto più fusti e lui terminase andare a queli jn quela fiada el farà leuar el sò stendardo d'oro cum la so arma al fanò a pope, et de presente tute le Galie se debia redure appreso lui, é andare à se soe poste, e faza dar arme in couerta, et ordene le sue pauexade à proua segondo uxantia, et lo resto de pauixi sia per imbrazar et andar per couerta, et per suso le pertegete sia meso schiauine segondo usanza et à la prima trombeta zascadun se debia armar, à la segonda leuar l' Insegna de San Marco et rinfrescarti i corpi. A la terza quando serà leuado à meza Galia el standardo quadro con la Insegna del nostro signor Jesu Christo all' hora ognun uada arditamente et come buon' ordene che una galia non impaci l' altra à inuestir i diti navilij ouer fuste e non se desparta dalla battaia fina 1' ultima sconfita.

Et perche molte fiade ocore che le Galie se separa una dall' altra, et squarase da misier lo capetanio, però lè de necesità dar ordene ò segno per el qual posa recognoserse dalle nostre Galie, una dall' altra si de zorno come de note come è dito qui de soto.

Se alguna Galia se smarirà de miser lo capetanio per poterla recognoser, sel sarà de zorno miser lo capetanio farà un fumo à prua, et uezando questo segno la Galia che sarà squarada, responda per si fato segno et poi farà leuar una bandera a pope a cauo de banda destra, et per el simel lui debba responder, et poi lui farà leuare una bandiera quara à prua à ladi senestro,

Likewise the Captain commands in case more ships are discovered and he is determined to go to them; in this case he shall order his own standard to be raised, the gold standard with his arms, at the lanthorn on the poop, and immediately all the galleys ought to repair close to him, and proceed each to her own post, and order the arms on deck and order their pavisades to the prow according to custom, the rest of the shields to go round the deck, and on the supports of the awning the galley slaves' clothes are to be put as is customary, and at the first trumpet each man is to arm himself; at the second to raise the ensign of Saint Mark and to take refreshments for their bodies. At the third, when the square standard with the ensign of Our Lord Jesus Christ shall be raised amidships each ship shall proceed boldly and in good order, so that one galley may not hinder another, to board or come up with the said ships or galleys and not to leave the battle until they are finally routed.

And as it often happens that the galleys are separated one from the other and are dispersed from the Captain, therefore he must necessarily give an order or signal of recognition by which they may be recognised by our ships one from the other by day as well as by night, as is mentioned below.

If any Galley shall stray from the Captain, in order to recognise it, if by day, the Captain makes smoke on the prow and seeing that signal the galley which had separated shall answer by the same signal, and then the Captain shall order a flag to be raised on the forward end of the poop on the right side; and with the same signal he is to answer and the Captain shall order et per el simel quela Galia debia responder, et poi lui farà leuar una bandiera quara à prua et per el simel questa Galia debia responder, e farà i diti segni, miser lo capitanio farà leuar l' Insegna di Misier San Marco, et cosi debia responder la dita Galia e sia ben prouezuda à non se acostar, sel nò cognosese bene i deti segni.

Item zonzandò mr lo capo in algun liogo...non uoiando che algun sopracomito faci butar i sò copani in acqua fara butar el suo e leuerà la soa bandera de uento, à cao de banda. E in questo caso algun no dieba butar lo suo, fia la deta bandiera sarà alzada, mà mouesta sara quela cadaun posi butar soto quela pena à lui parerà.

Item quando mr lo capitanio uorà, che tuti i soracomiti uegna à lui, el farà meter la so bandiera da uento in pope à la scaza inuerso prua, alora debia uegnir da lui, perche altrimenti bisognaraue mandar per cadaun.

to raise a square flag on the left side of the prow, and likewise that galley is to answer and make the aforesaid signal. The Captain will raise the Ensign of St Mark and this the galley ought to answer, and be very attentive not to go alongside if it does not well recognise the above signals.

Item the Captain, cruising in any place, ... not wishing any commander to lower his boat into the water, will launch his own boat and raise his flag on the windward side of the poop forward, and in this case no one shall lower his boat as long as the said flag is hoisted, and if any does so it shall be under the penalty which he thinks fit.

Item if the Captain wishes all the commanders to come to him, he will put his flag to windward, on the poop near the ladder, inclined towards the prow, and then they must go to him because otherwise he would have to send for them.

The Venetian orders contain no provision for calling a Council, but they include two flag signals for calling up the galleys to take orders. Possibly the Venetians, anticipating Drake, did not assent to the scriptural dictum that in the multitude of councillors is wisdom. In the Castilian Instructions there is not only provision for calling a council by day, by hoisting the royal pendant, but also for calling an informal council at night. In daytime the captain and a boatswain[354] from each galley had to come in a boat on board the Admiral, but at night each galley ranged up with the Admiral in turn, spoke with him, and then fell off again. Another signal not found in the Venetian Instructions is that for calling assistance; in the Castilian Instructions this is to be done by raising the royal pendant. There are two signals for discovery of a fleet in those instructions; if the fleet was recognised as an enemy the sighting galley hoisted the royal pendant and rushed off to tell the Admiral all about it, without attempting to denote by signal the number of ships, but if it was merely a strange fleet the sighting galley contented itself with hoisting a flag to the masthead and raising and lowering it as many times as there were ships. The first galley to sight land raised a flag to the masthead, kept it there a short time, and then lowered it. The recognition signal differs from that provided in the Venetian orders, but it contains the same serious defect found in most of the early recognition signals—the two ships simply copy one another. In the Savoy Instructions of

[354] Cada patron con un cómitre.

1366 it will be seen that there is a slight variation in the signals made by the two galleys, sufficient to betray any stranger not acquainted with the difference. One would have thought that the necessity for some such device would have been apparent to any seaman, for the use of an enemy's colours was a well-known artifice and nothing could be simpler than to copy exactly the signals of another ship.

For the early sixteenth century we have two important sets of signal instructions. One of these, the "Ordonnances et signes pour nauiguer jour et nuyt en une armée royale[355]," drawn up by Antoine de Conflans about the year 1515 for use in a fleet composed of sailing ships and galleys, is worth translation in full:

> Ordinances and Signals for navigating by day and by night in a navy royal, if his most Christian Majesty, whom God preserve, or other prince of the realm, should set out to the conquest of the Holy Sepulchre or other lands of the enemies of the Holy Catholic Faith, and the Ordinances and Chapters written below, which are for the recognition by day and by night of those who are of the party and of the company of the said most Christian king or prince; Also if other ships, either strangers or enemies, whether sailing ships, galleys, foists or other vessels, should be found among the said navy by day or night, they may be easily recognised by these said ordinances, which must be well kept and observed by the whole fleet and company of the said navy.

> And First:

> The King's ship, or that of his admiral and lieutenant if the said lord is not himself present, shall ordinarily wear the banner in the top called the "gabye" in the Levant; and this shall be the mark by which the royal or admiral ship shall be recognised by day; and by night, because the aforesaid banner can not be seen, the said ship shall carry on its poop a lighted lantern, such as is called a "fanal" in the Levant waters, which shall burn all night, so that the whole fleet can see it; and by this means the royal or admiral ship shall be recognised by all the fleet.

> Item, all the ships of the fleet, whether galleys or other vessels, shall come each morning to salute the King's or admiral's ship and to ascertain the watchword (mot du guet), and in the evening to learn the night-cry (cry de la nuyt); and in the evening they shall come and salute the said lord and his ship, and enquire what route and course he intends to follow, in order that if, through tempest or for other reasons, any vessel should lose itself by night, it will know what route to follow; and none of the said ships or galleys, except the king's or admiral's, shall carry a banner in the top, nor any lantern or beacon, except the Captain General of the galleys, who usually may carry the banner at the stern, and by night a stern lantern. If by chance bad weather

[355] Published with notes by Jal in the *Annales Maritimes et Coloniales 1842*, Part II, pp. 54 et seq.

should occur (which God forbid) and it is feared that the vessels may become separated from one another, the king will carry two banners by day and two lanterns by night, and each of his fleet one; and in the same way the Captain of the galleys and his fleet one other.

Item, no ship shall fail to change its course and go about when the said lord does so, and generally, each one shall perform the manoeuvre which the said lord shall perform.

Item, if the said lord wishes to speak with other ships he will put a banner at the stern, and each ship shall be bound to approach the said lord. And if the said lord wishes to speak with the galleys only he will put the banner in the admiral's stern gallery.

Item, let each one carry as much sail as seems good to him, and proceed at the same speed as the said lord and no more, so that he does not pass his said ship, under the penalty afore-mentioned or of being punished at his discretion. And also let each one take care to keep near the said ship.

Item, if any of the said ships or galleys see one or more sail, the ships shall show, as many times as they see sails, a banner in the top on that side on which they see the said sails, and the galleys shall show it on the mast-head[356]. Each one of them, whether ship or galley, shall keep it there until the captain[357] has replied with a similar signal.

Item, let no one, on pain of death, whether commanding a ship, galley or brigantine, chase any ship of any sort or condition without leave and licence of the said lord.

Item, let no vessel salute another whilst it is within sight of the said lord, on pain of corporal punishment, except the galleys, which shall salute the Captain as a mark of respect.

Item, if by day any of the said ships or galleys shall have suffered any damage (which God forbid) that one to which the accident has happened shall place in the top a pendant so as to be seen by the said lord. It shall fire one gun and shall keep the said banner flying until the other vessels have come to its assistance. In the case of a galley it shall fly the said banner at the masthead and shall fire one gun as already said, and each of the said ships shall approach that to which the accident has happened in order to render aid.

Item, if by chance the said ships have parted company, which God forbid, and meet again by day, the one to windward shall lower and raise the topsail once and fire one gun; and the one to

---

[356] Calcet.
[357] Cappitaine. He is thinking only of the galleys.

leeward shall lower and raise the said topsail once and fire two guns. In the case of the galleys, the one to leeward[358] shall twice draw up to the mast the lower end of the lateen yard and shall fire one gun; and the one to leeward shall peak the lateen yard (by drawing the upper end down to the corsia) and fire two guns, keeping the said yard arm to the corsia[359].

Item, if any of the said ships is in need of aid from the galleys it shall fire one gun and hoist a banner on the poop twice and the Captain of the said galleys shall then, if possible, go or send to it.

Item. [If any of] the said ships or galleys sights land [the ship] shall hoist a banner at the lower yard arm and the galley at the fore or at the after end of the lateen yard slung horizontally[360] on the side on which land is seen, and shall keep it out until the said lord has answered.

Item, if the said lord wishes the said ships to lower their boats he will place two banners at the poop and fire one gun, and immediately the said ships shall launch their boats and put out towards the said lord or where he shall wish them to go.

Item, if the said lord, being at anchor, wishes to make sail, he will place a banner at the edge of the top in addition to the ordinary banner, and will fire one gun, and everybody must thereupon return on board to hoist sail likewise.

Item, if by day one or several sail are sighted, and the said lord wishes the galleys to chase and speak with them, he will place a banner at each yard-arm and fire two guns.

Item, if the said lord wishes the whole fleet to chase he will place two banners at the said yard-arms, and also two more on the edge of the top in addition to the ordinary one, and he will fire four guns, and every ship shall be bound to carry the requisite number of sails.

Item, if the said lord and his fleet encounter enemy fleets where they must fight, they shall show all the ensigns and banners they have, so that each one may do his duty.

These articles will be changed every time that a fleet is set out, however the substance of them remains the same.

Here follow the arrangements and chapters drawn up for night-time.

And first

If the said lord is at sea, and he wishes to make sail, he will

---

[358] Soubz le vent, probably an error for "to windward."
[359] The gangway running along the galley amidships.
[360] La gallère ou care ou à la penne à demy pendant.

show two lanterns and will fire one gun, and he will keep the said lanterns showing until the others have replied to him with two other lanterns, but without firing guns; and each one shall be bound to get under way and make sail like him.

Item, if, being under sail, the said lord wishes to speak with the other ships, he will show two lanterns twice and twice conceal them; and the last time he will keep them showing until the others have replied by a similar signal, and each one shall be bound to go to the said lord; and if he wishes to speak with the galleys only, he will show a single lantern over the stern light, and if the brigantine is to come he will show two.

Item, if any of the said ships or galleys sight one or several sails it shall show a single lantern as many times as it sees sails, and shall betake itself to the said lord as soon as it can, and all the others shall do in like manner.

Item, if the said lord wishes to take off a bonnet, he will show three lanterns, one after the other, until the others have replied with three other lanterns, and each one shall be bound to do the same.

Item, if the said lord wishes to set a bonnet and crowd on sail he will show three lanterns one above the other and keep them out until the others have answered with a similar signal, and each shall be bound to crowd on sail to follow the said lord.

Item, if the said lord wishes to chase by night, he will show three lanterns in a row three times, and will fire three guns, and will keep the said lanterns showing until the others have replied by similar lanterns. And to enable them to recognise one another each ship shall carry four lanterns at the poop, and the said lord will carry three on each side of his stern light.

Item, if the said lord wishes to take in sail he will show three lanterns one above the other three times, and will fire one gun, and the third time he will keep the said lanterns showing until the others have replied by similar lanterns without firing guns.

Item, if the said lord wishes to come into port, he will carry two stern lights, one above the other, and will fire one gun, and each of the said ships shall be bound to follow him to the said port; and when they shall have followed him and anchored, the first ones must keep a lantern at the stern until they have all arrived in the said port, in order that they may not hinder one another; and when all the said ships have arrived they shall take in the said lanterns, and the stern light of the said lord alone will remain burning.

Item, if by night any accident shall occur to any one of the said ships (which God forbid) it shall show four lanterns at the stern and four at the bows, as it may be difficult to see all the said lanterns; it shall also fire two guns until the other ships shall come to its aid, whereupon the said ships shall be bound to come to its succour.

Item, if one of the said ships should have need of galleys, it shall fire one gun and keep a lantern at the poop until the said galleys have arrived, and the Captain of the said galleys shall be bound to go or send to it if it is possible.

Item, if it should happen that the ships part company by any chance (which God forbid) and they find their companions by night, the one to windward shall show six lanterns three by three and shall fire two guns.

Item, the one to leeward shall show four lanterns one above the other and fire four guns; and the watchword for the night shall be cried; and thus each one will be easily recognised without having to come right up with one another; and the said lord wills and commands that when the fleet thus part company and find one another by night, and some distance off find another ship not belonging to their company, none shall dare to fire at one another without first having made the above signals, as well by day as by night; and moreover, the said lord wills and commands that they shall, in addition, speak with one another.

The watchword or cry for the night, and all the other signals, as well for day as for night, are changed and are at the discretion and will of the lord and chief of the said fleet, with the council of master mariners and pilots, and with the aforesaid council and the assistance of this present collection, they can make use of as much as seems good to them.

The instructions just quoted are plainly an ideal set; they represent the best experience of the age, but there is no indication that they were ever actually employed at sea.

The other important set of instructions of the early sixteenth century is by no means so full as that of Conflans, but it was actually used at sea, and reappears in various guises until the middle of the century. It seems to have been first drawn up by Philippe de Cleves, to have been used by the Emperor Charles V in his voyage from Flanders to Spain in 1517, and finally to have been incorporated, with slight alterations by Jehan Bytharne, Gunner in Ordinary to the King of France, in his *Livre de Guerre tant par mer que par terre*[361] written in 1543. The flag signals, which Bytharne says he had himself seen made at sea, present no improvement on those already cited, and they may, as given by Bytharne, be summarised as follows:

---

[361] See *Book of War by Sea and Land,* edited by Sir J. K. Laughton in vol. I of *The Naval Miscellany* (Navy Records Society).

To assemble the Captains for Council or to speak to them. The Captains to bring their best pilot and most experienced officer.	A square banner tied in a weft[362] in the main mizen.
On sighting strange ships.	A square banner tied in a weft[363] halfway up the shrouds on the side on which the ships are seen.
If the strange ships are numerous, then	Two flags as above, one over the other.
If the Admiral, on receiving the above signal from one of the scouting ships, desires that they should go forward and reconnoitre.	A banner on the fore mast inclined forward.
All ships to chase.	A square banner between the main top and the small banner flown at the main topmasthead.
Sighting land.	A square banner in the main top inclined on the side on which land is seen.
Ship in danger.	Man in main top to swing banner round and round. Three guns in quick succession.

If we now turn to the contemporary instructions of the English navy as given by Audley in his *Orders to be used in the King's Majesties Navy by the Sea* (c. 1530)[364], we are at once struck by the primitive nature of the signals contained in them. They are as follows:

> Whensoever, and at all tymes the Admyrall doth shote of a pece of Ordinance, and set up his Banner of Councell on Starrborde bottocke[365] of his Shippe, everie shipps capten shall with spede go aborde the Admyrall to know his will.

> When and at all tymes the Admyrall will anker or disanker, he must shote a pece, that thereby the rest may know to do the same; and that no Shippe ride in an others walke, for in that is greate danger.

> If they saile by night the Admirall must beare a greate light in the stearne of his Shippe, and if his fleete be greate, the Admirall

---

[362] "À demy clouée."

[363] "à moitie pendant." Presumably there was some difference in these two methods of tying a flag in a weft, but it is not known in what this difference consisted. Perhaps "a demy clouée" meant that the fly was gathered into the hoist, while the other expression denoted that the flag was gathered up horizontally in the middle, the normal method of making a weft.

[364] *Harl. MS.* 309.

[365] quarter.

must carie ij lights; and the Vice Admirall one, and the said Admirall must make such Saile over night that all his fleet may kepe about him; perchanse ells in the morning a greate parte of his flete may be out of his sight, for everie Shippe saileth not alike.

If it chance any Shippe in the night fall in leake, or breake his maste, he may shote a pece of Ordinance, or ij to warne the flete he hath harme and in perall, to the entent he may have helpe, and the rest to tarie.

The Admyrall ought to have a swifte pynnes abord alwaies abrod to askrie so farre of that he may se the flete out of his toppe, and if he seeth any enemyes or any other sailes, geve knowlege to the Admyrall if they be any enemyes let him shote ij or iij peces of; in the meanetyme the Flete may put them self in order and councel before hand. Allwaies foreseing the pynnesse prease not so nighe the enemve that he might be apprehended, for by that the secrets might be knowne to the enemye, and evrie night he to cum into the flete agayne.

If in the night there chanseth any enemyes unlooked for to fall into the flete, he that first doth askrie the same shall shote of ij peces, and geve a token of ij fyers and by that token shal be understande that they be enemyes that be in the Flete. Yf they do flee, let everie man make after, and that Shippe that is nighest beare a light in his Stearnye that the rest may know whether[366] the enemye goeth, for otherwise they may lose them: and if he that giveth the chace, se not the fleete follow, let him shoote of a pece, that they may follow by his shotte, in case they should not see his light.

The Admyrall ought to have this order before he joyne battell wth the enemye that all his shipps shall beare a flagge in their missentoppe and himself one in the foremaste beside the Mayne mast, that everie man may know his owne flete by that token....

Scanty and insufficient as are these signals, and they leave everything to "councel" beforehand, there was no marked improvement on them until the days of the Commonwealth and the First Dutch War. The Instructions drawn up by Wynter[367] in the last year of Queen Mary's reign contain only one flag signal—the banner of council—one night signal for change of course, which is of interest as showing that the primitive cresset was, in 1558, still in use in the English fleet:

Item, in the night we do change our Course then the Admiral will bear a light in his Cresset for the space of one hour, whereby every Man may know what he ought to do; And all the night after none, and then he will show out a Lanthorn with a Candle light in the Mizon Shrowds.

one elementary recognition signal:

[366] whither.
[367] *Pepys MS.* 1266.

> Item, if any be separated as before said, and that they descry by fortune one another, to the end they may be assured that they are of one Company the one shall strike his foresail, and a Yaw[368], and to howse it and strike it in that sort, until he do think that the same be seen unto the other, and then shall the other answer him by striking of his foresail, and shooting of one good piece, so that by the signs they shall be certain the one of the other.

and one signal for use in fog, that seems as inefficient as the others:

> Item, if there do happen any great Mists, in such sort, that one cannot discern another, then according to the weather, or place we be in, we must order ourselves, that is to wit, if there be so room. The Admiral will strike his Sail, and shoot one piece then, whereby every Man may be warned to do the same, and if the Admiral will anchor, then he will shoot off two pieces, one after another, and strike the Sail incontinent upon the same, but if it so fortune that he can neither drive nor ride at Anchor, then every man mark well at the beginning of the mist what course the Admiral keepeth, and to do the same. And the said Admiral will within every Glass running shoot one piece for acknowledge, and because one may be the better warned of another, ye shall make noise with trumpets, drums, or knocking.

If any tactical instructions were issued to the fleet that engaged the Spanish Armada they have not been preserved to us, but there is no reason to suppose that they were—or would have been—any less rudimentary than those we have just considered. They may be taken to be represented by the "Rules in Sir John Hawkins his tyme" preserved among the State Papers of James I[369]:

> 5. Item that the fleetest pynassis doe waight still on the Admirall and be at hand yt he maye upon all occasions send them from shipp to shipp as hee shall see Cause.

> 12. Item that upon the settinge up of a flagge in the quarter of ye Admiralls shipp every shipp come and speak wh the Admirall.

> 13. Item that when the Admirall shall set up his flag of Counsell in the shrowdes That then every Captayne shall repaire to knowe his pleasure.

> 14. Item when the Admirall shall cause a pece of ordinance to be shot of and a flagge of Counsell to be put out upon the mayne yard then shall all the other shipp reporte to the Admirall and the Captaynes wh their Mr shall come in their boats aboard the Admirall.

> 19. Item If it fortune a strange shipp to fall into the fleet by night, that you dowbt them, you shall call unto them for the

---

[368] *Sic;* apparently the ship is to yaw, i.e. deviate from her course.
[369] *S. P. D. James I*, CLVII, 67.

watchword. And if he or they have not the same then you shall hange up two lights one above the other on the same side of the shipp wh you shall perceave them of, so as the rest of ye shipp maye have warninge accordingly.

There is no provision in these "Rules" for any communication by signalling. All orders are given either by word of mouth or by sending a message by a pinnace.

The Instructions[370] for the Cadiz Expedition of 1596, elaborate as they are in certain directions, provide few signals. There was, of course, the "Flag of Council," half-mast high against the mizen-mast: the royal standard for the "selected" council, and the St George for all captains and masters. Each squadronal admiral might call the captains and masters of his own squadron to his flagship for orders by removing the white pendant (with which all ships were provided) from his mizen yard and hanging it in the main yard "two men's height." If a strange sail was sighted the nearest ship might chase it, but not more than one was to do so unless the admiral of the squadron signalled for two or three to go, by hanging out two or three flags (presumably any flags that were handy) one over the other. If the squadronal admiral himself bore up and chased, all might follow unless the Generals (Essex or Howard) hung out the flag of council, when all were to give over and keep their course. As a recognition signal, a ship that had lost company was to strike and hoist the maintopsail twice, or in bad weather the main mizen twice or as often as they liked.

The Instructions issued on various occasions during the next fifty years present few points that concern us. They never contain more than two or three signals, and those only of the type with which we are already sufficiently familiar. It may, however, be of interest to note the various forms taken by the "Flag of Council." In the Orders drawn up by Raleigh in 1617 for his expedition to Guiana the form of this flag is not indicated, apparently any flag might serve the purpose:

> When the Admirall shall hang out a flagg in the main shrowdes, you shall knowe it to be a flagg of counsell; then come aboard him[371].

For the voyage of Prince Charles to Spain in 1623 and for the Cadiz Expedition of 1625 the arrangement was the same as in 1596—the royal standard for the Council of War, or select council of the principal officers, and the St George for a general council of all captains and masters—but in August, 1628, Buckingham substituted the Union, or, as he called it, the "Brittish," flag for the St George in calling the general council. In September of that year, however, the Earl of Lindsey was using the Union flag for the Council of War and the St George for the council of Captains and Masters. The orders drawn up by Pennington in 1631 and in 1639 present a fresh variation, the separation of the Captains from the Masters:

> 44. Whensoever you shall see the Brittish flagg spred in my myson shrowds, then all the Captains are to come aboard of me. If the

---

[370] *The Naval Miscellany* (Navy Records Soc.), vol. i.
[371] *S. P. D. James I,* xcii, 9.

Red Antient then both the Captains and Masters.

In 1635 Lindsey used the Union flag for the General Council, or Council of War, but the signal for captains and masters was altered to the red ensign, and this form was adopted by the Earl of Northumberland in 1636.

Before we proceed to consider the signals of the First Dutch War, which heralded a new era, it will be desirable to refer to those contained in the *Dialogues* of Nathaniel Boteler. Boteler had served as captain in the Cadiz Expedition of 1625 and in the Rochelle Expedition of 1627, and seems to have written the first draft of the *Dialogues* shortly after the latter event. Judging from the manuscripts that remain, he re-wrote parts of them at various times until 1634, but his remarks on signals remain practically unaltered[372], and may be taken to represent the ideal of English seamanship of that period. On comparing them with Conflans' suggested instructions of 1515 it will be seen that the English ideal was by no means a high one, yet it was not surpassed until the Commonwealth Instructions were issued in 1654.

Speaking in guise of a seaman "Captain," who is instructing a court "Admiral" in his duties, Boteler says:

> In the first place therfore, when the Generall entends upon such a daye to make out to Sea with his whole Fleete; a fitt Signall to expresse as much to every perticuler shypp may be, by causeinge his Topp-sayles to lie loose upon the Capps, very early that morneinge; and if itt prove to be hazie and darcke weather, soe that the fleete being great, or lieing scattered att an Anchor, may not well perceive it, Hee may then, about two or three houres before he begin to waye his Anchors cause fire to be given to a single Piece of Ordinance.
>
> Secondly, if a fleete being att sea, and occasions require a generall convention of the Captaines and Masters aborde the Admiralls shypp: A fitt signall to lett them know itt may be, to hang out a yellow flagge in the uppermost part of the Admiralls Maine Shrowdes: But if ther be entended only the comeinge aborde of the Counsell of Warre, then may ther be a blewe flagge hung out in the same place; for I conceive that this part is more proper then is the Missen Shrowdes, (though that be the most received place for this purpose) in regard that itt is more perceptable and may better be discovered.
>
> Thirdly, if the Generall shall finde cause, to cast about in the night (for if by daye, this asketh noe signall) besides the Light or Lanthorne, which every Admirall is to carry in the Poope, the most evidenceinge signe that I can thincke of may be, to put another light in the Maine-topp: And if Hee entend to lie a-Hull, to shewe two lights in the same place: If a-Trie, three lights, the which lights are soe to be carried untill itt be founde that the whole Fleete hathe

---

[372] The latest MS. appears to be Sloane MS. 2427; the earliest that the author has seen is in the Bodleian. It was from a MS. almost identical with the latter that the printed edition was published in 1685.

taken notice of itt, and answere itt accordingly.

Fourthly, If any Squadron or parte of the fleete, by beinge too forwards a-heade, shall be required to shorten sayle, and to attend the comeinge up of the Admirall; a Signe appropriated may be, to heave or wave an Ensigne abroade in the Admiralls Fore-topp, and to give fire to a great piece withall; And on the contrary, whensoever any of them keepe too farre a-sterne, to wave out the same flagge in the Missen-topp.

Fifthly, If upon the discoverye of any straunge fleete or Shyp, the Generall find itt fitt to have any of the Pinnaces, and best saylers of his fleete, to stand in with them, and to require them to come to speake with him; an apte signe may be to give fire to a piece of Ordinance or two out of his own chase, and withall to shewe a flagge in his Bolt sprites Topp.

Sixthly, Whensoever a Fleete shall meet with the Enemies fleete, and after due consultation aborde the Admirall, itt shall be found fitt to fight, the Admirall may take in his ordinary Ensigne from the poope of the shyp and hang out another all redd, which is tearmed the bloudy Colors; that soe all the fleete may dispose and order themselves to fall on upon the Enemie in such forme and fashion as they are before hand to be instructed in.

And thes are such necessary Causes, to require any signalls to be expressed by the Generall himselfe, out of his perticuler Shypp: It followes, to intimate in some other perticulers, wherin every perticuler shypp of the fleete is to doe the like; hereby as well to give notice to the Generall himselfe or any of the rest.

Admiral. And what are thes?

Captain. If any Shyp of a fleete shall discover any straunge fleete, or any Squadron of straunge Shypps, or any single Shyp whatsoever; itt being necessary that not only the Generall, but the whole Armadoe, should with all expedition, receive advertisement hereof. A convenient signall to this purpose may be, to shewe abroade some flagge in that part of that Shyp which pointeth most upon the discovered Straunger; and if it be a fleete that is soe discovered, then to hang out two flagges in the same manner, and withall to give to a great Gunne or two, that so notice may generally be taken of what is done.

Likewise, whensoever a fleete comeinge out of the Sea, expecteth a Landfall: the first Shyp of them that maketh Land is to give present notice therof to all the rest of the fleete; and this she is to doe, if itt be by daye, by shewinge her Colors abroade, though itt be (for the time) in the Maine-topp itt selfe, inclineinge and bendinge them towards that part whence Land is discovered; and if this discovery happen in the night, she is to shoote of two pieces of Ordinance and withall shewe a light abroade; and instantly cast about and stand off, that the residue of the fleete may take notice and beware.

If any Shyp of a fleete shall find her selfe in daunger of foundringe in the Sea, by springeinge of a leake, or any the like mischaunce; if this bee by daye shee maye shoote off three pieces of Ordinance, and withall cause a youncker to goe upp to the Mainetopp and shewe a waft: And if this happen in the night time; then to continue this shooteinge ever and anon of a single piece, and withall to shewe a light, that notice may be taken by the Gunne and her selfe found out by the light, and so relieved. And because ther may be many occasions wherby a fleete may be far dispersed, and yet afterwards gett togither againe, and that itt is fitt, that upon the first ken one of another, they may be knowne one unto another and soe noe mistakeinges ensue, an apt Signall to this purpose, may be by the puttinge out and takeinge in of a flagge soe many times one after another as shall formerly be agreed upon, or by the soe often strikeinge of a Topp-sayle or the like; the which they are to answer one unto another.

Boteler's suggestion of yellow and blue flags as signals for calling a Council is of especial interest as being the earliest proposal to use special flags for making signals. Until the year 1654, signals—at any rate in English fleets—were with two exceptions always made with the flags already in use for other purposes, that is, with the Flags of Command or Colours of Distinction, whose primary uses we have already discussed. These two exceptions are the red flag of war and the white flag of peace.

The red flag, or "bloody colours" as it was often called, and the white flag are not mentioned in any of the early instructions. They were, in fact, international signals and formed part of the traditional "Custom of the Sea" which was never completely codified and, except so far as it was gathered into such collections as the Rooles d'Oléron and the Consolado del Mar, can now only be recovered by the laborious process of collecting precedents.

The red flag, could we completely trace its descent, would no doubt be found to have sprung from the "scarlet cloak" which the ancient Greek navy seems to have borrowed from the Phoenicians, but we first meet with it, so far as English ships are concerned, in the document of *circa* 1299 referred to above[373] in which is set forth the injuries inflicted by the Normans on the shipping of England, Ireland and Gascony (then subject to the English crown). In April a fleet of English, Irish and Bayonne merchantmen set out from Portsmouth bound for Bordeaux. Off St Mathieu, on the coast of Brittany, they anchored. According to their own story, they were becalmed. News of their presence reached a fleet of 290 ships of Normandy, then loading wine in the river Charente. Leaving half their cargoes, in order that their sailing might not be impeded, the Normans fitted up fore and after castles and fighting tops at the mastheads and hoisted streamers of red sendal two yards broad and thirty yards long, called "baucans," as a sign that no quarter

[373] See p. 40.

would be given[374]. A southerly wind having now sprung up the Normans fell upon the other fleet, only to receive a thorough beating. In refusing to give up the spoils taken on this occasion, the allies explained to Edward I that when the "baucan" had been raised in an engagement of this kind no one could be held responsible for life or property taken[375].

Although the red flag was a recognised signal for combat among all European nations, it was not until the year 1647 that it was formally included in the English "Instructions." It remained in them until the year 1799.

In the West Indies, so Cleirac tells us, the Spanish flag of combat was blue: in European waters it was red, with the arms of Castile upon it.

The flag of peace, or truce, seems to have been adopted at sea about the end of the fifteenth century, but although it may be regarded from one point of view as a signal it will be convenient to defer our consideration of it until we come to deal with the flag incidents connected with the surrender of a ship[376].

(II) THE FIRST ENGLISH CODES[377]

It is evident from the foregoing sketch of the early history of flag signals that up to the middle of the seventeenth century the signals of the English navy were of the most elementary description. The first steps towards the introduction of a more efficient system were taken in 1647 when the "Right Honourable the Committee of the Lords and Commons for the Admiralty and Cinque Ports" issued "Instructions" on a more elaborate plan. The general instructions, dated 6th April, 1647, are preserved; but, unfortunately, the "Instructions for sailing," issued at the same time, which contained the signals, have not yet been brought to light. From the "supplementary instructions" preserved in the Harleian mss., and printed by Sir Julian Corbett[378], it may be inferred that the British navy was at length drawing on a level with the navies of France and Spain in respect to its method of communicating orders.

In 1653 a further great improvement was made[379], and a "code" of instructions, with the accompanying signals, now appears, issued "By the Right Hon-

[374] "lesqueles banères sount appelés baucans et la gent d'Engleterre les appelent stremers et celes banères signefient mort sans remède et mortele guerre en tous les lious où mariners sont."

[375] "nous ne sums tenus faire restitution ne amende si nulle chose eit esté fait ou prise par nous en ladite guerre; quar il est usage et ley de meer que de choses faites ou prises sur meer en guerre meisement ou ledit baukan soit levée ne doit estre fait restitution n'amende d'une partie ne d'autre." 'Baucan,' cognate with 'beacon,' must not be confused with 'bauçan.'

[376] See p. 196.

[377] This and the two following sections are in substance a revision of a pamphlet *Nelson's Signals, The Evolution of the Signal Flags*, written by me in 1908 and published for the Admiralty by H.M. Stationery Office. I am indebted to the Controller of that Department for permission to make use of it in this work.

[378] Corbett, *Fighting Instructions* (N. R. S.), p. 99.

[379] Possibly as a result of the first collision with the Dutch, Tromp appears to have been ahead of the English in the matter of signals.

ourable the Generals and Admirals of the Fleet," and signed by Blake, Deane, and Monk. The following were the flags to be used for signals: A weft of the ensign or jack, a pendant, and the three flags—red, blue, and white—already in existence as flags of command.

The signal to "Engage the enemy," doubtless that used by Monk in fighting Tromp, and by Blake in his last glorious action of Santa Cruz, was made "by shooting-off two guns and putting a red flag over the fore topmast-head."

This Commonwealth code was further expanded in 1665, under the guidance of the Duke of York, afterwards King James II. In a supplementary order of the same year, a red and white striped flag first appears as the signal to chase. In 1672 and 1673 the instructions and signals were further amplified and then printed, being possibly the first set of naval fighting instructions to be put into print.

In a finely bound manuscript copy of the 1673 Instructions, now in the Admiralty Library, which, from internal evidence, was prepared about 1689, we have the earliest surviving example of the "signal book" proper. Hitherto the signals had been embodied in the various Articles of Sailing and Fighting Instructions, the appropriate flag being merely described in the text of each article, but no diagram or coloured representation of the flag being given. In this MS. we have for the first time coloured drawings of flags arranged in order, with the meaning and place where hoisted against each in parallel columns, a convenient method of systematising the signals that was not followed in the official printed "Instructions" for a century.

The flags of the manuscript are as follows:

Union Flag.

The Standard.

Red Ensign.

Blue Ensign.

White Ensign.

Dutch Ensign (red, white, and blue in three horizontal stripes).

A flag striped red and yellow from corner to corner.

Red flag.

Blue flag.

White flag.

A "Jack coloured with colours." (This was a "Union Jack," or small Union flag.)

A pendant.

A flag striped red and white horizontally.

A flag striped red and white from corner to corner.

White with red diagonal cross.

In other copies of the 1673 Instructions the last four are omitted, but a flag striped yellow and white from corner to corner is mentioned as a signal for fire-ships.

The Instructions of 1673 formed the basis of the instructions for the next hundred years. They were issued in a revised form by Admiral Russell in 1691 when the following signal flags were added:

> Yellow.
>
> Striped yellow and white horizontally.
>
> Red and white.
>
> Genoese Ensign (similar to an elongated St. George's flag).

Russell's instructions were adopted by Rooke in 1703 with but slight modification of the articles and with no change in the flags.

The year 1714 saw the issue of the first printed "Signal Book." This was a private venture of one Jonathan Greenwood. The author justifiably boasts that he has "disposed matters in such a manner that any instruction may be found out in half a minute," and that he has "made it a pocket volume that it may be at hand upon all occasions." No doubt this duodecimo book was much more convenient than the folio size Instructions. Each signal is represented by a drawing of a ship flying the flag or flags of the signal at the proper place, the purport being added underneath, a method which appears to have been in use in the French navy at least 20 years earlier, for a Signal Book of 1693, containing De Tourville's signals arranged on this plan, was exhibited at the Franco-British Exhibition in 1908. Although the instructions were regarded as confidential the signals apparently were not, as the work is described as "designed to supply the Inferior Officers who cannot have recourse to the Printed Instructions."

The next "Signal Book" proper was again a private venture and was published by John Millan in 1746, "price 2s. 6d. plain and 4s. coloured." In this book the flags are set out along the tops of the pages, and the signals made with them are classified below, according to the different positions of the flags, with references to the numbers of the articles of the various Instructions—"Sailing," "Fighting," and "Additional"—in which the signals are laid down. The only new flags appearing here are the following:

> White cross on red ground.
>
> Red cross on blue ground.
>
> Blue and white in two horizontal stripes.
>
> Red and white in two horizontal stripes.

In a manuscript signal book of ten years later, in the Library of the Royal United Service Institution, we have the earliest representation of a "chequered" flag. This book is interesting. It contains Hawke's autograph, and is possibly the one in use by him when he "came sweeping from the West" at Quiberon. The following are the flags then first appearing:

Red, white, and blue in six horizontal stripes.

Spanish flag.

Blue and white in five horizontal stripes.

Red and white chequered.

Blue with six white balls[380].

Yellow and blue chequered.

Blue and white chequered pendant.

During the course of this—the "Seven Years'"—war a number of "additional" sailing and fighting instructions were issued by the Admiralty, to which the Admirals in command of fleets made some additions of their own. The advance made by the end of the war is indicated by a manuscript signal book dated 1762 containing the "General Printed and Additional Signals delivered out by Sir Edward Hawke." It illustrates the following flags:

Standard.

Union.

Red Ensign (called the "English Ensign").

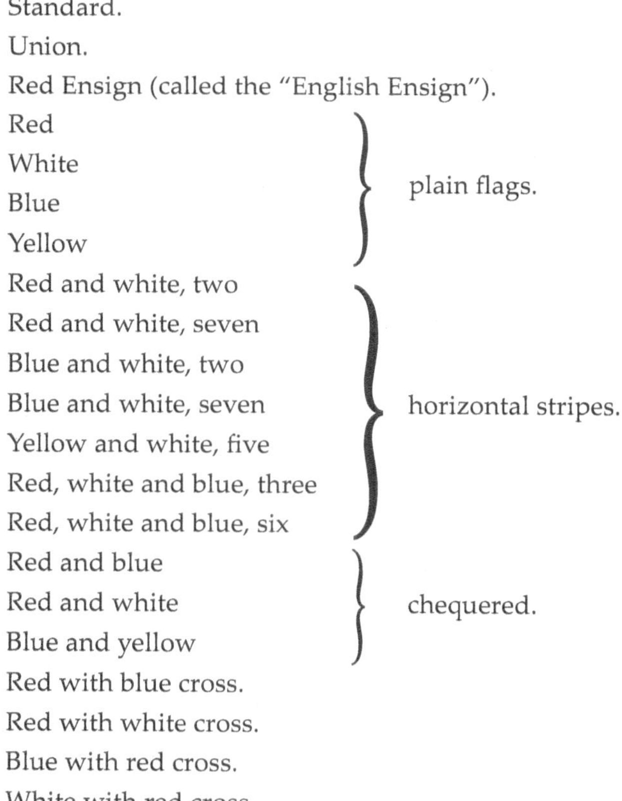

Red

White

Blue

Yellow

} plain flags.

Red and white, two

Red and white, seven

Blue and white, two

Blue and white, seven

Yellow and white, five

Red, white and blue, three

Red, white and blue, six

} horizontal stripes.

Red and blue

Red and white

Blue and yellow

} chequered.

Red with blue cross.

Red with white cross.

Blue with red cross.

White with red cross.

[380] Shortly after 1756 the white balls disappear, and a white square takes their place, the flag thus becoming what is now familiarly called the Blue Peter. By Rodney's time this flag at the mainmast head had become the signal to recall everyone to his ship, whence its present use to denote that the ship is about to sail.

White with blue cross.

Blue pierced with white square.

Spanish flag.

Red pendant.

Red and white striped pendant.

To which, though they are not illustrated, were added a blue pendant and a white pendant.

Development of signals henceforth became very rapid, and new flags had to be invented to keep up with them. This is well seen in the signal book used by Rodney in his memorable fight with De Grasse in 1782. Here we have, in addition to flags already mentioned, the following new ones:

Red and white, quarterly.

Blue and white, quarterly.

Red and blue, quarterly.

*Red and blue, two horizontal stripes.

*Blue and yellow, two horizontal stripes.

Blue, red, and white, three horizontal stripes.

Red, white, red, three horizontal stripes.

*Blue, white, red, three horizontal stripes (inverted Dutch Ensign).

Red pierced with white[381].

White pierced with red.

Yellow and blue, two vertical stripes.

White and red, two vertical stripes.

White with blue saltire.

Yellow with blue cross.

Blue and yellow in six horizontal stripes.

Eight pendants.

In addition to these the white and blue ensigns were also to be used for signalling purposes.

The flags marked * were also used inverted, as were also the two-striped red and white and blue and white flags already in use.

The signal to "Prepare for battle" was the red flag at the main topgallant masthead under the Admiral's flag.

To "Engage the enemy"; the same flag at the fore top masthead, just as in 1653.

"To come to a closer engagement"; the blue and white flag (two horizontal stripes) at the fore topgallant masthead under the signal for engaging.

[381] A flag is said to be "pierced" when it has a small square of another colour in the centre.

In this code we reach the culmination of the old system of signalling by means of a large number of different flags each having a different meaning according to the position in which it was shown.

(III) THE INVENTION OF NUMERARY SIGNALS

The development of tactics and fleet organisation and the consequent increase of the signals had been so rapid during the latter half of the eighteenth century that the old methods had become inadequate. In 1746 there were 16 flags in use to express 144 signals, by 1780 there were about 50 flags, each hoisted on an average in seven different positions, providing for about 330 signals. Twenty-five years later the Trafalgar signal book contained upwards of 400, not including those in Popham's Code.

So long as the signals were few in number, so that the flags could be made in a few strongly contrasted designs, and only the most prominent positions need be used for them, the old system had the advantage of simplicity, but when the signals multiplied, less conspicuous positions and less strikingly differentiated flags had also to be made use of, and simplicity gave place to complexity.

It must be remembered that flags at sea have to be distinguished not only when a fair breeze is unfurling them plainly to the view; they have also to be distinguished in a dead calm when they hang down along the halyards, and when distance and haze lend enchantment to the view but not to the signalman.

In order that the differences in the flags may be readily distinguishable at sea in any circumstances two conditions are essential—

(1) The colours must be quite unlike, so that they do not "merge" at a distance.

(2) The designs of the flags must be simple and not complicated.

In practice this limits the colours to the following: Red, blue, and yellow, with black and white. Moreover, it is found that when two of these colours are to be shown in one flag they should be of one of the following combinations: red and white, yellow and blue, blue and white, or black and white. But with so many as 40 flags it was impossible to adhere to these two rules.

The fact that no further development on old lines was possible was, no doubt, widely comprehended; for Admiral Sir Chas Knowles tells us that it was the Marquis of Hastings, an officer in the Army, then in America, who first advised him to "strike out something new." The first steps in the new direction were taken about 1778 by Kempenfelt, Howe, and Sir Chas Knowles, each acting more or less independently. There is no need to waste time in discussing the rival claims of these admirals to be the inventor of the numerary method, because as a matter of fact this method of denoting signals had been invented by Mahé de la Bourdonnais, 40 years before, for use in the struggle he was preparing to wage with us for the mastery of India and the East Indies. La Bourdonnais was one of the most brilliant and versatile officers that France has produced; but he was of somewhat obscure birth when compared with the high nobility who at that period officered the French navy, and he had been admitted to their ranks by a back door, having first served in the French East India Company. Fortunately for Great Britain, the jealousy of Dupleix and of La Bourdonnais' high-born brother officers thwarted his plans, and finally resulted in his recall to France. His signals seem never to have been adopted[382], but the system is described by Bourdé de Villehuet in his book, *Le Manœuvrier*, published in 1769, one of the classic works on tactics of the eighteenth century. It is evident from an extract in one of his letters to Lord Barham that it was from this source that Kempenfelt became acquainted with the system.

The claim of Admiral Sir Chas Knowles to have "discovered the signals by numbers" in 1778, which numeral signals he gave to Lord Howe on his arrival at Newport, Rhode Island, may therefore be dismissed, so far as discovery is concerned, but his claims to have "discovered the tabular flags (suggested by a chessboard)" may possibly hold good.

Sir Chas Knowles's signals were not adopted in the navy, but as we shall find "tabular flags" used in the Signal Books of Howe, it will be well to explain the two methods.

When a signal code has been drawn up and the signals have been numbered consecutively, the numbers may be represented by flags in two different ways.

The simple numerary method, that invented by La Bourdonnais and finally adopted by Howe for his principal signals, is to assign one flag to each of the figures 1, 2, 3, 4, 5, 6, 7, 8, 9, 0; so that by combining the flags any desired signal number may be rendered.

The other, the tabular method, for which Sir Chas Knowles claims the credit of invention, is more complicated. A chequered table like a chessboard is ruled out, each side having a convenient number of squares, 8, 9, 10, or more. Then, choosing the same number of flags, these are laid out in order along the top, commencing at the left-hand corner, and also down the left side. The signal numbers are then placed in the squares of this table.

There will then obviously be two flags corresponding to each of the numbers, the top flag being that at the head of the vertical column in which the particular number is found, and the lower one that at the left of the corresponding horizontal column. For example, supposing we have three flags, red, white, and blue, they might be arranged as below:

	Red	White	Blue
Red	1	4	7
White	2	5	8
Blue	3	6	9

The signal corresponding to 6 will then be a white flag over a blue one.

If the signals to be thus denoted number considerably more than 100, it is convenient to form the table of 10 squares to a side, giving 100 squares in all. The first 100 numbers will then be written in, and by the addition of suitable pendants to

[382] In his memoirs it is stated that in 1746 he had written a book on Signals and Naval Evolutions.

represent 100, 200, 300, etc., it will be possible to denote any signal number from 1 upwards.

The disadvantage of this method is that the individual flags have no fixed numerical value, and a reference to the table is necessary before the number represented by the combined flags can be ascertained, and *vice versâ*.

In spite of this drawback, this was the method first chosen by Howe for all his signals[383], and it was used by him in his second numerary code for those of his signals which were intended for the use of private ships when communicating with the flagships, the numeral signals of the La Bourdonnais method being in this code only used for the Admiral's orders to his fleet. In the 1799 Signal Book the tabular method was discontinued.

Some time before June, 1776, probably on being appointed to command the North America Squadron in February of that year, Howe had compiled a signal book on the old plan of single flags in particular positions, condensed from the "general signal book," and containing all the signals "likely to be needful on the present occasion."

The flags he employed were as follows, those marked * being also used inverted:

Union.

St George.

Red

Yellow

Blue   } plain flags.

White

*Red and white

*Red and blue

*Blue and white   } in two horizontal stripes.

*Red and yellow

*Blue and yellow

*Red, blue, white

*White, red, blue   } in three horizontal stripes.

Blue, white, red

A year or two later, probably in consultation with Kempenfelt, he drew up the first of his codes on the numerary system. The signals were divided into those for the Admiral and those for private ships. For the former a "table" of 16 squares on each side was employed with the following flags:

---

[383] Possibly because with a "table" of 16 squares a side he was enabled to make 256 signals, with two flags only to each "hoist," whereas by the simple numerary method he could of course only make 99 with less than three flags.

1. Yellow cross on blue ground.
2. Blue and yellow quarterly.
3. Blue cross on yellow.
4. Yellow.
5. Blue and yellow chequered.
6. White and red in two vertical stripes.
7. Red, white, and red in three vertical stripes.
8. Yellow and blue in two vertical stripes.
9. White cross on red.
10. Red and white chequered.
11. Red and white in two horizontal stripes.
12. Red and white quarterly.
13. Blue and yellow in two horizontal stripes.
14. Red.
15. Blue, yellow, blue, in three vertical stripes.
16. Yellow, blue, yellow, in three horizontal stripes.

The signals for "private" ships were mostly on the old plan of single flags in particular positions.

To express numbers, as in the number of ships seen, depth of water, latitude and longitude, a "table" of 10 squares each side was employed. The flags of this were as follows:

1. Union.
2. Red.
3. White.
4. Blue.
5. Red and white.
6. Blue and yellow.
7. Red, white, and blue.
8. Red pendant.
9. Yellow pendant.
10. Red, white, and blue pendant,

and a blue pendant to represent 100 for use in numbers from 101 upwards.

It will be noted that three of the most unsuitable of Rodney's flags, the quarterly red and blue, striped red and blue, and the red with blue cross, each of which would look like purple at a distance, had disappeared.

About the same date Kempenfelt produced his own numerary code. He tells

Lord Barham, in a letter dated March, 1781[384], that the plan he followed was not that he most approved of.

> That which I would have adopted—though most evidently the best—I could not get any of the Admirals or Officers of note to approve and countenance. I therefore followed in a great measure Lord Howe's mode, he being a popular character.

In this code the transition from the old to the new method is well seen, for each signal has, besides a signal number for use after the new method, a flag and position for use after the old, e.g.:

"Engage the enemy" could be signalled as No. 224 or by means of a red flag at the fore topmast head.

"Prepare for battle" by the same flag at the fore topmast shrouds, or as No. 226.

"Come to closer engagement" by a red and white flag (two horizontal stripes) at the main topmast head, or as No. 171.

A special signal was provided to denote that the numerary signals were going to be used for practice, when every ship was to note down the significations. Kempenfelt improved upon Howe in that he did not separate out the "Private ship" signals, but included all in one series of more than 400 numbers. The flags for signalling by the old method were mostly the same as those already in use. His "table" for the new method was of 10 squares a side, as follows:

1. Union.
2. Yellow.
3. Blue and yellow, chequered.
4. Red pierced with white.
5. White cross on red ground.
6. Blue cross on yellow ground.
7. Red and white, quarterly.
8. White and red in two vertical stripes.
9. Yellow and blue in two vertical stripes.
10. Red and white in four horizontal stripes.

With pendants for 100, 200, 300, 400, and 500.

Further development of this code ceased in 1782 on Kempenfelt's tragic end in the 'Royal George.'

---

[384] J. K. Laughton, *Letters and Papers of Lord Barham* (N. R. S.), ı, 340.

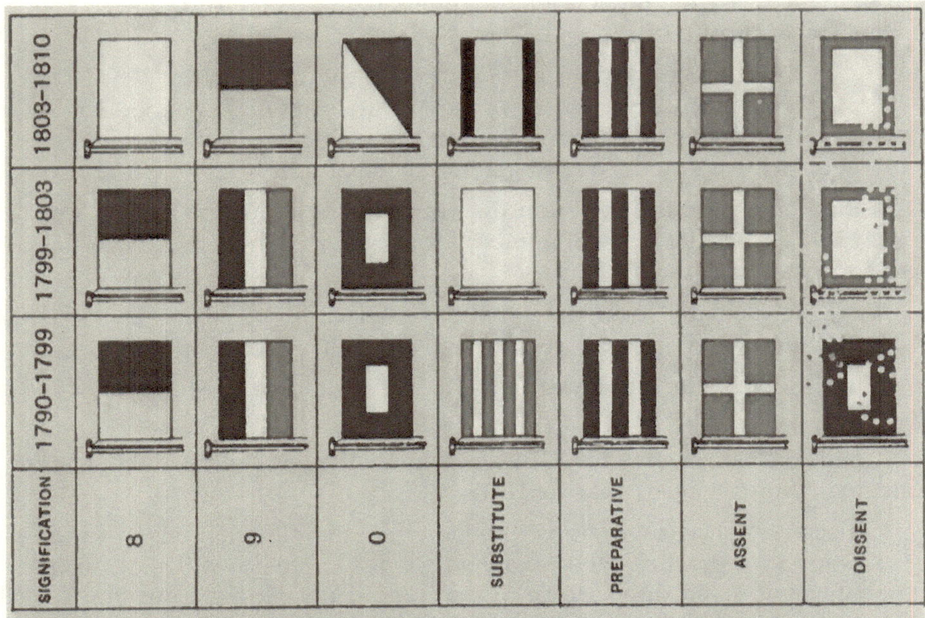

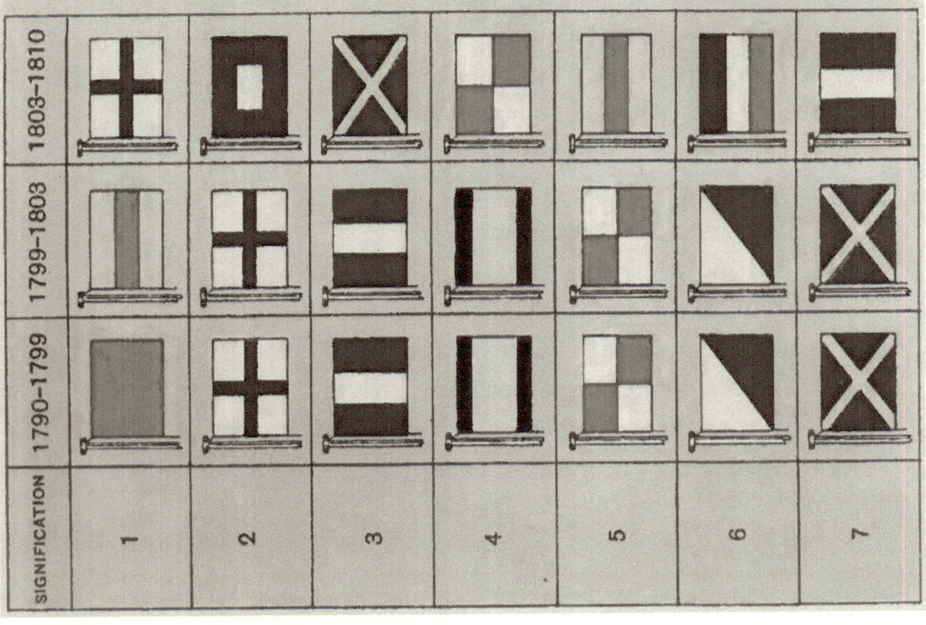

Plate XIII

Numerary Signal Flags, 1790–1810

From 1783 to 1788 Howe held office as First Lord of the Admiralty, and seems to have devoted part of his time to the improvement of the tactics of the Fighting Instructions and of their accompanying signals. He elaborated a new signal book, which he introduced into the navy on taking command of the Channel fleet. In this new book he abandoned the "tabular" method so far as the bulk of the signals—the Admiral's signals—were concerned, employing instead the simple numerary method, and for these numerals he chose the flags that were afterwards, in their transposed meanings, used at Trafalgar. For this reason, and because it was the code used on the "glorious First of June," and at Camperdown, and was the basis of those used at St Vincent, the Nile, Copenhagen, and Trafalgar, it is important to consider it in some detail.

This second numerary code of Howe, the *Signal Book for the Ships of War* of 1790, is a quarto[385] volume of 85 pages.

After three pages of explanatory instructions relative to the method of making the signals, distinctness, destruction of signal books in danger of falling into the hands of the enemy, etc., follow two pages relative to the triangular distinguishing flags of squadrons. We then come to the Admiral's signals—nearly 200 in number, commencing at 10. These were, as already stated, in the "simple numerary" system invented by La Bourdonnais, in which each signal number is represented by the numeral flags corresponding to the figures composing it.

The numeral flags, five of which—Nos. 2, 3, 4, 6, and 7—are new to us, are shown in the accompanying plate. Each of these numeral flags had, however, another signification when hoisted singly, as follows:

1. Enemy in sight.
2. Form in order of sailing by divisions.
3. Form established order of sailing.
4. Take and keep stations.
5. Engage the enemy.
6. Signal not understood.
7. To chase.
8. To anchor.
9. Leave off chase.
0. Negative answer.

In addition to these, the following flags were to be used:

White cross on red ground.—Affirmative answer.

White with red border.—Annul.

Union.—To call officers.

Blue and yellow chequered.—Rendezvous.

Yellow.—To distinguish signals made to the fireships.

---

[385] Hitherto the official books of Instructions and Signals had been of folio size.

White with red border and pierced with blue.—Transpose the numeral flags.

Red and white, yellow and blue, and their inversions.—For the four quarters of the compass.

Blue cornet[386].—First signal to be carried out in the manner denoted by the remainder.

Red and white striped.—Substitute. To repeat the flag next above it.

Blue and white striped.—Preparative.

White flag:—

    (1) Truce.

    (2) Open secret instructions.

    (3) Signal made herewith is to take effect after the close of day.

To illustrate the use of the two latter flags we may take Nelson's signal at Trafalgar, "Prepare to anchor after the close of day."

This signal consisted of four flags in one hoist:

Preparative.

No. 6
No. 3 } Anchor as soon as convenient.

White flag.

When a "Preparative" flag was hoisted with a signal it denoted that the order was not to be immediately obeyed[387]. If hauled down together with the signal, preparation was to be made to obey the latter directly the Admiral hoisted it again. If hauled down and the signal left flying, the latter was then to be carried into execution. Nelson had intended to hoist the signal to anchor (63) as soon as the fighting was over, with a view to securing his battered ships and their prizes against the bad weather he saw coming on, but Collingwood could not carry out the intention.

The white flag had, in the Admiralty copy of the 1790 book, four meanings. Alone, in battle, it denoted truce; hoisted at the fore topmast head it could be used to call in distant ships; when hoisted with other flags it signified that the signal denoted by them was not to be carried into effect until the day closed; and, finally, it denoted an order to open secret instructions. In the Signal Book of 1793 the two latter significations were denoted by a black and white flag, the former when black was uppermost and the latter when white was uppermost. In 1805 the white flag had the first and third of these meanings, besides denoting numeral 8.

The Admiral's flags and signals of Howe's second code, as used on 1st June,

---

[386] A "cornet" is a swallow-tailed flag.

[387] According to present practice no signal made with more than one flag is obeyed until the officer making it hauls it down.

1794, are reproduced in vol. 1 of *Logs of the Great Sea Fights* (Navy Records Society).

These Admiral's, or "Numeral signals," as they are called by Howe in contradistinction to his tabular "Signals by private ships," are grouped under various headings, beginning with "Battle," "Bear-up," "Bring-to," and going on to "Enemy," "Engage," "Line," "Order," "Sail," "Tack," etc.

We then have certain subsidiary pendant signals, of which the most important are: a chequered blue and yellow pendant to denote that accompanying numeral flags represented figures only, and a quartered red and white pendant to serve the purpose of a note of interrogation.

Now follow nine signals made with sails and guns, a quaint survival that disappears in 1799 [Except No. 1. This was No. 174 of the '99 Code, but could be made by the fore topsail if desired.] The following are their purports:

> 1. "To prepare for sailing," denoted by loosing the fore topsail, just as in Rooke's Instructions of 1703. 2. Every one to repair to his respective ship. 3. Recalling ships. 4. Unmoor. 5. Weigh. 6. Moor (denoted by "Main topsail loose in top"). 8. Cut or slip. 9. Fast on shoal.

We next have 14 signals for calling officers to take orders, made with the Union flag in different positions; a few signals to fireships, made with the yellow flag; 20 fog signals made with guns; and then the tabular signals for private ships. The "table" provided for these shows a slight variation on the usual form. It is not quite square, being 8 wide and 9 deep, as the first flag space on the left side is blank, so that the first row 1 to 8 is made by single flags. The flags used are:

1. Red.
2. Blue.
3. White over red, two horizontal stripes.
4. The same inverted.
5. Blue over yellow, two horizontal stripes.
6. The same inverted.
7. Union.
8. Blue, white, red, horizontally.

Stars are placed in the four squares whose flags would be one of the invertible flags over its own inversion, probably because there was only one flag supplied of each design, and the other squares are numbered 1 to 68. Sixty-one signals are given. We then have half a dozen signals with Jacks, Pendants, and Wefts, Signals for each point of the compass, ending with 11 pages of Night signals.

Perhaps the best testimony of the value of this book is given in the letter from Nelson to Howe in acknowledgment of his congratulations on the victory of the Nile:

8th January 1799.

It was only this moment that I had the invaluable approbation of the great, the immortal Earl Howe, an honour the most flattering a Sea-Officer could receive, as it comes from the first and greatest Sea-Officer the world has ever produced. I had the happiness to command a Band of Brothers; therefore night was to my advantage. Each knew his duty, and I was sure each would feel for a French ship. By attacking the enemy's van and centre, the wind blowing directly along their Line, I was enabled to throw what force I pleased on a few Ships. This plan my friends conceived by the signals (for which we are principally if not entirely indebted to your Lordship) and we always kept a superior force to the enemy[388].

Meanwhile, John McArthur, a purser in the navy, who had during the war of American Independence been frequently stationed to observe signals in the fleet and had therefore practical experience of the delays, difficulties and misunderstandings that occurred with the older methods of signalling by flags in particular positions, had been for many years at work on a new code which he submitted to the Admiralty in 1790. The basis of this plan was the old tabular system with two flags hoisted together or separately at the most conspicuous parts of the ship. The code contained upwards of 550 signals, with provision for an indefinite increase, and incorporated an ingenious device for continuously altering the numerical value of the flags. It was an advance upon any of the codes hitherto in use, but "some scruples of delicacy intervened in the adoption of any new plan of signals which would supersede that of Earl Howe's numerary code," and it was not adopted. Nevertheless, it attracted the attention of Hood, then the Senior Sea Lord, and on his appointment to command the Russian armament in 1791 he made McArthur his secretary. McArthur then turned his attention to re-arranging Howe's signals "by simplifying the form with Indices for facilitating their being made and understood, and engrafting in the body and instructions many new ideas and instructions of his own." Howe approved of the alterations, and the revised code was then printed and issued to Hood's fleet. This "new arrangement" was introduced by Hood in 1793 into the Mediterranean and continued to be used there until 1799. It was the signal book in use at the Battles of St Vincent and the Nile. In it the values of Howe's numeral flags, as shown in Col. 1 of Plate XIII, were transposed as follows: 1 became 4; 2, 9; 3, 7; 4, 2; 5, 6; 6, 0; 7, 8; 8, 5; 9, 3; and 0, 1. The tabular flags were also transposed, 1 becoming 8; 2, 7; 3, 5; 5, 3; 6, 2; 7, 1; 8, 6; while 4 remained of the same value.

(IV) THE VOCABULARY SIGNAL BOOK

With the compilation, in 1790, of Howe's second signal book, we have the end of that system, or want of system, which is especially noticeable during the American War of Independence, under which the signals used in each fleet or squadron varied with the idiosyncrasies of each individual commander-in-chief.

---

[388] Nicholas, *Letters and Dispatches of Lord Nelson*, iii, 230.

Henceforth, although it was usual for the admiral commanding each fleet to add a few of his own devising, the bulk of the signals were, so to speak, stereotyped in form, and were in general use throughout the British navy.

In 1799 the *Signal Book for the Ships of War* was increased in size to 167 pages by the addition of an index to the signals and the inclusion of the printed instructions. The "Private ship" signals were placed at the end of the "Admiral's signals" and numbered consecutively after them, so that the "tabular" flags disappear, and all signals are henceforth made by the simple numerary code, the total number being increased from about 260 to 340.

It will be seen from the plate of numeral flags that Howe's numerals were continued in the 1799 book with only two slight modifications: No. 1, instead of being a plain red flag, became yellow, red, yellow, in three equal horizontal stripes, and the substitute became plain white. But his arrangement was simplified. The half black and white flags were done away with as unnecessary, since their meanings could equally well be expressed by those remaining.

In addition to the signal book, each commander-in-chief compiled for his own fleet a tabular "pendant board," on which two pendants were assigned to the name of each ship of his fleet. By this means he was enabled to address any of the signals to a particular ship, without making the command general to the whole squadron. For example, Nelson, at Trafalgar, before making general his favourite signal, "Engage the enemy more closely," addressed it particularly to the 'Africa,' which, having become separated over night, found herself at a distance from the two columns, and, just before the commencement of the action, was sailing near to the enemy's van, on an opposite and parallel course. This he did by hoisting flags Nos. 1 and 6, together with the pendants appropriated to the 'Africa's' name on the "pendant board."

But a code for signalling or other purposes is like a language; if the language is what we call "dead," i.e. if words have ceased to be added to it, it is of little use for expressing every-day needs. Similarly, if the navy is not stagnating, continual amplification of tactics or of every-day details necessitates an increase in the range of conversation between the Admiral and his fleet. Although at the time of the battle of Trafalgar the signal book was only six years old, it had already had its range of signals increased by upwards of 80 additions, made in manuscript, on such varied matters as:

412. "The ships or vessels chased have separated on different courses."

280. "Send for fresh beef immediately."

291. "Engage the enemy as close as possible."

This last is the third signal provided for close engagement, the others being "Engage the enemy more closely," expressed either by No. 16 (the signal Nelson favoured), or by the red pendant over the quarter-red and white flag.

The need for a more flexible method of communication than that of set sentences had long been felt. Rodney and Howe had both found it impossible, in face of the enemy, to make their instructions clear to their captains, and even without this distraction, in bad weather, when ships could not get near enough for the voice to carry from one to another even with the assistance of the speaking trumpet, or when the roar of the gale rendered speech of no avail except within a range of a very few feet, while the launching of a boat was out of the question, much inconvenience had often been felt. Even when verbal communication was possible, much time was lost in closing near enough to make it.

The steps to remedy this impediment—to make, as it were, the flag-language more civilised, so that it might express refinements of thought in one direction and little every-day wants in another, to increase, that is, its scope of expression from that of a child to that of a grown man—were first taken by Sir Home Popham.

It may be that in this matter, as in so many other inventions, the first to make some practical use of an idea got that idea at second hand[389]. However this may be in Popham's case, it is clear that the labour of perfecting the invention and what is perhaps equally important, of persuading others that it was really worth a trial, was undertaken by Popham alone. For twelve years the books which he produced were privately printed by him, and from the free-handed way in which he gave them to his brother officers when urging them to try this code, it is probable that he carried out his propaganda at some pecuniary expense to himself. The idea that dominated it was to provide parts of speech and let the users make their own sentences whenever those in the signal book did not suffice. It was the step from a "Traveller's Manual of Conversation" to a dictionary of the language.

Popham tells us that his *Telegraphic Signals, or Marine Vocabulary* ("telegraphic" being, of course, used thirty years before the invention of the electric telegraph, in its primary sense of writing at a distance) was originally compiled in 1800, to facilitate the conveyance of messages from Popham's ship, the 'Romney,' off Copenhagen, to Admiral Dickson, off Elsinore, when that officer, with a squadron of ships, was giving additional weight to the British Ministers' arguments with the Danish Court. "Its utility was in that instance so obvious and so generally allowed by the Captains of the North Sea Squadron that Sir Home Popham conceived it might be brought into more extensive practice."

The first edition of this code consisted of nearly 1000 words chosen by Popham from the dictionary as most useful for naval purposes. In 1803 a second part, consisting of nearly 1000 less useful words, and a third part, consisting of nearly 1000 "sentences most applicable to military or general conversation" were added. To prevent the signal numbers from becoming unduly high, derivations were grouped with their root-word, e.g. expedite, expedited, expediting, expedition, and expeditious were each expressed by No. 270, it being left for the receiver to determine the exact word by the context. Further, "In verbs, the number, person, tense and mood" had to "be applied to the sense of the sentence." When the exact word was not in the vocabulary, the one most nearly synonymous was to be adopted, but "should it be of any consequence to use a word not in the vocabulary,"

---

[389] Richard Hall Gower, an officer of the East India Company's fleet, suggested in the 2nd edition of his *Treatise on Seamanship*, 1796, the use of a dictionary with the words numbered consecutively from 1 upwards under each letter of the alphabet. The letter and number were to be shown on a large board.

it could be spelt by the numerical alphabet, which was known by the numbers 1 to 25. It may be noted, as the solution of the conundrum that has puzzled many in spelling out "duty" in Nelson's celebrated signal that in this alphabet, not only are I and J treated as one letter, but V precedes U.

Thus, in the preparation for that signal, when Pasco told Nelson that "confides" was not in the vocabulary, he suggested the "one nearest synonymous," namely, "expects," as this latter could be expressed by three flags in one hoist, while "confides" required 11 flags in eight hoists. "Duty," however, had to be spelt[390]. The sentiment of the signal had been sufficiently spoilt by the substitution of "expects" for "confides"; the further substitution of "best" or "utmost" would have hopelessly ruined it.

When the words of the message had been chosen from the vocabulary and their corresponding numbers written down for the signalman's guidance, it remained to translate them into flags. To do this required nine flags to represent the figures 1 to 9, and one flag to represent the cipher. It was convenient to add one or two substitute flags to say "ditto," in case not more than one flag of each numeral was available, with two flags for "yes" and "no."

Popham found all these flags already provided in the 1799 *Signal Book for the Ships of War*, but the thousands he expressed thus: numbers between 1000 and 2000 by a ball or pendant placed above the "hoist," or group of three flags representing the hundreds, tens, and units; and numbers above 2000 by a similar ball or pendant placed below the "hoist." This was done to avoid unduly increasing the "substitute" flags, as one set of numeral flags was often all that was available, and for the same reason such numbers as 333, 888, 2222 were omitted from the code.

All that was now wanted was a flag to denote whether the signal hoisted was to be deciphered by the Signal Book or by the Vocabulary Code. For this purpose Popham designed a flag divided diagonally into white and red to be used as a "preparative" or "telegraph" flag, with all signals made in his code. This was hoisted before the message started, and hauled down when it finished.

Such were the signal books in use at Trafalgar, and in the hands of a man like Nelson, who did not keep his tactical ideas to himself, but discussed them freely with his captains during the months of watching and preparation, they proved amply sufficient for the purpose.

But suppose the books were captured by the enemy; how then? In such an event, which all captains were told to guard against by throwing the books overboard if there was any probability of their ship being captured, the most effective precaution was to change the whole of the signal numbers, both in the general signals and in the vocabulary, but this was a heavy task.

A less effective method was to transpose all the flags. It was less effective since, *ex hypothesi*, the enemy had the signal books, they had therefore only to note the colours of the flags which preceded some easily recognised manoeuvre, such as

---

[390] The hoists were: Telegraph flag; 253 (England); 269 (expects); 863 (that); 261 (every); 471 (man); 958 (will); 220 (do); 370 (his); 4, 21, 19, 24 (duty). In the hoist for 220 the second flag was the "substitute," duplicating the numeral "2."

"Make more sail," "Bear up and sail large," to discover what flags were now being used to indicate the signal numbers which they saw against that signal. A little patience and ingenuity would then supply the key to the changes in the flags, whereas if all the signal numbers were irregularly transposed, each signal would have to be re-constituted separately by the enemy.

About fifteen months before Trafalgar the 12-gun schooner, 'Redbridge,' commanded by a Lieut. Lemprière, who, to judge by Nelson's remarks about him, was not particularly efficient, was captured by some French frigates off Toulon. Such a small ship, commanded by an officer of such subordinate rank, was not allowed the confidential signal books, but Lemprière had, in common with many other junior officers, obtained a surreptitious copy for himself—one of those little manuscript and hand-painted signal books one sees in museums, or occasionally picks up in second-hand book shops.

This book Lieut. Lemprière had neglected to throw overboard, and when, later on, one of Nelson's scouts, looking into Toulon harbour to see if the French were getting on comfortably, found the captured 'Redbridge' just outside, the latter made the signal for the scout ship to anchor; but fortunately the officer in command was a little sharper than the 'Redbridge's' late commander had been, and the net was spread in vain.

Directly Nelson learned this he changed the flags and reported the matter to the Admiralty. On the 4th November, the Admiralty, despite the objection of Lord Keith that a change of signal numbers would be better, issued a circular letter to all commanders-in-chief telling them to alter their numeral flags in accordance with a painted copy enclosed with the letter. These are the flags shown in the third column of the plate. Further, as their Lordships had reason to apprehend that Lieut. Lemprière was not the only officer under commander's rank who had obtained a copy of the signal book, the strictest injunctions were to be given that such improper proceedings were not to take place in future, and existing irregular copies were to be impounded.

The flags in use in the Mediterranean were changed in numerical value in accordance with the Admiralty order on the 16th January, 1804, and these new numeral flags were the ones used at Trafalgar, and, in fact, until the end of 1810[391].

We have seen that Howe's second code, first in its original form, next as re-arranged by McArthur, and finally as simplified and expanded for the 1799 Signal Book, in each case with practically the same numeral flags, sufficed, when supplemented by Popham's Vocabulary, for the navy's needs throughout the most sustained and strenuous struggle that until the recent war had ever fallen to its lot[392].

Towards the close of this period, however, Popham, who seems to have devoted all the time not required for his professional duties, or for defence against the attacks made upon him, to the improvement of his code[393], brought out a greatly

---

[391] See the last column of Plate XIII.

[392] In 1808 the 1799 book was reprinted, and the manuscript additions incorporated, but its form was not changed.

[393] He produced in 1804 a signal code for the East India Company's ships.

enlarged and improved vocabulary, which is best described in his own words:

> The present edition is wholly new cast and composed; very considerably enlarged by additional materials; and, as I trust, improved by a distribution of those materials which was intended to increase the facility of reference.

> It consists of nearly 6,000 primitive words, exclusive of the inflexions of verbs, &c., making in all upwards of 30,000 real words; the sentences have also been extended to about 6,000, with 1,500 syllables, a Geographical Table, a Table of Technical Terms, a Table of Stores and Provisions, and a Spare Table for Local Significations.

With so large a number of signals the limitation in the number of flags that can be conveniently hoisted at a time made itself at once felt, and Popham found himself compelled to abandon the "simple numerary" method. Taking the limit of convenience at three flags, the ten numeral flags of the Admiralty Signal Book would suffice for only 999 signals. Popham, therefore, after calculating the number of combinations available with various sets of flags, chose 23. These, which were mostly of his own design, he denoted by the numbers 1 to 9 and the letters A to O. With these 23 flags the number of available combinations is as follows:

Singly	23
Two at a time	506
Three at a time	10,626
Total	11,155

So that upwards of 11,000 signals could be made using no more than three flags in one hoist.

Hoisting four flags at a time, the number of possible signals with 23 flags is increased by 212,520, making 223,675 in all, sufficient for the most exhaustive vocabulary. If this code had been invented seven years earlier, Nelson could have made his signal in precisely his own words, the first three of which would have been as follows: England, 69B; confides, 5I3; that, B67. Curiously enough, Popham, in 1812, seems to have preferred "confides" to "expects," for the former was one of "most needed" words and could be made by three flags, whereas "expects" was No. 6138 and required four.

In demonstrating the extensive use to which his code could be put, Popham gives one or two amusing illustrations, apparently in all seriousness. Thus:

FA1	Have you an idea
G647	a change of ministers is about to take place

* * * * *

52A	Certainly
8BF	not

G643   ministers are gaining strength

* * * * *

BOE   Your

AC8   sister

852   married

85F   to

C87   a Lord of the Admiralty

This vocabulary, published in 1812, was such an evident improvement that it was issued to the fleet in 1813.

In 1816 it was revised by Popham and re-issued by the Admiralty as an official Vocabulary Signal Book. Eleven years later the signal books were again revised and re-cast in three volumes: —

1. The General Signal Book, containing evolutionary and battle signals, to which the numeral flags were henceforth appropriated.

2. The Vocabulary Signal Book, containing words and general sentences, to which were appropriated the alphabetical flags, now increased to 21 by the addition of P, Q, R, S, T, V, and Y.

3. Night and fog signals.

In 1882, W was substituted for V and slight alterations were made in some of the flags, and in 1889, when the signal books underwent a more extensive revision, the alphabetical series was completed by the inclusion of all the letters, and a series of numeral pendants was added. The flags thus finally established in 1889 remain in use to this day. It may be observed that they contain a number of survivals from Howe's Code of 1790, four indeed with their original significance. They are as follows:

(1) An alphabetical series, in which many of the flags are of the same design as those in the International Code (see p. 187) but with different significations, as follows:

A   flag, diagonally striped yellow & red   = Y   of Internat[l] Code

B   flag, white, bordered with blue & pierced with red   = W of Internat[l] Code

C   flag, divided diagonally yellow, blue, red & black   = Z   of Internat[l] Code

D   Pilot Jack (Union Jack with white border[394])

E   flag, divided horizontally blue, white, blue   = J   of Internat[l] Code

---

[394] During the war this flag was altered to one divided vertically yellow, red yellow, in order to obviate the use of the Pilot Jack as an ordinary signal flag.

F	flag quarterly yellow & black	= L	of Internat[l] Code
G	flag divided vertically white, black, white		
H	flag, yellow with black ball	= I	of Internat[l] Code
I	flag, blue with yellow saltire	=	Numeral 7 of 1790
J	pendant, divided vertically white & red		
K	flag, divided horizontally yellow & blue		
L	flag, white with red saltire	= V	of Intern[l] Code
M	pendant, divided horizontally red, yellow, red		
N	pendant, divided horizontally yellow, blue, yellow		
O	flag, divided diagonally red & yellow	= O	of Intern[l] Code
P	pendant, blue with white cross		
Q	pendant, red		
R	pendant, yellow with red cross		
S	pendant, divided vertically blue & yellow		
T	pendant, blue with white ball	= D	of Intern[l] Code
U	burgee, divided vertically white & blue	= A	of Intern[l] Code
V	flag, white pierced blue	= S	of Intern[l] Code
W	flag, yellow	= Q	of Intern[l] Code
X	pendant, striped vertically black & yellow		
Y	pendant, white with red border		
Z	flag, chequered blue & white	= N	of Intern[l] Code

Affirmative   }   as in 1790 (see Plate XIII)
Preparative   }   as in 1790 (see Plate XIII)
Negative   flag, white with 5 black crosses

(2) A series of numeral flags:—

1 as No. 5 in 1790

2 as No. 2 in 1790

3 flag, chequered yellow & blue

4 as No. 9 in 1790

5 flag, divided horizontally red & white

6 as No. 8 in 1790

7 as No. 8 in 1790

8 flag divided vertically red, white, blue

9 as "Dissent" in 1790

0 as No. 0 in 1790

(3) A series of numbered and special pendants:—

1 divided vertically red, white, blue

2 divided horizontally red, white, blue

3 white with red cross

4 striped vertically white & red (16 stripes)

6 white with 2 black crosses

7 divided quarterly white, black, yellow, red

8 red

9 white with red ball

0 divided vertically yellow & blue

Interrogative divided quarterly red & white

Answering divided vertically red & white

Guard, red with white cross

Numeral, chequered blue & yellow

Church, as No. 2 but with St. George's Cross in chief.

These pendants are all of a different shape from those employed in the alphabetical series, being more narrow and elongated, and cut off square at the end, whereas the former are almost equilateral and might perhaps be more correctly designated as "triangular flags."

The "substitutes" used are as follows:

1st.	(repeating the 1st. flag or pendant of a "series")	the Affirmative flag
2nd.	(repeating the 2nd. flag or pendant of a "series")	Answering pendant
3rd.	(repeating the 3rd. flag or pendant of a "series")	No. 2 pendant
4th.	(repeating the 4th. flag or pendant of a "series")	No. 0 pendant
1st.	(when using the numbered pendants)	Interrogative pendant
2nd.	(when using the numbered pendants)	Answering pendant

With these we have probably reached the final development of form so far as flag signals are concerned, for wireless has taken the place of visual signalling to such an extent that it is not likely that circumstances can now arise that will necessitate any radical recasting of the flag signal system.

(V) COMMERCIAL CODES

Some elementary flag signals, notably that for a pilot, were in use among merchantmen at least as early as the fifteenth century, but the first attempt to supply a code of signals suitable for merchant ships appears to have been that made by Sir Home Popham in 1804, when, at the request of the East India Company, he compiled a book of "Commercial and Military Signals" for the use of the ships in their service. In this book the "military" element preponderates, as might be expected from the circumstances of the time at which it was drawn up. The signals relate almost exclusively to the fighting and manoeuvring of ships sailing in convoy. After the peace, in 1817, Captain Frederick Marryat drew up what may be regarded as the precursor of modern commercial codes. It was in six parts, each in the simple numerary system, with a distinguishing flag to indicate the part to which the signal related. The parts were as follows: 1. Names of men-of-war. 2. Names of merchantmen. 3. Ports, headlands, etc. 4. Sentences on various subjects. 5 and 6. A vocabulary adapted from Popham. This signal book went through ten editions before the author's death in 1848.

In 1855, owing to the enormous increase in communication by sea, and the adoption of an official number for every merchant ship imposed by the Merchant Shipping Act of 1854, the need for a much more ample code had become urgent, and the Board of Trade appointed a Committee to draw up a new one. This committee reported that an efficient code "ought to provide for not less than 20,000 distinct signals and should, besides, be capable of designating not less than 50,000 ships, with power of extension if required." They further stated that "a signal should not consist of more than four flags or symbols at one hoist," and pointed out that under this condition the ten numerals without repeaters would make only 5860 signals, or 9999 signals with three repeaters. They therefore abandoned the numeral system and chose 18 flags which, by using two, three, or four flags together, allowed of 78,642 permutations. These 18 flags, which embodied most of those already in use in Marryat's Code unchanged, or with slight alteration, were designated by the letters of the alphabet except a, e, i, o, u, x, y, z, the vowels being omitted because "by introducing them every objectionable word composed of four letters or less, not only in our own but in foreign languages, would appear in the code in the course of the permutation of the letters of the alphabet."

The flags adopted were as follows:

    B red burgee (flag with swallow-tailed fly)

    C pendant white with red ball

    D pendant blue with white ball

    F pendant red

    G pendant divided vertically yellow and blue

    H flag divided vertically white and red

J   flag divided horizontally blue, white, blue

K   flag divided vertically yellow and blue

L   flag divided quarterly blue and yellow

M   flag blue with white saltire

N   flag chequered blue and white

P   flag blue pierced with white square (the blue Peter)

Q   flag yellow

R   flag red with yellow cross

S   flag white pierced with blue square

T   flag divided vertically red, white, blue

V   flag white with red saltire

W   flag blue bordered white pierced with red square,

and an "Answering Signal" or Code Pendant divided vertically red and white in five stripes. In 1857 this "Commercial Code of Signals for use of all Nations" was issued by the Board of Trade, and it sufficed for the needs of the next thirty years, the name being changed to International Code about 1880. At the end of that period the Board of Trade appointed a Committee to bring it up to date and to consider whether a system of night signals should be added to it. In 1899 this Committee submitted a revision of the Code "which differed from that then current only in the omission of certain signals which had become obsolete and the substitution of certain other signals for which modern developments had created a demand." The criticisms of the foreign maritime powers upon this book led, however, to a complete revision and recasting of the old code for reasons which the Committee summarise in their final report[395] in 1896 in the following words:

> Since the old Code of signals was first issued there has been a very considerable increase in the average speed of vessels belonging to the Mercantile Marine, owing both to the larger percentage of steamers as compared with sailing vessels and to the greater speed to which steamers now attain. Vessels consequently remain within signalling distance of one another and of signal stations for a much shorter time than was the case 40 years ago, and it is necessary that an efficient Code of signals should provide the means of rapid communication. In a Code, such as the International Code, in which signals are made chiefly by means of flags, rapidity of communication can best be secured by reducing to a minimum the number of flags required to make the signals, since every additional flag in a hoist involves delay in bending on the flags on the part of the person making the signals and delay in making out the flags on the part of the person taking in the signals, and to enable this to be done without the number of signals in the Code being reduced, it was necessary to provide an increased number

---

[395] *Parl. Paper* C 8354 of 1897.

of two or three flag signals by adding additional flags to the Code.

The number of signals which can be made by permutations of 18 flags, no flag being used more than once in the same hoist, is as follows:—

One-flag signals	18
Two-flag signals	306
Three-flag signals	4,896
Four-flag signals	73,440
Total	78,660

The number of signals actually provided in the old Code which can be made by the Code flags is:—

One-flag signals		4
Two-flag signals		215
Three-flag signals about		4,500
(*a*) Four-flag signals, excluding those representing the names of places and ships, about	8,700	
(*b*) Four-flag signals representing the names of places, about	3,400	29,600
(*c*) Four-flag signals representing the names of ships, about	17,500	
Total about		34,319

The following is the number of signals which can be made by means of the 26 flags which we have adopted, no flag being used more than once in the same hoist:—

One-flag signals	26
Two-flag signals	650
Three-flag signals	15,600
Four-flag signals	358,800
Total	375,076

Moreover, by using the Code pennant over and under one or two flags of the Code, the following additional signals made by not more than three flags are obtainable:—

Code Pennant over one flag	26
Code Pennant under one flag	26
Code Pennant over two flags	650
Code Pennant under two flags	650

Total   1,352

It will therefore be seen that by the adoption of the eight additional flags, many of the more important signals which have at present to be made by three-flag hoists can be converted into two-flag signals, and that all the four-flag signals (excluding those representing the names of places and of ships) in the old Code can be made by three-flag signals, while between 3,000 and 4,000 new signals to be made by hoists of not more than three flags can be added.

The abolition of all four-flag hoists for general signals will very greatly increase the *Rapidity* with which communication can be held by means of the International Code of Signals.

It will also tend to secure another essential in efficient signalling, viz., *Accuracy*, for every flag added to a hoist affords an extra risk of mistake, both in bending on a wrong flag and in reading off the flags in the hoist incorrectly.

In addition to the gain of rapidity and accuracy of signalling, the inclusion of the eight new flags has, as we have already stated, afforded the means of providing a large number of signals which do not appear in the current Code, and we have availed ourselves of this possibility to the extent of adding some 4,000 new signals.

Moreover, the fact that under the proposed scheme there is a flag to represent every letter of the alphabet has enabled us to arrange for a system of spelling proper names and words not appearing in the Signal Book, which we regard as less cumbersome than the Alphabetical Spelling Table which is at present in force.

These advantages appear to us to be so important that we have not hesitated to increase the number of flags to be used, although the step involved the abandonment of the Code suggested by us in 1889 and the preparation of an entirely new Signal Book.

The letters omitted from the alphabet in 1855 were now added, the objection which had led to their omission on the former occasion being regarded as a "sentimental rather than practical objection," though the Committee took care to eliminate objectionable words as far as practicable.

The flags now added were:

A Burgee divided vertically white and blue

E Pendant divided vertically red, white, blue

I Flag yellow with blue ball

O Flag divided diagonally yellow and red

U Flag divided quarterly red and white

X Flag white with blue cross

Y   Flag striped diagonally yellow and red in ten stripes

Z   Flag divided diagonally in 4 triangular parts, yellow, blue, red, and black.

At the same time the F and L flags were slightly altered.

> We have altered the flag F from a red pennant with a white ball on it to a red pennant with a white cross, as the flag at present in use is liable to be mistaken for Flag D (blue pennant with a white ball on it), and we have altered flag L from a flag of yellow and blue quarterly (the blue squares being at the top left-hand and bottom right-hand corners) to a flag of yellow and black quarterly, the black squares being at the top right-hand and bottom left-hand corners. Our chief reason for making this alteration is that in a calm it is difficult to distinguish the present flag L from flag K.

Certain of the above flags are used singly with special significations, viz. A by H.M. ships on full speed trial, B to signify that explosives are being landed or discharged, C as affirmative, D as negative, P to denote that the ship is about to sail and S as signal for a pilot, while L is used in the United Kingdom to indicate infection from cholera, Yellow fever or plague, and Q is generally used aboard to denote liability to quarantine.

Signals made with two flags are urgent and important. Of the three-flag signals those from ABC to AST relate to the compass; from ASU to AVJ to money; from AVK to BCN to weights and measures; BCO to BOZ to decimals and fractions; from BEA to CWT to auxiliary verbs and phrases; while the general vocabulary occupies the permutations from CXA to ZNV. The Code flag over two flags serves for Latitude and Longitude, Divisions of time, and the Barometer and Thermometer, and the Code flag under two flags from UA to ZY provides a numeral table. The geographical names of places are signalled by four flags from ABCD to BFAU, while the permutations from CBDF to CZYX are used for an alphabetical spelling table. This completes the flag signals of the Code, but it contains in addition a number of Distant Signals, Semaphore Signals and Morse Code Signals.

Combinations from GQBC onwards are used for the names of ships, which will be found in separate publications.

This new Code was published in 1899 and brought into force on 1st January, 1901, the old Code being used concurrently with it until the 31st December of that year. It has now reached the seventeenth edition, and a complete revision of it, which will probably entail the alteration of many of the flags, is occupying the attention of an International Commission, but it will be several years before this is brought into use.

In making a signal, a ship first hoists her ensign with the code flag under it, and if necessary the distinguishing signal of the vessel or station with which she desires to communicate. On seeing this signal the ship (or station) addressed then hoists the "Answering Pendant" (i.e. the Code flag) at the "Dip," that is, some little distance below its position when hoisted "close up" to the block at the masthead or yardarm through which the signal halliards are rove. The first ship then hoists her own distinguishing signal, consisting of the four letters appropriated to her name, and then proceeds with the signal she wishes to make. When the first hoist is noted down and translated in the ship receiving the signal, this ship hauls the answering pendant "close up" to show that the signal is understood and keeps it there until the signalling ship has hauled that hoist down; the answering pendant is then again lowered to the "Dip" until the next hoist is disposed of, and when the ship signalling has finished, she hauls down her ensign to indicate that the message is at an end.

Among signals of distress by means of flags—which from their nature are of international use and common to both men-of-war and merchant ships—the earliest appears to have been made by tying the ensign in a knot in the middle, or making a weft as it was called. Another, which appears to have been in use in the seventeenth century, was to invert the ensign; this, of course, could not be done with those ensigns (such as the modern French) which are symmetrical in design. The signal appears sometimes to have been given by placing the ensign in an unusual position, such as at the main topmast-head or in the shrouds. An instance in which the ensign was placed inverted in the shrouds will be found on page 202.

CHAPTER VII
CEREMONIAL AND OTHER USAGES

THE student who has wandered along the by-paths of early military and naval history may perhaps have been struck by the fact that although he met not infrequently with instances of the devotion and respect with which the soldier regarded his military ensigns he met with no similar examples in naval affairs. He might at first be disposed to attribute this to the fact that the histories he had read were not the work of professed seamen, but upon reflexion he would more probably be disposed to infer that, except in the ship of the Commander-in-Chief, there was at sea nothing to correspond to the military insignia. The examination into the early history of the flag which we have endeavoured to carry out in the first chapter of this book leads us to the conclusion that until the thirteenth century there was no equivalent of the military ensign in use at sea, and the early history of the salute at sea tends to confirm this view.

The Ordinance[396] drawn up by King John in 1201, which required all ships and vessels to strike and lower their sails at the command of the King's ships, makes no mention of a flag, and although the striking of the sails was perhaps primarily intended not so much as a mark of respect as a practical means of ensuring that the ships in question should render an effective submission to the will of the king's officers, the omission is at any rate of some significance. An instructive commentary upon the relative significance of the acts of striking sails or flags is afforded by the account of the taking of two Spanish ships by the 'Amity' of London in 1592[397]. These merchantmen had fallen in with each other off the south-west coast of Spain, and apparently each side had determined to make prize of the other. The Spaniards were displaying a flag with the arms of the King of Spain, which caused the English to "judge them rather ships of warre then laden with marchandise." After a long fight the English ship gained the advantage,

> willing them to yeeld, or els we should sinke them: wherupon the one would have yeelded, which was shot betweene winde and water; but the other called him traiter. Unto whom we made answere, that if he would not yeeld presently also, we would sinke him first. And thereupon he understanding our determination, presently put out a white flag, and yeelded, and yet refused to strike their own sailes, for that they were sworne never to strike to any Englishmen.

Evidently the striking of the sails was an act of greater submission than the

[396] Twiss, *Black Book of the Admiralty*, I, 129.
[397] Hakluyt, *Voyages*, VII, 103.

display of the flag of truce, and its persistent survival until the year 1806 as part of the ceremony required when the salute was exacted by H.M. ships is a clear indication that it must have been originally the most essential part of that ceremony. When Pennington was given his instructions as Admiral of the Narrow Seas in May, 1631, he was told:

> If in this yor imployment you shall chance to meete in the Narrowe Seas anie ffleete belonging to anie forraine Prince or State you are to expect that the Admirall and cheefe of them in acknowledgmt of his Mats Soveraignty there shall strike their Topsayle in passing by, or if they refuse to do it you are to force them thereunto[398],

but no instruction was given him in regard to their flag, and the Treaty made between Cromwell and the Dutch at the close of the First Dutch War in 1654 required the latter not only to haul down their flag when rendering the salute, but also to lower the topsail (*vexillum suum e mali vertice detrahent et supremum velum demittent*).

After Trafalgar the British Naval Power stood at such a height that it was felt that no loss of prestige could then arise from the abandonment of the claim so tenaciously insisted on for many centuries, and the instructions to naval officers to exact the salute were quietly dropped out of the *King's Regulations* where they had, for many years, appeared in the following terms:

> When any of His Majesty's Ships shall meet with any Ship or Ships belonging to any Foreign Prince or State, within His Majesty's Seas, (which extend to Cape *Finisterre*) it is expected that the said Foreign Ships do strike their Topsail, and take in their Flag, in Acknowledgement of His Majesty's Sovereignty in those Seas; and if any shall refuse or offer to resist, it is enjoined to all Flag Officers and Commanders to use their utmost Endeavours to compel them thereto, and not suffer any Dishonour to be done to His Majesty. And if any of His Majesty's Subjects shall so much forget their Duty, as to omit striking their Topsail in passing by His Majesty's Ships, the Name of the Ship and Master, and from whence, and whither bound, together with Affidavits of the Fact, are to be sent up to the Secretary of the Admiralty, in order to their being proceeded against in the Admiralty Court. And it is to be observed, That in His Majesty's Seas, His Majesty's Ships are in no wise to strike to any; and that in other Parts, no Ship of His Majesty's is to strike her Flag or Topsail to any Foreigner, unless such Foreign Ship shall have first struck, or at the same time strike her Flag or Top-sail to His Majesty's Ship.

An adequate presentment of the history of the salute at sea would claim a volume to itself, and is indeed rather outside the scope of the present work, but it may be remarked that in the sixteenth century (and probably at an earlier date, though evidence of this is lacking) the requirement of the salute—in itself a mere

---

[398] *S. P. D. Chas I*, cxcii, 3.

passing ceremony—was expanded into a demand that no foreign ship or English merchantman should fly any flag at all when in the presence of any of H.M. ships of war. This point of view, as understood by the seamen of the late Elizabethan and early Stuart period, is set forth in the *Observations* of Sir Richard Hawkins published just after his death in 1622:

> One thing the French suffered (upon what occasion or ground I know not) that the English always carried their flag displayed: which in other partes and Kingdomes is not permitted; at least in our seas, if a Stranger Fleete meete with any of his Majesties ships, the forraigners are bound to take in their flags, or his Majesties ships to force them to it though thereof follow the breach of peace, or whatsoever discommodity. And whosoever should not be jealous in this point, hee is not worthy to have the commaund of a Cock-boat committed unto him: yea no stranger ought to open his flag in any Port of England, where there is any Shipp or Fort of his Majesties; upon penaltie to loose his flagg and to pay for the powder and shott spend upon him. Yea, such is the respect to his Majesties Shippes in all places of his Dominions, that no English ship displayeth the Flagge in their presence, but runneth the like danger, except they be in his Majesties service: and then they are in predicament of the Kings Ships.

*   *   *   *   *

> In Queene Maries Raigne, King Philip of Spaine comming to marry with the Queene, and meeting with the Royall Navie of England, the Lord William Howard, High Admirall of England, would not consent that the King in the Narrow Seas should carrie his Flagge displayed until he came into the Harbour of Plimouth.

> I being of tender yeares, there came a Fleete of Spaniards of above fiftie sayle of Shippes bound for Flaunders to fetch the Queene Dona Anna de Austria, last wife to Philip the second of Spaine, which entered betwixt the Iland and the Maine, without vayling their Top-sayles or taking in of their Flags, which my father, Sir John Hawkins (Admirall of a Fleete of her Majesties Shippes then ryding in Catt-water) perceiving, commanded his Gunner to shoot at the flagge of the Admirall, that they might thereby see their error.

The instances in which this point of view was impressed upon foreign ships and English merchant ships are numerous.

The following example of the ceremonious manner in which the salute was sometimes voluntarily rendered outside the "Narrow Seas" is of special interest. It occurred during the expedition to Algiers in 1620, under Sir Robert Mansell:

> The one and thirtieth of October, in the morning wee turned into the Road of Gibraltar, where were riding at anchor two of the King of Spaines ships of warre, the Vice Admirall of a Squadron

> with the Kings Armes in his fore-top and another, who so soone as
> they perceived us weighed their Anchors, set sayle, and comming
> Lee-ward of our Admirall, strooke his flag, saluting him with
> their small shot and great Ordnance, after haled him with voyces;
> our Admirall striking his flag, answered them with voyces, gave
> them his Ordnance and small shot, all the Fleet following in order.

Before the legislative union of the two kingdoms, the salute was exacted by English men-of-war of ships of the Scottish navy. In June, 1706, the 'Royal William,' one of the three small ships that then comprised the Scots navy, put into Tynemouth, whereupon the commanding officer of H.M.S. 'Dunwich' fired "a sharp great shot" at her and complained that her commanding officer was displaying a broad pendant in English waters. In his letter reporting the incident to the Lord High Admiral of Scotland, Commodore Gordon adds that the commander of H.M.S. 'Bonaventure' had told him "that he should be sorry of meeting me without the Island of May, since he had orders from the Board of England to make our frigates strike and salute[399]."

Closely connected in idea with the lowering of the flag in salute and as a mark of respect to a stronger power is the lowering of it as a sign of submission and surrender in action. Its application to this purpose seems comparatively modern and to have been really an extension of the salute. In naval warfare among the ancients and during the middle ages submission was often of little use; the only safe thing to be done by those who saw that they would be beaten and cared to save their lives was to take to flight. Prisoners, except a few likely to be of value for ransom, were usually disposed of summarily by being thrown overboard, for there was little room for them in the early ships and none at all in the galleys. It will be remembered that Chaucer says of his "Schipman": "If that he foughte and hadde the heigher hand By water he sente hem hoom to everyland." When Hubert de Burgh's men in 1217 agreed that so soon as they had boarded Eustace the Monk's ship one of their number should climb the mast and cut down the flag, they did not imagine that this would indicate surrender; the object they had in view was to confuse the remaining enemy ships by depriving them of the mark by which they could recognise their leader's ship.

Until the use of great ordnance had been sufficiently developed at sea to enable an enemy ship to be overcome at a distance, it is obvious that the dispute for the mastery could only be settled by hand-to-hand encounter. In these circumstances there would be no need of any method of indicating surrender other than by a personal appeal for quarter on the part of the vanquished crew, and indeed, the vanquished would hardly have the time or opportunity of removing the various flags placed along the bulwarks or flown from the masthead as a preliminary to such an appeal. But when it became possible for the ship to be destroyed from a distance, some method of indicating a wish to surrender on terms became necessary. This appears to have first been provided by displaying a flag of truce, a practice that was no doubt adopted about the beginning of the sixteenth century from the usages of land warfare where it had been current for many centuries. The

---

[399] Grant, *The Old Scots Navy* (N.R.S.), p. 337.

following instance of its employment at sea occurred during Sir Richard Hawkins' voyage into the South Sea in 1593-4. In April, 1594, Hawkins' ship was caught at a disadvantage in the Bay of San Mateo. The crew were not over-anxious to fight, and talked of surrendering. Hawkins harangued them: "Came we into the South Sea," he asked, "to put out flagges of truce? And left we our pleasant England, with all her contentments with intention and purpose to avayle ourselves of white ragges?" After some fighting, which their neglect of proper preparations rendered useless, the captain of the ship "presently caused a flagge of truce to be put in place of our Ensigne, and began to parley of our surrendering[400]." It will be noted that the colours were hauled down and the white flag then hoisted on the ensign staff.

This method of indicating a wish to surrender was evidently the general practice at this period, for in the same year, during an attack upon a carrack by the Earl of Cumberland at Terceira, some of the crew of the carrack who had had enough fighting waved a flag of truce and called out to the English to save their lives, but the captain ordered them to take in the flag of truce, for he had determined never to yield while he lived. In the time of the First Dutch War the striking of the colours formed part of the outward symbolism of surrender, but not the whole. According to Captain Joseph Cubitt's account of the Battle off the Texel on 31st August, 1653, some of the Dutch ships "that had lost all their masts struck their colours and put out a white handkerchief on a staff, and hauled in all their guns[401]." It may be concluded from this that the mere hauling down of the colours was not in itself considered sufficient to indicate that the ship desired to take no further part in the fight, nevertheless it is clear that as great importance was attached to the capture of the flags as to the capture of a regiment's colours on land, for the States General published a list of rewards[402] offered to their "soldiers at sea" which included an offer of 1000 guilders to him who should "fetch off and deliver up" the flag of the chief admiral, 500 guilders for a subordinate admiral's flag, 250 guilders for a jack, 150 guilders for a flag from the mizen, and 50 guilders for a stern ensign.

The process of surrender is illustrated by Captain John Smith in his *Accidence for Young Seamen*[403] in the following words:

> They hang out a flag of truce ... hale him amaine, abase or take in his flag, strike their sailes and come aboard with their Captaine, Purser and Gunner, with their commission, coket, or bils of lading.

By the time of the Second Dutch War (1666) the mediation of a flag of truce appears to have become unnecessary, for Van de Velde's picture of the surrender of the 'Royal Prince,' Admiral Ayscue's flagship which ran aground on the Galloper during the Four Days' Fight, clearly shows the lowered ensign and a man at the main masthead in act of lowering the admiral's flag. Van de Velde was present at the action, so that there can be little doubt but that the details are correct. From this

---

[400] *The Observations of Sir Richard Hawkins, Knight, in his Voiage into the South Sea*, p. 155.

[401] *S. P. D. Inter.*, xxix, 11.

[402] *First Dutch War* (N. R. S.), v, 319.

[403] 1626, reprinted with additions as *A Sea Grammar* in 1627 and 1653.

date the lowering of the colours appears to have been sufficient.

But perhaps the principal reason for the disuse of the white flag at sea lay in its ambiguity. On the occasion above referred to, Ayscue was Admiral of the White Squadron, and the 'Royal Prince' was displaying a large white flag at the masthead and an ensign which was almost entirely white save for a small St George's cross in its upper corner. In such circumstances the display of another white flag would have been liable to misunderstanding. A like ambiguity would have arisen in the French navy, where from 1661 until the Revolution the ensign was plain white, and it may be noted that in 1794 during the attack on Martinique the French fired on a flag of truce sent by the English, and explained their action later as being due to a mistaken supposition that it was intended for the colours of their late rulers the Bourbons; whereupon it was agreed that in future ships bearing flags of truce should have the enemy's flag at the bow and their own national colours at the stern.

The plainest and most unmistakable method of indicating surrender is to hoist the enemy colours above one's own, and this was the course adopted by some of the Spanish ships which surrendered at Trafalgar, although others appear to have hoisted the white flag after hauling down their own colours[404]. Modern practice, however, recognises the hauling down of the colours accompanied by the cessation of fire as sufficient; the victors on taking possession then hoist their own flag above the enemy flag as a sign of capture.

It is evident from an incident that occurred during the capture of the Island of Goree by Commodore Keppel in 1758 that the precise significance of hauling down the flag was in doubt even at that comparatively late date. The fire of the British Squadron was so overpowering that the enemy's flag was hauled down and the fire thereupon ceased.

> A lieutenant being ordered ashore, attended by the Commodore's Secretary ... was surprised on being asked before they quitted the boat on what terms the surrender was "expected." The lieutenant astonished at this question asked if they had not struck their flag, intimating an unconditional submission resting merely on the clemency of the victor? He was answered "No: lowering of the flag was intended only as a signal for a parley."

The action was thereupon renewed and finally the Governor ordered the regimental colours to be dropped over the walls as a signal of surrender at discretion[405].

The captor's flag is not hoisted above the colours of a neutral vessel seized for breach of blockade or similar reasons; in such a case the captor's flag (if hoisted) should be hoisted in another part of the ship.

The custom of "half-masting" the flag, that is, of lowering it to a position halfway or more down the flagstaff as a sign of mourning, does not seem to be very an-

---

[404] The 'Bahama' (Sp.), the 'Argonauta' (Sp.) and the 'Achille' (Fr.) indicated their surrender by displaying Union jacks from the deck.
[405] Charnock, *Biographia Navalis*, v, 318.

cient, but it is probably older than the seventeenth century. The earliest instance in which I have met it occurred in July, 1612, on the occasion of the murder of James Hall by the Esquimoes during the first expedition in search of the North-West Passage in which Baffin took part, when the 'Heart's Ease' rejoined the 'Patience' with "her flag hanging down and her ancient hanging over the poop, which was a sign of death." On entering the Thames two months later the 'Heart's Ease' again lowered her flag and ensign "in token and sign of the death of Mr Hall," so that it was at that date well understood to signify the death of the commanding officer of a ship. It was the custom in the navy after the Restoration to observe the anniversary of the execution of Charles I in a similar manner, for Teonge twice records the fact in his Diary:

> 30 Jan. 1675. This day being the day of our King's marterdome wee shew all the signs of morning as possible wee can, viz. our jacks and flaggs only halfe staff high;

and again:

> 30 Jan. 1678. A solemn day, and wee keep it accordingly with jacks and pendents loared halfeway.

Evidently the practice of half-masting the flags was well understood both in the English navy and in the merchant service, but it is doubtful if it became a universal custom until comparatively modern times. The 'Black Pinnace,' which brought the body of Sir Philip Sydney from Holland in 1586, had black sails, but the illustration in the contemporary account of his funeral[406] shows the flags at the masthead, and the Danish ship which brought over the Duke of Richmond's body in 1673 had a "black Flagg at his Main Top Masthead and black colours[407]." Black as a sign of mourning is of great antiquity, and a black sail was used for this purpose among the ancient Greeks, but a black flag was used by Drake at Cartagena in 1585 as a sign of war to the death, and was commonly adopted by pirates with a like meaning. It was never used in the navy in the sinister connection in which it is used ashore; an execution in one of H.M. ships was signalised by the display of a yellow flag at the masthead.

We may conjecture that the original signification of the lowered flag was the passing away of the authority which that flag connoted.

> After the battle of Lepanto in 1571 the fleet of Don John entered Messina "the galleys gay with all their flags and streamers and towing their prizes with lowered colours."

There were several ways of treating the flag of a captured ship during the seventeenth century. It might be hung below the ensign of the captor on his ensign staff, hung over his stern spread upon a spar or trailing in the water, hung over the stern of the captured ship in like manner[408], or kept to "dress ship" with. When

---

[406] Reproduced in Corbett, *Drake and the Tudor Navy*, i, 363.

[407] *Pepys MSS.* Narborough's Journal, 9th September, 1673. This ship was actually fired at for not striking the flag on coming near the fleet!

[408] The practice of towing captured galleys stern foremost with their flags trailing in the water was in vogue as early as the end of the thirteenth century.

Captain Heaton was in command of H.M.S. 'Sapphire' during the First Dutch War,

> he took so many prizes that on a festival day the Yards, Stays,
> backstays and shrouds being hung with Dutch, French, Span-
> ish and Burgundian colours and pendants variously intermixed,
> made a beautiful show, and raised the courage of all belonged to
> her[409].

The practice of hoisting numerous flags in token of rejoicing is so ancient and so widespread that it may be regarded rather as the result of a primitive instinct than the outcome of any formal symbolism, but it may be noted that, although the display of numerous flags by ships in harbour on holy days and days of national rejoicing was allowed, and in some cases even enjoined by authority, the display at sea of "ostentatious bravery" was usually interpreted to indicate some warlike or provocative action on the part of the ship indulging in it. This was certainly the case until the end of the seventeenth century, but with the dawn of the eighteenth a more law-abiding, or perhaps we should say more civilised, spirit began to prevail upon the sea, and these primitive methods of displaying the red rag to the bull began to go into disuse. The practice of displaying flags upon occasions of rejoicing, however, gave rise from time to time to unpleasant incidents between ships of different nations from the indiscriminate use of all the flags in a ship, including national flags of other nations, in the desire to make a fair show; for until the nineteenth century was well advanced both men-of-war and merchantmen carried very few signal flags, which are the only flags over whose relative precedence when hoisted in "dressing ship" no offence can be given.

Prior to 1889 it was usual in the Royal navy for one of the junior officers to draw up a scheme for "dressing ship" on ceremonial occasions for the approval of the captain, but since that date the order of the signal flags, some 60 in number, has been laid down in the Signal Manual so that uniformity is secured, the national ensign (or ensign of a foreign power if the occasion warrants the use of this) being exhibited only at a masthead.

The modern practice, for all ordinary occasions, is to hoist the national colours in the morning and to keep them up until sunset, but innumerable references to hoisting or "heaving out" the colours indicate that in earlier days this was not the custom, and that they were only hoisted at sea when there was some special reason for so doing. There was a routine for hoisting the flag in harbour in the time of Elizabeth, for the orders for Drake's fleet in 1589 and the "Brief Noates" of John Young *circa* 1596 both contain an article to this effect, those absent without leave at the time being deprived of their "aftermeal," but the hour at which the ceremony took place is not stated. The practice at the end of the eighteenth century, as related by Wm Spavens[410], Pensioner on the Naval Chest at Chatham, was as follows:

> At sunrise every ship in the fleet hoists her colours viz the
> ensign and jack, unless it blows hard and the yards and top masts
> are struck, in which case the colours are not hoisted but when
> some vessel is coming in or passing; and at sunset they are again

[409] Gardiner, *First Dutch War* (N. R. S.), i, 23.
[410] *The Seaman's Narrative*, 1796, p. 127.

struck or hauled down; at half past 7 o'clock the drums begin to beat and continue till 8, when the ship on board of which the Commander in Chief hoists his flag, fires a gun.

We do not know when this practice of hoisting the colours at sunrise was first instituted, but it is not older than the seventeenth century. In 1844 the time was altered to 8 A.M. from 25th March to 20th September and 9 A.M. from 21st September to 24th March. If there is sufficient light for the ensign to be seen, it is hoisted earlier or later than these hours, if the ship is coming to an anchor, getting under way, passing or meeting another ship, approaching a fort or town, etc.

The use of false flags as a means to deceive or entrap an enemy is probably as old as the flag itself. We have already had an example of the application of a similar ruse in the case of the Greek and barbarian standards in the year 480 B.C., but perhaps the earliest instance upon record of the use of flags at sea for this purpose occurred about the end of the twelfth century when Frederick of Sicily was a little boy (*dum ... Fredericus Sicilae Rex esset puerulus*). The Pisans had fitted out twelve ships and galleys and set out to attack Messina, which they tried to blockade. One night the citizens discovered that four of the galleys were off the Pharos, or lighthouse. They fitted out two galleys under Walter of Ferrara with picked crews, and hoisting Pisan flags (which presumably would be visible near the lighthouse) they fell upon the Pisans and took two of the galleys. Many instances of the use of false flags, either to avoid scaring an unsuspecting prey or to escape the notice of a stronger enemy, might be culled from the sea literature of the sixteenth and seventeenth centuries, one of the most interesting being the following, taken from Captain Wyatt's account of Dudley's voyage in 1594-5:

> But this before mentioned Spaniarde perceavinge the imminent dainger ensewinge and seinge noe way to avoyde it ... made triall of a thirde, which was to worke theire safetie by desaitefull pollecie, a fitt subject for base objects to worke strainge stratagems, yett the usuall occupation of Spanish practises. Being in this dilemma, and driven withall to this forced conclusion by necessite, they bore up with us puttinge forth an English flagg, keeping his men soe close that they might not soe much as seeme to bee Spaniards. But wee seinge her to be a flibote standinge with us, bearinge in her top the English collers, supposed them at the least to be some Irishmen bounde for Lisborne.... But beinge noe sooner past us, and perceavinge that if wee should cast aboute after them, wee might hasarde the bouldginge of our selves, beinge a shipp of soe great a burden, and withall soe neare the Rock, they then begin to disclose themselves, abusinge that most contemptuouslie which before they had most safelie, although craftelie, used for their safegarde, by takinge their English flagg, by whom they had theire safe pass, from their top and hanging it at theire sterne most disdainefullie[411].

Among more modern instances, one that is almost classic occurred in January,

[411] *The Voyage of Robert Dudley to the West Indies* (Hakluyt Soc.), II, 3.

1797, when five large East Indiamen under the orders of Lennox, master of the 'Woodford,' met a French squadron of six frigates off Java. Lennox immediately hoisted the flag of a British admiral and made imaginary signals, and by this means deceived the French into thinking that they were in presence of a number of British men-of-war; with the result that they withdrew and the East Indiamen escaped capture.

There is no clear pronouncement of International Law as to what is and what is not lawful in the use of false colours, and publicists are by no means unanimous upon the subject, but the following instance is given by Halleck[412] as an example of what should not be allowable:

> In that year (1783) the 'Sybille,' a French frigate of thirty-eight guns, Captain le Comte de Krergaron de Soemaria, enticed the British ship 'Hussar,' twenty guns, Captain J. M. Russell, by displaying an English ensign reversed in the main shrouds, and English colours over French at the ensign staff. She was also under jury-masts, had some shot holes, and in every way intimated herself to be a distressed prize to some of the British ships. Captain Russell at once approached to succour her, but she immediately, by a preconcerted and rapid movement, aimed at carrying away the bowsprit of the 'Hussar,' raking and then boarding her. This ruse de guerre, of so black a tint, was only prevented taking full effect by the promptitude of Captain Russell, who managed to turn his ship in such a way as only to receive half the raking fire. He then engaged with the 'Sybille,' and, on eventually capturing her, publicly broke the sword of the French captain, who he considered had sullied his reputation by descending to fight the 'Hussar' for above thirty minutes under false colours, and with signals of distress flying. "She" (the 'Hussar'), said Captain Russell, "had not had fair play, but Almighty God had saved her from the most foul snare of the most perfidious enemy." He confined the captain of the 'Sybille' as a State prisoner. It appears that the latter was subsequently brought to trial by his own Government, but was acquitted.

It is, however, now generally agreed that ships of war may hoist false colours for the purpose of deceiving the enemy, provided that their proper national colours are substituted for them before any hostile act is committed. As regards the use of neutral colours by merchantmen seeking to escape capture, it will be remembered that during the late war the Germans claimed this as a violation of the law, but the British Government contended that it was a legitimate *ruse de guerre*, and had been recognised in the past as not entailing a breach of international law.

A few remarks may be offered upon the various methods of fastening the flag to its support. In the earliest times it seems to have been nailed to its staff, and while it was small and easily portable this entailed no inconvenience. Afterwards it became customary to form a socket of canvas, buckram, or other stout material

[412] *International Law*, I, 568.

to which the hoist was sewn, and which was slipped over the staff from the top. This method was only convenient for the smaller flags, and with larger ones it appears to have been usual to sew a band of canvas down the hoist and attach a number of ribands to this by which the flag was tied to the staff. Finally, the flag was sewn to a piece of rope which could be made fast at the ends to halliards running through a block or sheave in the cap at the top of the staff, but at first these halliards were, in the case of masthead flags, taken only down to the top, not to the deck, so that a sailor had to ascend the mast whenever the flag was taken down or put up, or when any signal had to be made aloft. Thus, during the battle with the Dutch off Lowestoft on 3rd June, 1665, the Duke of York

> ordered the signal to be given for the whole fleet to tack, but the sailor who had got up the mast to give the signal was so long about it that before he could let the flag fly Opdam had with his van bore up round.... This little accident lost above six hours.

No doubt it was "accidents" of this nature that led, at a later date, to the introduction of longer halliards reaching down to the deck[413]. After the introduction of the driver or spanker boom about 1790 the ensign staff on the poop had to be removed in three-masted ships when the ship was under sail, and the ensign was then hoisted at the "peak" or outer end of the gaff by which this spanker sail was supported, the halliards passing from the poop through a small block made fast at the extremity of this spar. This continued to be the position for the ensign when the ship was at sea until the abolition of sails brought it again to its original position.

It remains to say a few words about the sizes of flags. The "baucan" streamer of *circa* 1293 was 30 yards long and 2 yards wide at the head. In 1337 the streamers range from 14 to 32 yards in length and were from 3 to 5 "cloths" wide. It is not known what the width of a "cloth" was, but it was certainly not the full width in which the cloth was made in the loom, which would have been 54 inches or more. Probably it was about one yard, for the banners were 1¾ yards long and 2 "cloths" wide, and we know that these were rectangular and rather deeper in the hoist than they were long in the fly. In the time of Elizabeth the streamers were from 12 to 28 yards long and 2 to 3 yards broad at the head, rather less in size than those of 1337, but the banners had increased in size and some were 5 yards long and 4½ yards deep. In 1623 ensigns were of 9 to 18 "breadths," flags 5 to 24 "breadths" and pendants 8 to 24 yards long. This "breadth" was probably 11 inches, for in 1664 the material was being woven in widths of 23 inches and then cut in half. Pepys, at a somewhat later date, tells us that

> it is in general to be noted that the Bewper of which Colors are made being 22 inches in breadth, and the half of that breadth or 11 inches going in ordinary discourse by the name of a Breadth when wrought into Colours, every such breadth is allowed about half-a-yard for its Fly.

By this rule the largest ensigns in 1623 were 27 feet long and 16 feet 6 inches deep,

[413] The date is not known, but it was after 1672. Cf. Narborough's Journal, 29th May, 1672: "A seaman set at the Foretopmasthead with the Flagg of Defiance loose in his arms ready to hoist."

and the largest "flags" (i.e. masthead flags) 36 feet long and 22 feet deep. In Pepys' time the ensign or flag of a first rate was 26 breadths and 14 yards in the fly, while the jack was of 14 breadths and 7 yards fly, and the pendant 3 breadths at the head and 32 yards fly. The "distinction" pendant as used in the Downs was broader and shorter, being of 5 breadths and 21 yards fly. The Lord High Admiral's flag was 24 or 22 breadths and 12 or 11 yards fly. In 1708 the ensigns had slightly increased in size and varied from 10 to 30 breadths, but the "breadth" was then nearer 10 inches than 11. An ensign of 26 breadths in 1709 was 14 yards long and the Union canton was 189 inches by 117 inches. In 1742 ensigns were from 16 to 34 breadths and 9 to 17 yards long, and jacks were from 6 to 16 breadths and 3 to 8 yards long.

These were truly enormous flags, and towards the end of the eighteenth century the sizes seem to have suffered a gradual reduction. In modern times the "breadth" has been reduced to 9 inches, and the largest ensigns are not more than 22 breadths, but the relative length of the flag has been slightly increased. Thus the largest ensign of 1742 was 51 feet long and 28 feet deep; the largest modern ensign is 33 feet long and 16½ feet deep. The largest Union flag is now 18 breadths, i.e. 27 feet by 13 feet 6 inches, while pendants vary from 3 to 20 yards in length. The proportions of the crosses in a modern Union flag are as follows:

St George's Cross	{	red	$\frac{1}{5}$ of width of flag
	{	white border	$\frac{1}{15}$ of width of flag
St Andrew's Cross		white	$\frac{1}{10}$ of width of flag
St Patrick's Cross	{	red	$\frac{1}{15}$ of width of flag
	{	white border	$\frac{1}{30}$ of width of flag

It may be observed that the white "fimbriation" of the St Patrick's cross, required by the rules of heraldry to prevent the colour red from touching the colour blue (white being a "metal": silver) is now taken from the width of the red, reducing that from $\frac{1}{10}$ to $\frac{1}{15}$. The two crosses, St Andrew's and St Patrick's ought, however, to be of equal width, and the fimbriation of the latter should therefore be taken from the blue ground.

In the white ensign the St George's cross in the fly is $\frac{2}{15}$ of the width of the flag. In the red and blue ensigns the Union canton now occupies one-fourth of the flag; in the white it is, of course, slightly smaller owing to the space occupied by the large St George's cross.

The pendant at the masthead of one of H.M. ships is a sign that the ship is in "commission"; that is, in active service under the command of an officer of the Royal Navy holding a commission from the Crown or the Lord High Admiral or the Commissioners for executing that office. It is not flown in ships in reserve. In ships flying the flag of an Admiral, or a Commodore's broad pendant, the Admiral's or Commodore's flag is in itself sufficient indication that the ship is in commission, and the pendant is not flown in those ships. It is, however, not struck when a captain hoists a Senior Officer's pendant.

It is difficult to say when the custom of hoisting a pendant on commissioning the ship became established. Mainwaring, writing about 1623, speaks of the pendants as serving solely "for a show to beautify the ship," and Boteler, ten years later, knew them only as used for this purpose or as a means of distinguishing the squadrons of a fleet[414]; but from 1661 onwards there was, in addition to the three squadronal pendants with red, white or blue fly, a fourth with the fly striped red, white and blue. This was the distinctive pendant of all H.M. ships in commission which did not form part of a fleet divided into squadrons by the red, white and blue squadronal colours.

The first step towards the recognition of the pendant as the distinctive sign of a man-of-war was taken by the Proclamation of 1661, which assigned the Union pendant to H.M. ships only, and the next by the Proclamation of 1674, which forbade merchantmen to fly any pendant whatsoever; but although the use of a pendant was thereby confined to men-of-war, it does not seem to have been the custom at that time to fly it continuously. It is clear from the Diary which Teonge, the naval chaplain, kept during his service in the Navy from 1675 to 1679, that the pendant was only hoisted—with the jack and ensign—when the ship wished to make her nationality known; or was preparing to fight; or on days of rejoicing, when pendants were hung from every yardarm; but the significance of the pendant seems to have been generally recognised at that date, for in the account which he gives of the launching in 1676 of a brigantine by the Knights of Malta, he says that after the religious ceremony, "they hoysted a pendent to signify shee was a man of warre, and then at once thrust her into the water."

Although it was not until 1824 that the King's Regulations for the Navy contained any instruction that ships in commission were to fly a pendant, it is probable that the practice of flying a pendant continuously in H.M. ships in commission was established about the end of the seventeenth century, for the first edition of the Regulations (1731) contained a direction to Captains "to husband the Ship's Colours, and not to keep them abroad in windy weather, the Pendant being a sufficient mark of distinction," from which it is clear that the latter was then flown continuously. The practice in the Navy at the beginning of the nineteenth century is given by Captain Basil Hall[415] in the following words:

> In the mean time I must proceed to put my ship in commission. The first thing to do is to get hold of one of the warrant-officers to "hoist the pendant," which is a long slender streamer, having a St George's cross on a white field in the upper part next the mast, with a fly, or tail, either Red, White, and Blue, or entirely of the colour of the particular ensign worn by the ship; which, again, is determined by the colour of the Admiral's flag under whose orders she is placed. The pendant being hoisted shows that the ship is in commission, and this part of the colours is never hauled down day or night. At sunset, when the ensign is hauled down, a smaller pendant three or four yards in length, is substituted for the long one, which, in dandified ships, waves far over the stern.

---

[414] See p. 119.
[415] *Fragments of Voyages and Travels*, 3rd Series, vol. III, p. 6.

Ships in ordinary[416] hoist merely an ensign.

According to modern practice the pendant is hoisted at 9 a.m. on the day on which the ship is "commissioned" and is kept flying night and day (unless an Admiral's flag is hoisted in her) until she is "paid off." At the present day the regulation size is strictly adhered to, even in "dandified ships"; but it is a common practice for ships abroad, when ordered to return home to pay off, to hoist a very long narrow pendant, apparently as a sign of rejoicing. This pendant, which is of course not officially recognised, is made by the signal staff out of white bunting which they have "acquired" in the course of the commission, and is usually of such length (150-250 feet) as to reach from the masthead to the water, even when inclined at a considerable angle from the perpendicular, but in some instances it is much longer and it has been known to reach 1400 feet. A bladder filled with air is fastened at the end to keep it buoyant when trailing on the water.

It was at one time the custom to fly the Union flag at the masthead of any of H.M. ships in which a foreign personage of importance was embarked. The two following examples are typical of this usage, which is now obsolete. When William Prince of Orange came to England in 1677 to marry the Princess Mary, the royal yacht which brought him over carried this flag at the masthead while he was on board; and in 1689 Admiral Russell, who had embarked the Queen of Spain in his ship at Flushing and conveyed her to the Downs and thence to Corunna, flew the Union flag at the main topmast-head during the time the Queen was on board his ship. In modern times the personal standard of the Prince or the Queen would have been flown, but it is clear from these and similar examples that the wearing of a foreign flag at the masthead of one of H.M. ships would at an earlier period have been regarded as an intolerable act of humiliation.

Analogous to this usage was the flying of the Union flag at the main when the Lord Lieutenant of Ireland, Governors of Colonies, or Ambassadors were embarked, but this mark of honour was not permitted in the waters of the English Channel or in the presence of an Admiral's flag. In 1821 the Lord Lieutenant of Ireland was granted the use of a special form of the Union flag bearing in the centre a harp on a blue escutcheon, and in modern times the Governors General or Governors of Colonies or Dominions may, when afloat, fly a Union flag bearing the badge of the Colony in the centre.

* * * * *

In this account of the history of British flags I have not dwelt upon the immaterial or emotional aspects of these important national emblems; partly because this seemed somewhat foreign to the aim I had in view; partly because this side has been sufficiently illustrated in other works. There is, however, one aspect which may receive an illustration here. Among the privileges and duties of which a British flag has for so many centuries been an outward emblem, not the least in value has been that of freedom. Towards the end of 1769 Lord St Vincent, then plain Captain Jervis, was in the Port of Genoa in H.M.S. 'Alarm.' Two Turkish galley slaves temporarily released from their chains were walking on the mole near their

---

[416] I.e. in reserve.

galley when they caught sight of one of the 'Alarm's' boats. They jumped into her and wrapped themselves in the British colours, claiming their freedom. The Genoese guard removed them by force, part of the boat's pendant being torn away in the struggle. Jervis demanded of the Doge and Senate of Genoa that the officer of the guard should bring the slaves with the fragment of the colours and make a formal apology on the quarter deck of the 'Alarm.' When this had been done, Jervis "asked the slave who had wrapped the pendent round his body what were his sensations when the guard tore him from the pendent staff. His reply was that he felt no dread for he knew that the touch of the royal colours gave him freedom." And upon this note I must make an end.

INDEX

Symbols

Æthelstan *31*

A

Admiral *Vi, 9, 10, 24, 43, 53, 56, 59, 60, 62, 63, 65, 66, 67, 77, 78, 79, 80, 81, 82, 83, 84, 85, 86, 87, 88, 89, 90, 91, 92, 94, 95, 96, 97, 98, 99, 101, 103, 104, 105, 106, 110, 117, 118, 119, 122, 123, 124, 125, 127, 139, 147, 151, 157, 158, 159, 161, 162, 166, 168, 169, 170, 171, 175, 176, 177, 179, 180, 194, 196, 197, 198, 204, 205, 206*
Admiralty Flag *81, 84, 85*
Agrippa *12*
Alexander The Great *9*
Amadeo Of Savoy *115*
Anchor *81, 82, 97, 159, 161, 176*
Anchor Flag *80, 83, 85, 86, 104*
Anthony Anthony *42*
Antioch *18, 19, 21, 34, 35*
Antoine De Conflans *152*
Aradus *7, 8*
Arms Of France *72, 77*
Arms Of Ireland *50, 74, 140*
Artemisia *10*

B

Baldwin *19*
Banner *2, 33, 56, 72, 157*
Banner Of Council *42, 77, 144, 147, 158*
Banner Of Richard I *5*
Battle Of The Standard *5, 32, 47*
Baucan *4, 164, 203*
Bauçan *3, 21, 164*
Bayeux Tapestry *14, 21, 31, 39*
Bayonne *40, 163*
Blue Ensign *94, 103, 121, 122, 124, 125, 126, 130, 131, 133, 134, 135, 137, 138, 139, 140, 141, 165*
Blue Flag *12, 91, 97, 104, 124, 165*
Bohemond *18, 19, 21*

Bombay Marine *125, 126*
Bristol *43*
Bruges *40*
Brutus *12*
Budgee Jack *58, 128*

C

Calais *Iv, 42, 129*
Captain John Young *117*
Carroccio *25, 26*
Chansons De Geste *19*
Charles Ii *75, 83, 136, 138, 139*
Colours Of Distinction *113, 163*
Comitus *24*
Commercial Codes *187*
Commonwealth *49, 58, 62, 63, 64, 73, 74, 80, 83, 84, 92, 94, 124, 132, 158, 161, 165*
Consecrated Flag *15*
Constantine *13*
Constantinople *17, 25*
Count Of Flanders *40*
Crescent *7, 9, 10, 11, 142*
Cross *21, 45, 53, 63, 64, 67, 68, 70, 71, 91, 103, 104, 105, 110, 111, 112, 122, 126, 132, 134, 136, 138, 186, 204*
Cult Of St George *34*

D

Danes *13, 16, 31*
Don John *115, 199*
Dover *6, 40, 44, 67, 129, 139*
Dragon Standard *16, 31, 33*
Dressing Ship *200*
Duke Of Buckingham *55*
Duke Of Clarence *85*
Duke Of York *65, 81, 83, 165, 203*

E

Earl Howe *178*
Earl Of Essex *59, 88, 117*
Earl Of Northumberland *83, 161*
Earl Of Pembroke *80, 85, 103*
Early Flags *2*
Early Flags *3*
Edward I *Vii, 33, 34, 36, 37, 39, 40, 45, 164*
Edward Iii *38, 41, 72, 77, 87*
Egypt *7, 114*

S

Sandwich *39, 44*
Saracens *5, 18, 19, 22*
Semeion *2, 9, 142*
Sidon *7, 8, 10*
Signum *2, 5, 10, 11, 15, 19, 21, 24, 31, 32, 35, 143*
Sir Edward Hawke *168*
Sir George Rooke *101*
Sir Home Popham *180, 187*
Sir John Hawkins *78, 116, 159, 195*
Sir John Pennington *56, 59, 91*
Sir Nathaniel Boteler *60*
Sir Richard Hawkins *195, 197*
Sir Roger Strickland *96, 111*
Sizes Of Flags *203*
Squadronal Colours *71, 94, 95, 103, 105, 111, 113, 117, 120, 123, 124, 138, 205*
Standard *Vi, Vii, 2, 4, 5, 7, 20, 21, 22, 31, 32, 47, 63, 64, 69, 72, 73, 76, 79, 81, 83, 92, 97, 103, 118, 119, 165, 167*
St Andrew *4, 38, 45, 48, 50, 53, 55, 63, 69, 70, 74, 91, 112, 131, 132, 133, 204*
St Columba *45*
St Cuthbert *33*
St Edmund *4, 33, 36, 37, 38, 40*
St Edward *3, 33, 36, 37, 38, 40, 42*
St George *Vi, Vii, 4, 6, 19, 22, 23, 24, 31, 32, 33, 34, 35, 36, 37, 38, 39, 40, 41, 42, 43, 49, 50, 53, 55, 56, 63, 64, 68, 69, 70, 71, 74, 77, 78, 79, 80, 83, 86, 88, 89, 90, 91, 101, 103, 105, 108, 109, 112, 118, 120, 121, 122, 124, 126, 128, 131, 132, 133, 134, 138, 139, 140, 147, 160, 171, 198, 204, 205*
St John *21, 32, 33*
St Katherine *42*
St Margaret *48*
St Mark *23, 24, 25, 151*
St Mary *41, 42*
St Maurice *13, 31*
St Nicholas *42*
St Patrick *48, 49, 50, 70, 71, 131, 204*
St Peter *13, 21, 32, 33, 42, 45*
Streamers *41, 43*
St Wilfred *32, 33*

T

Tabular System *178*
Tancred *18*
Tenterden *43, 44*
Trafalgar *124, 169, 175, 176, 179, 181, 182, 194, 198*
Triangular Flag *16, 30*

Lector House believes that a society develops through a two-fold approach of continuous learning and adaptation, which is derived from the study of classic literary works spread across the historic timeline of literature records. Therefore, we aim at reviving, repairing and redeveloping all those inaccessible or damaged but historically as well as culturally important literature across subjects so that the future generations may have an opportunity to study and learn from past works to embark upon a journey of creating a better future.

This book is a result of an effort made by Lector House towards making a contribution to the preservation and repair of original ancient works which might hold historical significance to the approach of continuous learning across subjects.

HAPPY READING & LEARNING!

LECTOR HOUSE
LECTOR HOUSE LLP
E-MAIL: lectorpublishing@gmail.com